Changing for GOOD

Changing for GOOD

SUSTAINING SCHOOL IMPROVEMENT

Melissa Evans-Andris

CORWIN
A SAGE Company

For information:

Corwin
A SAGE Company
2455 Teller Road
Thousand Oaks, California 91320
(800) 233-9936
Fax: (800) 417-2466
www.corwinpress.com

SAGE Ltd.
1 Oliver's Yard
55 City Road
London EC1Y 1SP
United Kingdom

SAGE Pvt. Ltd.
B 1/I 1 Mohan Cooperative
    Industrial Area
Mathura Road, New Delhi 110 044
India

SAGE Asia-Pacific Pte. Ltd.
33 Pekin Street #02-01
Far East Square
Singapore 048763

Library of Congress Cataloging-in-Publication Data

Evans-Andris, Melissa, 1952-
Changing for good : sustaining school improvement/Melissa Evans-Andris.
    p. cm.
Includes bibliographical references and index.
ISBN 978-1-4129-6868-3 (cloth)
ISBN 978-1-4129-6869-0 (pbk.)
    1. School improvement programs. 2. Educational leadership. I. Title.

LB2822.8.E853 2010
371.2′07—dc22   2009027816

09 10 11 12 13 10 9 8 7 6 5 4 3 2 1

Acquisitions Editor:	Debra Stollenwerk
Associate Editor:	Julie McNall
Production Editor:	Veronica Stapleton
Copy Editor:	Codi Bowman
Typesetter:	C&M Digitals (P) Ltd.
Proofreader:	Dennis W. Webb
Cover Designer:	Karine Hovsepian

Contents

List of Tables and Figures

Acknowledgments

Numerous people contributed in significant ways to the production and publication of this book and the study that underpins it. I wholeheartedly thank my colleague, Wayne Usui, who urged me to pursue the study, competently oversaw the quantitative analyses, and assisted me in qualitative data collection. We spent countless hours in a conference room recollecting stories from the field, discussing our insights, and pondering outcomes. I thank him for his enthusiastic support and mentoring not only during the years of this project but also over my entire career. I am grateful to other friends, scholars, and colleagues including Brian Powell, Steve Clements, Betty Lou Whitford, and Cynthia Negrey who encouraged me through this project by giving me sound guidance, providing useful comments, and asking thought-provoking questions. I deeply appreciate the work of the graduate assistants who helped manage literature reviews, data collection, storage, and tracking, especially Katalina, Jill, Linda, Karen, and Josh. Thanks to Autumn for prompt, accurate transcription and sharp insight regarding interview data and to Jonetta and Lisa, who helped me navigate the complexities of the federal grants process. Finally, I thank anonymous reviewers and Corwin Senior Acquisitions Editor Debra Stollenwerk for her support, assistance, and patience in helping this project reach completion.

From the beginning of the study, I looked forward to traveling the state, visiting schools. I approached it like a series of adventurous road trips, and I was rewarded on many levels. First, I became better able to grasp the enormity of undertaking school reform at the local, state, and national levels. Second, I met a professional goal of providing state policymakers, district and school officials, and others with insights developed over the life of the project. As a researcher and scholar, I was deeply satisfied when one school administrator said he viewed my efforts as "part of the solution rather than part of the problem." Third, the experience was personally rewarding in that I made many friends along the way, like a bus driver who took me up the district's back roads on his route, a principal who called me long distance to alert me to expect bad weather when driving to her school, another principal who invited me to hike a nearby mountain trail with her, and an entire eighth-grade class that I had the honor of hosting at our university's planetarium when they traveled to my city on their class field trip. These new friends and dozens like them gave hours of their time to help me "get it right" in understanding how their schools approached the awesome task of sustaining improvement.

The study on which this book is based was funded by Grant #R305T010812 from the U.S. Department of Education, Office of Educational Research and Improvement (OERI), Field Initiated Study. Further, the study could not have been conducted without cooperation from the University of Louisville and the Kentucky Department of Education. The book incorporates portions of an article titled "Comprehensive School Reform and Student Achievement in Kentucky Middle Schools", by Melissa Evans-Andris and Wayne M. Usui published in the *Middle Grades Research Journal,* Volume 3, Number 2, Summer 2008. The data presented and the views expressed here are solely the responsibility of the author.

Finally, I dedicate this book to my family, who traveled every step of this journey with me. I appreciate the unwavering interest of my parents, John and Gene Evans, in each story of school improvement. I depended on our children, Janey and Johnny, who contributed significantly to this effort, each in their own talented way. I thank my husband, John, for all that he does.

Corwin wishes to thank anonymous peer reviewers and recognize the following for their editorial insight and guidance.

Randel Beaver
Superintendent
Archer City Independent School
    District
Archer City, Texas

Beth Madison
Principal
George Middle School
Portland, Oregon

Pamela Quebodeaux
Principal
Calcasieu Parish School System
Lake Charles, Louisiana

Dr. Stephen Clements
Associate Professor of Political
    Science
Chair, Department of Business,
    Economics, and Political
    Science
Asbury College
Wilmore, Kentucky

Brian Powell
James H. Rudy Professor of
    Sociology
Indiana University
Bloomington, Indiana

About the Author

Melissa Evans-Andris is an associate professor of sociology at the University of Louisville in Kentucky. Her interests include the sociology of education, work and occupations, and qualitative research methodologies, particularly as they relate to schools and teaching. Her research focuses on school reform, sustainability of school improvement, and teacher quality. She authored a book titled *An Apple for the Teacher: Computers and Work in Elementary Schools.* Most recently, she directed two research efforts, including Comprehensive School Reform, Educational Dynamics, and Achievement in Kentucky Middle Schools, and A Research Study of the Kentucky Teacher Internship Program Pilot Project, which tracked the experiences of new teacher-interns during their first three years on the job. She is active in local and statewide discussion forums related to school improvement and reform.

Introduction

In the fall of the third and final year of their funding cycle through the federal Comprehensive School Reform (CSR) program, I arrived in the front office of a large middle school to observe educators and learn about their experiences with their reform model. The secretary alternated between answering the phone, chatting with a guard, and shouting instructions to someone over a walkie-talkie. While she talked on one phone, the school's reform facilitator picked up another line and placed an order for flowers to be delivered to a funeral home. Then she looked over at me and said, "We got our test scores last week. We went down again." About that time, the principal—the third in three years—rushed by. She apologized that she couldn't talk as she was heading to a meeting at central office about implementing a new program in the school. She said she would tell me more about it later, and with that, she was out the door.

That week, I saw little evidence of classroom teachers employing instructional strategies promoted by the school's reform program. Rather, I observed classes across all content areas where much instructional time was devoted to homework review, worksheets, copying information from a chalkboard, independent reading, and off-task conversation. The little time spent in direct instruction was interrupted frequently by messages over the intercom system, disciplinary actions, or other unrelated activities.

Late in the week, I attended an afterschool faculty-training session held by a representative of the school's reform program. Originally, the meeting was to be on Halloween but teachers complained, and thus, it had been rescheduled. Even so, only the principal and 6 teachers from a faculty of 27 attended. The presenter delayed starting the session for about 10 minutes in hopes that additional teachers would arrive. When no one else came, she distributed multiple handouts for the audience to read and discuss. The teachers snacked, read a little, and chatted among themselves. The principal left after she ate. Rather than focusing on the session's topic of persuasive writing strategies, much of the discussion digressed to a host of topics including recipes, Halloween costumes, regulations and scoring of writing portfolios required in the state's annual assessment, and other minimally or unrelated matters.

As the meeting drew on, I began to reflect back on the week. I had learned that assessment scores had declined, and with the blessing of the district, the principal already was entertaining the idea of another reform. I observed few signs of changed behavior or interest in the present reform program among teachers. The program's afterschool training session was poorly attended. Few faculty members came, the principal left early, and the school's program facilitator did not come at all. Teachers who attended showed little interest; rather, they were distracted by more pressing interests such as assessment standards. The presenter tolerated off-task conversation throughout most of the session. When considering the life course of the reform model in this school over the last several years, it seemed that nearly everyone I had encountered that week already had dismissed it as "another reform effort" that didn't stick.

Throughout my career, I have been fascinated with innovation and reform efforts in schools. Presenting a new policy, tool, or strategy into an educational setting and then watching how people respond to it, how it becomes defined by users over time, and how it affects users and schools is captivating to me. In this book, I focus on why and how practitioners embrace and sustain change rather than disregarding it and allowing it to fade away, as the school in this example.

Understanding school reform and its sustainability has held my attention for nearly two decades beginning with an examination of computer implementation in the mid-1980s when schools acquired desktop computers in record numbers. A new statewide policy enabled schools despite size, socioeconomic status, and urban or rural location to obtain reserves of computers. I followed the introduction and implementation of the technology over the next 10 years while dozens of educators shared with me their goals, frustrations, and visions for this innovation and its application in the classroom.

As I learned more about how teachers defined and used computers and the extent to which teaching was affected by the technology, I honed a sharp understanding regarding the implementation and the effects of this technological change in schools. I determined that despite the massive acquisition of computer technology in schools across the state, principals and teachers did not perceive it as useful to their jobs (Evans-Andris, 1996). Consequently, the extent to which it became integrated and sustained as an instructional tool was minimal. Moreover, its application in classrooms nationwide has not changed dramatically since that time (Cuban, 2001).

COMPREHENSIVE SCHOOL REFORM

In the 1990s, a new type of school reform at the national level caught the attention of educators, sociologists of education, and others. Funded by the federal CSR program, thousands of schools implemented schoolwide reform models over the last decade. Targeting Title I or high-poverty schools, particularly those identified as low performing, and serving all students rather than subgroups, an underlying notion is that schools will be more effective when they adopt a unified, coherent, whole-school approach to increase student and school performance, rather than adding fragmented programs or investing in personnel dedicated to small groups of students in pullout programs (Berends, 2000). Policymakers and reform model developers commonly assumed that users would embrace and integrate reform components into their daily work routines. Yet despite the potential for lasting improvement, outcomes involving whole-school reform in many schools have not have been widespread or sustained. In schools like the one described earlier, implementation appeared to be disrupted by any number of factors such as the succession of principals, the pressure of assessment, ineffective professional development linked to the reform program, disinterest or disenchantment of faculty, and the lure of newer reforms.

Indeed, as I learned more about CSR, its potential for spawning improvement intrigued me. The program infused struggling schools with additional funds, most of which went toward purchasing a research-based model for whole-school reform. I, like many others, wondered if improvement would take hold and, if so, how long it would last.

Even though the nature of the reform is fundamentally different, I applied what I had learned about the implementation and sustainability of instructional innovation with computer technology to begin asking new questions about the conditions necessary to effectively introduce, implement, and sustain school reform models in low-performing schools. What goals guided reform, and how was it supported at each level in the overarching structure of the education system? Who were the *champions of change*, and what strategies did they employ to promote, manage, and sustain reform efforts? What was the nature of teacher commitment during reform? What was the relationship between reform program implementation and patterns of school performance and student achievement over time? Finally, to what extent did schools prepare for and sustain improvement strategies after their federal funding for reform expired?

PURPOSE AND FOCUS OF THE BOOK

The purpose of this book is to deepen understanding and identify strategies to inform practice regarding the implementation, effects, and sustainability of reform that schools nationwide grapple with. Many of the questions I posed have gone unanswered or unexplained in the literature on school reform generally and the literature on whole-school reform specifically. To answer them, this book examines how one major federal educational improvement policy played out at the school level as educators shaped and sustained reform efforts. Using the CSR program as a case in point, the book explicitly describes and analyzes variations in experiences and outcomes linked to the following:

- Conditions leading schools to seek reform
- Characteristics of district contexts in which reform is implemented
- Patterns of leadership in reforming schools
- Ways that reform implementation affects teachers' work
- Factors contributing to schools' propensity to sustain improvement strategies

The examination of these issues as they relate to school reform provides insight about their effects on the school environment as well as on participants. Further, it lays the foundation of a conceptual model for sustaining reform that identifies what shapes the change process and contributes to sustained improvement.

This book addresses concerns and questions held by a wide range of educational stakeholders, such as state and district administrators and school practitioners who are engaged directly in reform efforts or contemplating reform, particularly with externally developed, whole-school models. Practically, it determines and makes recommendations about what districts and schools, along with state departments of education and reform developers, can do to enhance the potential of reform and its sustainability on the organizational climate of schools, the work of teachers, and the experiences of students. The book also addresses the interests of educational policymakers at the federal, state, and local levels who shape and fund policy directed at broad scale school reform.

The book features cases from the research that exemplify successful, strategic practice for educators seeking to improve and sustain change efforts in their schools and districts. These are summarized in the Recommendations for Educators section found in Chapter 8. From this, educators may develop more effective policies and practices involving reform implementation and management to optimize its lasting positive effects on schools, teachers' work, and the learning experiences of students.

At a more theoretical level, the book speaks to the concerns of scholars, researchers, and instructors of education, especially those interested in organizations, accountability, and reform, by examining the implementation and sustainability of change in schools to develop a more holistic model of reform sustainability at the K–12 level. It also offers a detailed methodology and discusses ethical and practical issues involving field research.

RESEARCHING REFORM SUSTAINABILITY IN SCHOOLS

Unlike most studies about school reform, this book provides an intimate detailed view of the microdynamics of reforming schools and reveals outcomes grounded in their day-to-day experiences. Quantitative research on reform readily identifies patterns and causal linkages or effects, but typically, it is not able to provide rich explanations about patterns of change or capture the decision-making processes that led to them. Few studies of CSR are qualitatively based or longitudinal, yet such a research methodology best addresses the questions and purpose guiding this book.

Thus, data collection for this study involved ethnographic data from extensive field observation, in-depth interviews, and document analysis in 18 CSR-funded schools over three years and quantitative analysis of a larger sample of 74 schools over six years. The study specifically considered factors including school organization and climate, leadership and support for change, and commitment and professional development in relations to the schools' propensity to implement reform strategies, realize gains, and sustain change. The schools were located in Kentucky, served a seventh-grade population and were identified in 1998 as low performing based on their index scores from the state testing system. The Kentucky experience provides an interesting case because, like many other states, it had exerted increasing standardization and pressures related to assessment and accountability but also provided various support systems that in some respects, may have poised schools for further assistance toward improvement with comprehensive school reform models.

The ethnographic portion of the study provides the basis for this book. Beginning in the 2001–2002 school year, the last year of the CSR three-year funding cycle, and again as a follow-up two years later, in the 2003–2004 school year, a full five years after schools had begun reform with CSR, my colleague, Wayne Usui, and I collected data in each of the 18 CSR-funded schools. We observed in classrooms and other areas around the school that promised to provide information pertaining to its reform experiences. We devoted extensive amounts of time in these settings and focused on patterns of model implementation in the school and classrooms, climate, leadership, attitudes of teachers and others toward reform, instructional practices and indications of model adoption and effects, and efforts toward sustainability.

We conducted in-depth interviews with principals, teachers, in-school program facilitators, district administrators, and other key informants, and then reinterviewed most of those respondents two years later, totaling more than 250 interviews. Respondents shared their accounts of how the school selected and gained a comprehensive reform model, how they viewed their role and the role of others in the process of change, how they went about implementing specific model components into their schools and work routines, and finally, how they arrived at decisions about whether the school would sustain reform efforts. They also discussed the lasting effects of the reform model on their work and teaching strategies. Analysis of the second wave of qualitative data enabled us not only to detect changes but also to capture the attitudes, sentiments, and reflections of educators about their experience. Importantly, it also provided the opportunity to make determinations about how schools decided whether to sustain improvement efforts involving a school reform program and with what outcomes. The study's multimethod design allowed us to collect and balance accounts from different stakeholders and decision makers and to compare patterns identified in the third year against those from the first. The Resource section provides a more in-depth account of the field methods. Though the findings are not generalizable, they may substantively and theoretically inform schools and districts elsewhere as they undertake improvement efforts related to promoting and sustaining reform.

ORGANIZATION OF THE BOOK

In contrast to schools like the one described earlier that demonstrated poor practices and seemed unlikely to sustain improvement efforts, it is more instructional and informative to examine schools that are changing for good—that is, schools that are sustaining reform efforts. The book highlights organizational conditions that led those schools to sustain their programs in their entirety or some aspects of the reform experience rather than dismiss them after the expiration of CSR funding. It traces their experiences as they selected, implemented, and continued reform efforts after the funded three-year period. Though patterns may vary, the book reveals that schools are more likely to consider reform efforts as a lasting part of the educational landscape when they have or develop (1) a state context that promotes reform; (2) district support for reform; (3) strong leadership distributed across administration and faculty; (4) commitment among teachers to their profession, to their school, and to improvement; and (5) a belief among users that their reform efforts are having a positive effect in the school. Taken together, these themes provide a sound basis for a model of introducing and sustaining school improvement, which will be presented in Chapter 1.

The book is organized around these themes. The first two chapters lay the contextual groundwork for examining school reform. Specifically, Chapter 1 discusses the challenges of implementing and sustaining school reform. It provides an overview of school reform policies at the national level over two decades, including CSR and No Child Left Behind, which attempted to move school improvement in coherent, integrated ways. It identifies goals, successes, and failures of these policies and raises questions pertaining to the potential sustainability of change in schools. The chapter then defines the concept of sustainability and considers factors that may promote lasting or sustainable improvement in schools. Chapter 2 moves the discussion of school reform to the state level. It establishes the context for reform by reviewing the state's educational infrastructure resulting from the previous reforms and its emphasis on high-stakes testing. It discusses how the state shaped the CSR program by structuring the proposal and adoption process. It then describes 18 CSR schools and the five whole-school reform models they implemented.

The next four chapters identify and discuss factors that led to dramatically different outcomes in terms of sustaining school improvement over time. Chapter 3 argues that active district support is critical to school reform and its sustainability. It highlights two districts that offered schools strategic support and wide-scale cooperation through budgeting assistance, strong leadership, technical expertise, and opportunities for networking and information sharing.

Chapter 4 maintains that distributed leadership is a key component of sustaining change in schools. It recognizes expertise and encourages meaningful input in decision making among educators who may or may not hold formal leadership roles in their schools. The chapter illustrates this by examining the roles of the principal, the program facilitator, and teacher leaders in two reforming schools, and concludes that schools promoting distributed leadership are more likely to engage in reform that endures.

Chapter 5 explores the ways schools successfully generate teacher commitment to sustained improvement and to enhance professional capacity. It traces the experiences of two schools to demonstrate effective strategies such as creating effective common planning time, gaining teacher input for purposes of goal setting and decision making, expanding and enhancing professional growth and leadership opportunities, and involving teachers in collaborative opportunities in and beyond the school.

Chapter 6 recognizes the importance of school performance in a period of heightened emphasis on federal- and state-imposed assessment and accountability standards but goes further to reveal important, qualitative ways schools benefited from the reform experience. The chapter identifies and discusses real and perceived gains in schools since the beginning of CSR funding. Several schools demonstrated growth on standardized test scores, leading them to believe their reform programs were working. Schools celebrated other positive effects or spillover associated with their CSR grant. The chapter concludes that educators' perceptions of gains linked to the reform experience reinforced their commitment to sustain school improvement and reform efforts.

Chapter 7 identifies four patterns exhibited by schools five years after their adoption of a whole-school reform, ranging from sustaining reform models with alternative funding to no sustainability, and explores the decision-making process that guided the schools. Finally, Chapter 8 explains how factors explored in previous chapters are linked to the four patterns of sustained school improvement. It presents a theoretical model for sustaining school reform that builds on the themes from the previous chapter. It discusses policy-related implications and presents substantive recommendations to maximize the effects of improvement efforts in schools and enhance the educational opportunities of students.

1

Sustaining Change in Schools

Our bone of contention in education is that they [educational decision makers] never keep things long enough to really improve before they switch gears again. It was hard to take mandates for change very seriously. The older teachers used to say, "Don't worry. This will only be around a couple of years and then they will do something else." But when we went into this reform, it helped knowing it was for a long term and that we had funding for at least a few years. It made teachers think, "Well, this is going to be around for a while." We took it more seriously.

—A classroom teacher

Sustaining reform efforts in schools has long posed a challenge to policymakers, educators, and others. Indeed, numerous innovative educational policies have been introduced over the last century but despite various attempts to improve schooling, organization, curricular content, and instructional strategies have remained relatively stable over time. Although history suggests that lasting change is difficult to achieve, there is little agreement about why reform efforts may fail to incorporate enduring improvements in schools or classrooms.

To understand the complexity of sustaining school reform, this chapter provides an overview of major reform policies in recent decades that have attempted to address educational improvement in a comprehensive, coherent fashion. It considers their impact and raises questions regarding the lasting effects of such measures. The chapter discusses the term *sustainability* and presents alternative explanations of what promotes sustainable change in schools. Finally, it proposes a model of sustainability that is fleshed out in the remainder of the book.

TWO DECADES OF REFORM POLICIES

Several important national school reform policies over the last 20 years continue to shape the educational landscape today. Beginning in the mid 1980s, in response to the highly critical report A Nation at Risk by the National Commission on Excellence in Education (1983), state governments immediately began more actively developing and strengthening educational policy for their jurisdictions. Changes established standards for improvement in curriculum and accountability and related miscellaneous areas such as instructional time, core requirements, and graduation standards (Desimone, 2002; Furney, Hasazi, Clark-Keefe, & Hartnett, 2003; Malen & Fuhrman, 1991). Typically, these state efforts reflected a piecemeal approach to school improvement and had little impact in changing either how teachers taught or what and how students learned.

Realization that increasing standards and regulations, like previous waves of reform, would not achieve broadscale upgrading of the educational system led policy analysts to argue that barriers stemming from fragmentation and incoherence characterizing educational policy *itself* likely prevented significant, lasting improvement in most schools (Malen & Fuhrman, 1991). Smith and O'Day (1991) assertively recommended that policymakers establish "coherent, progressive, long-term strategies to achieve challenging common goals and outcomes" (p. 237). Hence began a movement toward educational coherence through systemic reform that has continued since that time. Analysts and scholars envisioned such reform would necessitate a comprehensive approach to integrate change throughout the educational system. It would require the school to establish a central vision to unify common goals and efforts pertaining to teaching and learning. It would also depend on a talented, stable, and committed staff; rigorous curriculum; engaged students; and parent involvement. Accordingly, this would entail organizational change involving both top-down and bottom-up approaches, a shared vision of goals, instructional program coherence, and a restructured governance system (Newmann, Smith, Allensworth, & Bryk, 2001; Smith & O'Day, 1991).

Recognizing the potential of a systemic, coordinated approach to school reform, an education summit held in Charlottesville, Virginia, in 1989, established national education goals around which subsequent school improvement efforts could focus. These targeted improving (1) school readiness, (2) performance on international achievement tests (especially in math and science), (3) high school graduation rates, (4) adult literacy, (5) teacher quality, (6) safety and discipline in schools, and (7) workforce preparation (McAndrews, 2006). Shortly after this, in 1991, America 2000 was passed as a reform strategy to achieve those goals. The New American School (NAS) Development Corporation was founded as part of that initiative. This public-private partnership, funded by businesses and foundations, was charged with developing an innovative improvement model for schools that would address the national goals identified earlier and operate at relatively the same cost as traditional schools (McAndrews, 2006). To fulfill its mission of identifying break-the-mold innovative models for schools, it awarded $150 million during the 1990s for the development and dissemination of eight whole-school reform models. This represented a shift away from reform strategies developed in state or local educational agencies to coherent reform programs created and provided by groups or organizations outside these educational agencies.

The movement toward an integrated, holistic approach to school improvement was further reinforced through the Improving America's Schools Act (IASA) of 1994 (Goertz, 2005), a reauthorization of the Elementary and Secondary Education Act of 1965. State educational systems introduced a host of initiatives that reinforced educational resources, services, and decentralized decision making. For example, regional centers coordinated resources and assistance to districts and schools in their geographic areas and, in some cases, functioned as an information clearinghouse between state and local agencies. The formation of site-based councils localized decision making at the school level.

Components of Title I of the IASA called for states to expand their infrastructure of support for low-performing schools, particularly those with high concentrations of students who are at risk of low achievement and dropping out. Such schools historically are resilient to improvement strategies. In a review of research, Land and Legters (2002) identify individual and family at-risk indicators including poverty, race or ethnicity, limited English proficiency, low education of mother, and single-parent families. Based on similar indicators, Natriello, McDill, and Pallas (1990) estimated that at least 40% of children in the United States were at risk of school failure, and according to Lee and Burkam (2002) and a report released by the National Center for Educational Statistics (Lippman, Burns, & McArthur, 1996), this figure has increased since that time. When examining school performance as it relates to socioeconomic characteristics of students, research consistently finds that schools with high concentrations of students eligible for the free or reduced-cost lunch program (a commonly used proxy for socioeconomic status [SES]) have lower performance scores. Further, resources promoting high performance in schools are unevenly distributed. Specifically, when compared to high-SES schools, schools with high concentrations of poverty tend to have less funding, a less experienced and less qualified faculty, a less expansive and less rigorous curriculum, and so forth.

To better support low-performing and high-risk schools, assistance teams comprised of distinguished educators, personnel from state education agencies, and others formed to help schools with planning and instructional guidance. Many states were unsuccessful establishing support services in a timely fashion, whereas others already had such systems in place. Not surprisingly, some services had more impact that was positive on school improvement than others (Billig, 1997). A study of school support teams revealed great variation across states in the composition of teams, the degree to which they were operational, the way they functioned, and with what success. Some teams provided intensive, frequent assistance to schools, whereas others were far less functional and only remotely familiar with schools in their jurisdiction (Billig, Perry, & Pokorny, 1999).

Further, IASA broadened the application of Title I funds to support schoolwide projects in qualified schools, recognizing that the most effective improvement strategies provided services to whole schools rather than pullout services targeting individuals or classrooms (Billig, 1997; Desimone 2002; McAndrews, 2006). These efforts resulted in an expanded and integrated infrastructure to support schools with the common goal of guiding and reinforcing coherent, comprehensive school improvement.

Comprehensive School Reform

In 1998, the Obey-Porter Bill provided financial incentives through the comprehensive school reform ("CSR" as "demonstration" was later dropped from the title) program for schools, particularly Title I schools identified as being in the greatest need of improvement, to enhance student achievement by implementing CSR programs or models. Whole-school reform gained increased attention and momentum in part because of this program. In addition to the externally developed reform models sponsored earlier by NAS, the design and implementation of other whole-school reform programs proliferated. By the end of the 1990s, states had approved nearly 300 such models (Whitmore, 2000) and more than 10%of public schools nationwide had contracts for design-based assistance (Olson, 2000).

For nearly a decade, thousands of schools nationwide implemented schoolwide reform through the federally funded CSR program. To qualify for CSR funding, legislation stipulated that a reform model must integrate 9 components and then later added 2 other criteria for a total of 11 components. It must demonstrate (1) measurable goals and benchmarks for student achievement; (2) support by school faculty; (3) effective research-based methods and strategies; (4) a comprehensive design with aligned components; (5) professional development; (6) meaningful involvement of parents and the community; (7) external technical support and assistance;

(8) in-school support for faculty and staff; (9) a plan for the evaluation of implementation; (10) identification of how other resources will be used to coordinate, support, and sustain the school reform; and (11) strong evidence that it will improve the academic achievement of students. Cavell (2002) argues the success of the reform models does not depend on any one of these components but how they integrate to present a comprehensive plan for school improvement.

No Child Left Behind

Three years after the establishment of CSR, the No Child Left Behind Act (NCLB) of 2001 was passed representing a large-scale reform effort to improve the achievement of all students by assessing student performance, identifying gaps, and tracking progress toward the goal of reaching proficiency by 2014. The act also called for enhanced teacher quality in schools by requiring that all teachers be certified and teach *in field*. By targeting achievement, accountability, and teacher quality, NCLB was designed to promote further consistency and coherence among state policies.

Most notably, NCLB emphasizes assessment and accountability whereby achievement in reading and math is measured annually for students in Grades 3 through 8 and once in high school. Science achievement is tested less frequently. Then using those scores, achievement gaps based on poverty, race and ethnicity, special needs, and so forth are documented and the progress of each school toward its adequate yearly progress goal is tracked. Schools that repeatedly do not meet their progress goals may be identified as being in need of improvement and become subject to a host of strategies to reverse poor-performance or close achievement gaps (Karen, 2005).

Proponents commend NCLB because it requires states to collect and report data at the student level. This requirement draws attention to achievement gaps among subgroups so schools can promote learning for all students. This is especially important given the dramatic growth of minority populations in schools over the last 30 years. Most significantly, they argue that NCLB has promoted gains in student achievement and made progress in closing the achievement gaps between white and minority students (Fuller, Wright, Gesicki, & Kang, 2007).

On the other hand, opponents view NCLB as a questionable and burdensome federal mandate that requires public schools to comply with unrealistic regulations and requirements. NCLB's focus on assessment and accountability imposes a narrow lens on educational endeavors that may undermine real school improvement at the classroom level (Lewis, 2002; Whitford & Jones, 2000). Although the legislation assumes that states and districts have or can develop capacity in instructional, technical, and financial support to assist schools in their attempts toward improvement

(Goertz, 2005), critics argue otherwise. For example, the cost of annual testing alone poses staggering costs to states, even though the federal government subsidizes a portion of the expense. Further, states and districts do not have the human or fiscal resources to provide sufficiently for the increased number of schools that qualify for assistance under the NCLB guidelines (Goertz).

Finally, with careful analysis of trend data from 1971 to 2004, using scale scores from the National Assessment of Educational Progress (NAEP), researchers detected slight gains in reading among fourth graders in the late 1990s that flattened after NCLB. Scores for eighth graders remained relatively unchanged across time. Math scores for both grade levels showed modest increases but for twelfth graders remained flat and then actually dropped slightly in 2006. When comparing the NAEP scores of African American students against those of whites, the data reveal that the achievement gap narrowed from 1971 to 2002 but showed no further progress since then (Fuller et al., 2007). Because it has not resulted in gains in overall student achievement, has not made progress in closing the achievement gap, and does not build capacity for permanent improvement, Fullan (2005) charged that NCLB presents impossible goals, offers only temporary solutions, and is likely to fail.

Although much of the scrutiny surrounding NCLB has targeted its federal oversight, accountability mandates, performance sanctions, requirements for teacher quality, and lack of sufficient funding, other aspects of the legislation explicitly encourage schools to strengthen instruction and build capacity through rigorous research-based mechanisms for improvement (LeFloch, Taylor, & Thompson, 2005). Thus, interest in the effectiveness of whole-school reform models heightened as researchers determined whether they represented a viable opportunity for schools to implement externally developed, scientifically proven strategies in an integrated fashion to support progress toward proficiency. Initially, NCLB provided increased funding for CSR. In 2002, CSR was authorized as Title I, Part F, of the Elementary and Secondary Education Act when the CSR program and Title I came together under the same legislation. Its goals continued to focus on improvement for schools, particularly those considered low performing, high poverty, or high risk for other reasons. By 2002, nearly 6,000 schools nationally had received CSR funding. Of those, 70% were high poverty, 40% were Title I, and 25% were low performing (Borman, Hewes, Overman, & Brown, 2002).

Effectiveness of Comprehensive School Reform

The effectiveness of comprehensive or whole-school reform models on school performance and student achievement is widely debated. The early research traced the initial stages of whole-school reform dating from the 1990s and focused on identifying promising programs for scaling-up, which is the transition from pilot or test status affecting few schools to implementation on a large-scale basis across either regions or nationally (Ross, Sanders, & Stringfield, 1998). Some NAS models indeed represented valid opportunities for performance growth in schools, but determinations about the effectiveness of others were compromised because of methodological inconsistencies and researcher bias (Pogrow, 2000).

The next phase researched the first cohort of schools that received funding in 1999 through the federal CSR program. It focused largely on the relationship of reform model adoption to school performance or student achievement. The findings of that research were mixed. Some studies revealed that the models had positive effects on school performance generally or on individual curricular-content areas specifically (Berends, 2000; Kirby, Berends, & Bodilly, 2002; Slavin, 2002), whereas others concluded that, in fact, few of the existing reform models demonstrated strong evidence of effectiveness through rigorous research (Pogrow, 2002; Whitmore, 2000; Zhang, Shkolnik, & Fashola, 2005). Few studies found a significant relationship between CSR and gains in school performance. Those that did commonly determined that effects of the models were small and limited to improvement in only one or two content areas. In seeking explanations for those findings, research then began exploring more intently the experiences of CSR-funded schools over time, beginning with model adoption through the three years of federally funded program implementation.

Whether schools implementing the reform models show gains is tied to intensity or how much the model's strategies are used, which, in turn, is affected by patterns of introduction, model adoption, and the faculty's fidelity to the model (that is, how closely they follow the model's guidelines and strategies). Improvement also varies based on duration or number of years of implementation in the school setting. Zhang et al. (2005) examined student achievement in math and reading as it related to reform model implementation and found that student achievement in CSR schools was lower compared to non-CSR schools in the first three years. During that time, students in CSR schools made greater gains, particularly in math, but not at a significant level. However, once the researchers controlled for intensity and duration of implementation (three to five years) they found that achievement in CSR schools was greater relative to the comparison schools. In another study, researchers tracking the effects of a whole-school reform model for up to five years in one school district found that by the fifth year, the effects on math gains had diminished and the effects for reading reversed from positive to negative (May & Supovitz, 2006; May, Supovitz, & Perda, 2004).

Only recently has the literature begun to address issues of sustainability of such reform efforts (Datnow, 2005; Evans-Andris & Usui, 2004b; Taylor, 2005). How does a school determine whether it is willing or able to continue to use a whole-school reform model once external funding expires? What support is necessary for schools to finance the reform models or otherwise continue to practice reform strategies consistent with those models? What patterns of leadership are effective to prepare and enhance the ability of teachers and others to sustain change? What factors contribute to a faculty's propensity to sustain reform efforts? Finally, to what extent do strategies characterizing comprehensive reform models persist in schools after federal funding expires? This book addresses these and other related questions.

SUSTAINING REFORM

Change in schools is considered sustained when it persists, endures over time, and has an ongoing effect on classroom practices (Berman & McLaughlin, 1978; Datnow, 2005). Datnow (2005) notes sustainable change requires consideration of contextual factors beyond the school itself, specifically those characterizing the state and district. She and others maintain that districts reinforce its continuation when they make decisions and design strategies to incorporate the change into standard operating procedures relating to budget, personnel, instructional programs, and facilities planning. When this occurs, the change becomes established or *institutionalized*; that is, it achieves both classroom assimilation and district incorporation (Datnow, 2005; Berman & McLaughlin, 1978).

Commonly, it is assumed that successful innovations are self-sustaining. However, in reality, continuation more likely is tenuous, even among programs that show instructional effectiveness. As long ago as the mid 1970s, a RAND study, commonly referred to as the Change Agent Study, examined the implementation and sustainability of nearly 300 federally funded projects in schools over four years and demonstrated that the adoption of projects did not ensure successful implementation. Further, the successful implementation of projects did not guarantee continuation of change over time (Berman & McLaughlin, 1978). Fullan's (2005) account of a more recent large-scale reform effort in England revealed similar findings. Schools showed significant gains in the first three years of implementation, but these were not sustained at an acceptable level after that.

Like other innovations in schools, most studies pertaining to whole-school reform or CSR-funded programs find that most often they are not sustained and are even less likely to become institutionalized. Reports show that attempts toward sustainability of reform models range from 25% to 35% of schools (Datnow & Stringfield, 2000; Evans-Andris & Usui, 2004b; Taylor, 2005). In research involving the implementation of whole-school reform models in nearly 400 schools, Taylor (2005) found that about one-third of the schools discontinued a relationship with their reform model provider within three years. Further, when schools were sorted based on reform trajectories by years of implementation, he found that 35% of schools institutionalized the change. Yonezawa and Stringfield

(2000) tracked eight schools over eight years and determined that only three had continued to sustain school improvement strategies to the extent that they were approaching *full institutionalization* of those reform efforts. Consistent with reform efforts in previous decades, these early findings demonstrate that although models touting comprehensive reform may exist in thousands of our nation's schools, improvement, particularly that which is lasting, is more elusive.

ORGANIZATIONAL CAPACITY AND SUSTAINING CHANGE IN SCHOOLS

This book seeks to determine what aspects of the reform process promote sustainable change in schools and identify ways of introducing and shaping change in schools organizationally to optimize the possibility of its sustainability. Although some aspects of schools follow more traditional patterns, it is also useful to consider those aspects that make them unique from other organizations. In fact, Ingersoll (2003) and Tyack and Cuban (1995) argue that many reforms fail because they do not consider this. The literature identifies factors associated with effective organizations to include strong leadership (Fullan, 2005), worker commitment (Ingersoll, 2003), and a climate conducive to innovation and improvement (Kanter, 1983). As they fend off pressure to change and innovate, researchers attribute the underlying stability of schools to increased bureaucratization (Bidwell, 2001), the organizational need for legitimacy (Meyer & Rowan, 1977), the loosely coupled administrative arrangement (Weick, 1976) between the technical or teaching core and the administrative core, or the social isolation of teachers (Lortie, 1975). Ingersoll (2003) examines the paradox of workplace conditions related to the professionalizing status of teachers and factors such as autonomy that contribute to their job satisfaction in the face of pressures exerted from organizational control and accountability.

The chances of a reform surviving increase when educators perceive it to be relevant and effective in addressing their organizational circumstances, concerns, and needs. Indeed, reforms commonly undergo some modification on their implementation as users adapt or tailor them to fit their setting (Datnow, 2005; Slavin, 2008). Datnow, Hubbard, and Mehan (2002) describe how teachers socially constructed the meaning of their schools' reform programs by adapting them to accommodate organizational constraints such as scheduling and staffing and to make them more consistent with their pedagogical views. Effective reform modification and adaptation depend on the extent to which schools give "voice" to their faculties and respect their professional autonomy, decision-making capacity, and problem-solving ability. However, Bidwell (2001) argues that increased bureaucratization has insulated schools from instructional change by constraining innovative informal problem-solving networks among teachers in which effective modification of reform might develop.

Reform must target change at the curricular and instructional levels to take hold, produce positive gains, and survive (Desimone, 2002; Newmann et al., 2001; Smith & O'Day, 1991). Newmann et al. argue that effective reform promotes coherence in instructional programs that is "guided by a common framework for curriculum, instruction, assessment, and learning climate and that is pursued over a sustained period" (p. 299). Schools must also become *learning organizations* to support classroom teachers as they seek to improve their instructional practices. Learning organizations, according to Giles and Hargreaves (2006), are schools marked by innovative structures and processes that promote professional capacity of teachers and enable them to respond effectively to changing external conditions. The teachers described at the beginning of the introduction to this book balked at attending a training session. That it was held after school, poorly attended, and delivered in a mediocre, mundane way may have contributed to its ineffectiveness. Most teachers likely perceived it to be irrelevant to their needs and concerns in the classroom. Darling-Hammond and McLaughlin (1995) explain that high-quality professional development provides classroom teachers with effective methods, materials, and knowhow. It bolsters knowledge sharing and critical inquiry among teachers. This, coupled with school support, will produce reflective and responsive instructional practices and success for diverse learners. Yet innovative professional development and other mechanisms that help teachers not only cope with but also thrive under conditions of change commonly are absent (Lieberman, 1995). Schools become successful learning organizations when they provide high-quality professional development, support information sharing among communities of practice (Coburn & Russell, 2008; Darling-Hammond & McLaughlin, 1995; Giles & Hargreaves, 2006), redefine the traditional roles of principals and teachers (Spillane, Halverson, & Diamond, 2001), and promote opportunities for active learning (Garet, Porter, Desimone, Birman, & Yoon, 2001).

Finally, change must build capacity at all levels to be sustained. Reform involving systemic change throughout the entire educational arena including the state, the district, the reform program providers, the school leadership, and the classroom teachers has the greatest chance of survival. Borman, Carter, Aladjem, & Le Floch (2004) define capacity as the ability of the stakeholders to "undertake transformative school improvement efforts" (p. 114) and note that it is not evenly distributed across districts and schools. Fullan (2005) maintains that reform programs commonly fail to take hold largely because *whole-system* capacity has not been built into the system of change. He argues that the commitment to and development of a culture of reform throughout the entire system is critical to the quest for continuous and sustainable improvement in schools. The various dimensions of change presented here all point to the need to view reform and its sustainability in a more holistic, systemic, integrated way.

TOWARD A MODEL OF SUSTAINABILITY

The failure of past reforms to significantly improve educational systems illuminates the need for a clearer understanding of how intense efforts to change may lead schools to sustain improvement over time. Taken together the arguments suggest that reform has the greatest chance of succeeding when it is carefully planned, managed, and otherwise supported throughout the educational system. Maximizing organizational capacity will increase the likelihood of sustaining change. This points to a conceptual model of reform sustainability comprised of five components. First, reform must be embedded in a sound organizational infrastructure that provides a supportive atmosphere and actively promotes a common direction for change by integrating rather than isolating various improvement efforts. Schools also must have district leadership and support, effective leadership at the school level that promotes rather than restricts the professional autonomy and capacity of teachers and teacher commitment that is reinforced by effective professional development. Finally, educators must believe that what they are doing is working. In other words, they must perceive that their efforts are having a positive effect. I discuss each of these next.

1. State Infrastructure

A sound state infrastructure establishes a supportive context for lasting improvement at the school level. The state educational agency establishes a vision for change and frames externally initiated reform policy ways that increase its potential to address that vision (Smith & O'Day, 1991). It becomes knowledgeable about various strategies to improve curriculum, instruction, and accountability efforts already underway in districts and schools and shares that knowledge with them. It provides support for improvement in a coherent, integrated fashion by establishing and availing financial and technical resources to reinforce the efforts of districts and schools. Finally, it facilitates school improvement in a manner that respects and further enhances the decision-making capacity of the local educational agencies.

2. District Support

Districts may provide or reinforce organizational capacity in schools by providing leadership and support for sustainability of change. The district may also incorporate or establish strategic procedures related to budgeting, personnel issues, resources, instructional programs, professional development, and so forth (Berman & McLaughlin, 1978; Fullan, 2005; MacIver & Farley-Ripple, 2008). They may also facilitate a network of support and information sharing among reforming schools and others, which is essential for lasting improvement (Moffett, 2000). Finally, districts may protect, buffer, and support schools as they face demands emanating from other sources such as the state and community levels that inhibit growth, innovative practice, and the sustainability of improvement measures (Datnow, 2005; Louis, Febey, & Schroeder, 2005).

3. School Leadership

Strong organizational leadership, particularly when it is distributed at all levels, may be a fundamental ingredient promoting sustainability of change (Fullan, 2001, 2005; Newmann et al., 2001; Spillane, Halverson, & Diamond, 2001). Principals are a critical source for such leadership, and schools may rely on faculty "champions" (Beath, 1991; Evans-Andris, 1996; Kanter, 1983) to actively promote coherent, sustainable change and lasting innovative behavior. Schools able to develop and recognize distributed leadership may be more likely to cultivate teacher commitment to reform efforts that endures over time.

4. Faculty Commitment

Strong leadership may promote worker buy-in or commitment during the innovative process, which is critical to the success of organizational change (Kanter, 1983). Further, studies reveal that participation in decision making in ways that affect the school increases teacher satisfaction (Ingersoll, 2001). Even so, the relatively high level of autonomy (Becker, 1970; Bidwell, 1965; Hanson, 1981; Lortie, 1975), loose coupling among teachers and school administrations (Weick, 1976), and growth of the administrative core (Bidwell, 2001) demand careful consideration of the ways teachers shape their workplace and the degree of support and commitment they may demonstrate throughout the implementation process (Daft & Becker, 1978; Hanson, 1981; Hargreaves, 1994; Hodson, 1991; Lipsky, 1980).

Related to faculty commitment is professional development. Change in schools necessitates a rethinking about the ways teachers teach and students learn (Whitford & Jones, 2000). In this context, teachers are encouraged to be *reflective practitioners* (Schon, 1987) who establish and build a tacit knowledge base through ongoing inquiry and analysis (Lieberman & Miller, 1990). Professional development is most effective when it is content based, offers strong pedagogical strategies, and provides opportunities for educators to develop professional communities and then build on that culture of support in and across schools for peer learning and information sharing (Coburn & Russell, 2008; Johnson et al., 2004; Lieberman & Miller, 1990; Little, 1993). Reform programs that garner commitment, facilitate and enhance opportunities for professional development, and promote quality learning experiences are most likely to be sustained.

5. Gains—Perceived and Real

Reform efforts that render gains may positively reinforce organizational tendencies for sustainable change. A fundamental premise of assessment and accountability systems is that standardized achievement scores reflect educational performance and school quality. Ingersoll (2003) points out that test scores are presumed to be a best measure to evaluate the effects of school characteristics on organizational effectiveness. They are often used at the expense of other gains such as increases in school climate, improved social relations, the acquisition of innovative instructional strategies, and student engagement (Desimone, 2002; Ingersoll, 2003). Reform efforts may be sustained when educators perceive a link between those efforts and gains including increased student achievement as well as others that are defined more broadly, such as improved school climate, the acquisition of effective instructional strategies, and additional positive spillover effects.

School reform should be viewed as an innovative process that will be most successfully implemented and sustained when the organizational structure and occupational climate of schools is conducive to change and innovation. This requires a strong state infrastructure, district support, school leadership that spans traditional boundaries, high faculty commitment coupled with effective professional development, and a positive school climate that recognizes and celebrates gains realized by reform efforts.

The next chapters begin to unravel the complexity surrounding the issue of reform sustainability by examining the CSR experience in Kentucky schools. The CSR program funded whole-school reform to penetrate and improve the performance of schools serving many students who were at risk of low achievement and dropping out. Even so, high-risk, low-performing schools most eligible for reform may be least likely to demonstrate the organizational characteristics identified in this chapter. Understanding how these factors play out differently in schools is critical to understanding the potential for lasting effects of reform efforts. Chapter 2 defines the state infrastructure and context for school improvement.

2

Setting the Stage for School Reform

When you look at the whole system, with everything that is going on in our state to support schools, I don't see any reason for schools to backslide. Comprehensive school reform (CSR) should be a vehicle for schools to improve, and the state is expecting schools to continue this progress long after CSR funding. We have so much to help schools here. It has always been our intention with this reform program that low-performing schools will have support. The state is really focused on building capacity in the district and school. That to me is the reason there shouldn't be any failures.

—State education administrator

When schools contemplate the adoption of improvement measures, it is important first to consider how external conditions or influences may shape their efforts. Several factors outside the local school system may affect the change process. These include the extent to which the state educational agency (SEA) provides an infrastructure to support change, how it shapes the reform process, and the compatibility of the reform's goals with the culture, priorities, and needs of local schools. Defining the state educational context in which schools pursue reform measures is essential to understanding the process of improvement.

This chapter begins by reviewing the infrastructure of support and context for reform established by Kentucky's SEA. Against this backdrop, it then examines how the SEA structured the CSR movement. It also describes the reform models and their aspects that were salient to school decision makers. The chapter determines that the state structured the initial phases of reform adoption to poise schools for improvement in ways that involved administrators and teachers in decision making by requiring them to identify goals, generate faculty buy-in, and select reform programs they believed would address their priorities.

Increasingly, as systemic reform expands, SEAs are called on to build educational capacity in districts and schools and facilitate change at the local level. In this context, Lane and Gracia (2004) identified four ways that SEAs affected the implementation of the federal CSR program in their jurisdictions. These included whether states integrated funds and supports with other initiatives for improvement, the amount of funding provided to reforming schools, SEA leadership capacity as indicated by turnover and shifts in state personnel overseeing the reform program, and support strategies provided to schools prior to and during reform implementation. Their premise was the more consistent input of SEAs, the higher implementation would be in schools.

The most promising support strategies of SEAs encourage educators at the local level to participate in meaningful decision making, that is, make decisions that shape their actions at work or the direction in which their workplace is moving. Participation in decision making allows workers to be an active part of the organization and may increase their sense of esteem and empowerment. Teacher participation in decision making contributes to a more positive school climate, greater job satisfaction, and ultimately, results in higher retention (Ingersoll, 2001). Desimone (2002), Borman, Hewes, Overman, and Brown (2002), and others point out that teacher participation in decision making is integral to the adoption and implementation of improvement strategies and the success of school change, including change involving CSR. Further, in a RAND study examining the experiences of schools over the years of whole-school reform implementation, Berends, Bodilly, & Kirby (2002b) found that teachers were more likely to understand the reform process and achieve higher levels of implementation when they felt they had gone through a well-informed decision-making process about their school's participation in the proposal and selection of a reform model.

The adoption of a reform model involves both information gathering and decision making (LeFloch, Zhang & Herrmann, 2005). Engaging teachers in the mission of information gathering and fact finding prompts them to take an active part in generating choices from which they can determine the most promising action. Once viable options are identified, teachers can express their preferences through a democratic voting process to demonstrate faculty buy-in. In theory, a vote of support reflects a faculty's willingness to adopt and use a certain reform model, to allocate school resources to it, and to modify the school's staffing structure when necessary to accommodate requirements of the program. Underlying the notion of buy-in is the premise that teachers perceive a need for change to begin with (Cotner, Hermann, Borman, Boydston, & LeFloch, 2005; Muncey & McQuillan, 1996). A longitudinal study of CSR over five years found that the voting process can contribute to higher levels of program implementation (LeFloch Taylor, & Thompson, 2005). However, this sign of buy-in is not always legitimate (Datnow, 2000).

Further, although successful reform implementation requires strong teacher input and support (Borman et al., 2002), Datnow and Castellano (2000) found that the level of initial support of teachers did not guarantee their fidelity to the reform model they selected. Although reasons for this are not explicitly addressed in their study, it may be that characteristics of the reform model itself explain, in part, the difference between initial support for reform and subsequent fidelity to a reform model. For example, Borman et al. (2002) found that models having prescriptive designs, effective professional development, and support or follow-up by model providers were implemented at higher levels and commonly showed greater effects, whereas in another study, Newmann, Smith, Allensworth, and Bryk (2001) observed that reform strategies lacking instructional coherence were more likely to fail because they diffused faculty attention, enthusiasm, and effort. These studies suggest that a reform program's characteristics in relation to the unique needs, goals, and concerns of a school can influence outcomes. SEAs that provide relevant information about program characteristics to schools may improve their decision making during reform adoption.

Certainly, it seems that the state context may affect how reform is implemented and with what success. The state further may shape the reform process by the degree it actively provides support and direction to districts and schools as they undertake change. Finally, the features characterizing reform models may alter their compatibility with various school cultures and, thus, affect their capacity for change. The following section frames the educational infrastructure in Kentucky by reviewing practices related to the Kentucky Education Reform Act.

SCHOOL REFORM AND STATE INFRASTRUCTURE

Consistent with the standards-based movement occurring nationwide in the late 1980s, Kentucky began shaping legislation that provided the structural foundation for school reform. The state pushed beyond the call for curriculum standards to promote a broader systemic reform that resulted in the Kentucky Education Reform Act (KERA) of 1990, hailed by some policy analysts as the most comprehensive and far-reaching state-mandated education reform effort of recent decades (Pankratz & Petrosko, 2000). KERA called for new funding and recast education finance, governance, and curriculum in the state. It included a raft of instructional changes and additional supports such as extended school services, regional service centers, and family resource and youth service centers in schools serving high-poverty populations. Site-based decision-making school councils were formed. In theory, components of the reform plan would work together, in an integrated fashion, to buttress a new statewide system of education (hence, *systemic* reform). KERA represented a significant, nonincremental policy change in that it demanded comprehensive rather than piecemeal outlooks and was characterized by indivisibility in the political commitment and resources it required for success (Clements, 1998).

High-Stakes Testing

KERA also abandoned the state's standardized testing approach in favor of a new, performance-based assessment program that would better gauge student progress toward learning goals the state would set, and would be tied to an accountability system of rewards and sanctions for schools and districts. KERA architects asserted that performance-based assessments, combined with well-articulated outcome goals for different subjects and grade levels, and a robust, state-generated (but locally tailored) curriculum framework, which yielded school level scores tied to financial rewards and state sanctions, would adequately drive the statewide reform effort. They designed a high-stakes, *milepost-testing* system (Stecher & Barron, 2001) where certain subjects would be tested at selected grades. For example, seventh graders are tested in reading, writing, and science, whereas eighth graders are tested in math, social studies, and humanities/practical living.

The first assessment and accountability system under KERA borrowed heavily from the National Assessment of Educational Progress (NAEP) approach to testing, which combined a few multiple-choice questions with many open-ended response questions, as well as multiple assessment forms, such as writing portfolios. Educators worked with testing contractors to set performance standards for students, such that all test scores would be categorized as novice, apprentice, proficient, and distinguished—and the goal would be for all schools eventually to have children reach the proficient level. Student-level test results were aggregated to the school level and, in two-year cycles, were fed—along with nonacademic information—by formula into an accountability index. The index score was then used to indicate school improvement, which would be rewarded or penalized. Based on the school index score, a state goal was established that all schools would reach proficiency, indicated by an index score of 100, by 2014 (Poggio, 2000). However, KERA's first assessment and accountability system lacked vigorous statewide curricular guidance to ground it and left schools to struggle toward improvement on their own. Not until 1996 was the Kentucky Core Content for Assessment established to identify key concepts across course content areas that children would be tested on. After that, curricular alignment with core content expectations and testing began to occur (Clements, 2000).

In 1998, the assessment and accountability approach was revamped. The heart of the new system was the Kentucky Core Content Tests (KCCT), which retained the open-response, performance-based features of the previous system but also included multiple-choice questions from national norm-referenced tests. A new accountability index was generated, and schools had new baseline scores set. Through these and related changes, the Commonwealth Accountability Testing System (CATS) was designed to provide a more valid and reliable set of measurement tools for determining school progress (Poggio, 2000). Even so, rather than promoting promising new instructional practices as some aspects of KERA were designed to do, critics charge that the high-stakes assessment and accountability system undermines educational innovation and improvement by encouraging teachers to focus on teaching strategies such as test-taking skills to increase school accountability index scores (Whitford & Jones, 2000).

Low-Performing Schools

Under CATS, schools that scored below a minimum threshold on the accountability index and showed little progress toward meeting improvement goals over a two-year measurement cycle were identified as *low performing* and became eligible for certain resources to improve performance, such as additional funding and the assignment of a highly skilled or distinguished educator. A highly skilled educator (HSE) supports improved teaching and learning in schools through a number of strategies, such as building capacity among faculties, helping them to align curriculum with core content, and advising them on techniques to meet improvement goals on the accountability index, development of school improvement plans, and expenditures of money for school improvement. Low-performing schools also were subject to a *scholastic audit*, a procedure to scrutinize practices in the school and provide recommendations for school improvement measures. Finally, these schools had to submit a transformation plan about how they intended to improve.

After nearly a decade of school reform efforts under KERA, the performance of a great number of Kentucky public schools continued to be disappointing. For example, of the approximately 350 schools serving middle-grade students then, nearly 80 schools were low performing. Those schools were targeted for federal funding and additional reform assistance through the newly legislated CSR program.

OPPORTUNITY FOR IMPROVEMENT THROUGH COMPREHENSIVE SCHOOL REFORM

In 1998, the Kentucky Department of Education (KDE) notified approximately 140 schools of their eligibility to apply for funding for school improvement through the federal CSR program because of their low-performance status based on their 1996 through 1998 average index score on the state assessment and accountability system. Each school was invited to send representatives to an orientation meeting held by KDE to learn about the program, various whole-school reform models, and proposal procedures. This section discusses the decisions confronting schools as they determined whether to decline the opportunity for school improvement or pursue funding for a reform model.

Opting Out of Reform

Despite the additional funding that the CSR awards represented, many low-performing schools opted out of this new opportunity for improvement. Of approximately 75 schools serving middle-grade populations invited to pursue funding for reform through the grant application process, roughly 40 declined. The personnel at KDE charged with overseeing the grant application process hoped that schools would realize broadscale improvement resulting from the implementation of whole-school reform programs purchased with the federal funds. They found the low-response rate among eligible schools particularly troublesome. One former KDE employee recalled, "It bothered us that a number of eligible schools didn't even make an effort to apply. In one sense, it worked to our advantage in that we didn't have the problem of rejecting many schools. At the same time, however, the fact that they didn't have the wherewithal or the motivation to go ahead and seek this opportunity likely was indicative of why they had performance problems."

Principals who opted out of the application process reported they anticipated it would be an arduous proposal procedure or their schools did not have a realistic chance of winning a grant. One principal's observations also confirmed this. She explained that an information meeting held by KDE was well attended in the morning, but during lunch, she overheard many comments like, "We can make it on our own," or "We aren't going to do all this work." Attendance at the afternoon's session was reduced by more than half, suggesting that some participants lost interest in the prospect for school improvement as they learned more about the technicalities of the federal program and application process.

A survey conducted in rural schools across four south central states (including Kentucky) found that more than half of schools eligible for CSR funds did not apply because they were unaware of the program, application process, or particular models that would meet the needs of their school. Principals cited barriers including lack of resources such as qualified staff and time to prepare a proposal (Leopold, Childers, & Hawley-Rowe, 2000). Contradicting those findings, this study revealed that KDE gave schools the opportunity to become well informed about the CSR program and the more viable models to select from. Nevertheless, slightly more than half of eligible schools chose not to submit an application because of lack of interest or the work it would entail. They hoped to avoid investing time and energy in a process they perceived would not pay off with a CSR award. It is also likely that by resisting the push to apply for funding some schools hoped to protect their faculties from work overload. Clearly, the awards were not a sufficient incentive to entice these schools into the reform process.

The decision to decline the chance for funding was not always well received by district superintendents, and as a result, several schools admitted they begrudgingly submitted an application for reform primarily to appease their district administrators. A principal of one rural school who deliberately had declined the proposal process was contacted by her district superintendent and urged to submit an application. She remembered, "My superintendent wanted us to apply. Her thinking was, 'Okay, if you fall back into a scholastic audit, where is any documentation that you even tried? They are offering you $50,000 in a grant for school improvement and you are not even applying?'" Then, rolling her eyes, the principal continued, "The superintendent said, 'I am not *telling* you to apply, I am just telling you it would be *good management* for you to apply even though you may not get it.'" A similar circumstance occurred in another district where a principal explained that because of low test scores and lack of money, the school was expected to apply for *any* grant it might be eligible for. She said, "First of all, we were an embarrassment to our county because of low CATS scores. Our superintendent was very unhappy with us and told us, 'You *will* write a grant application.' So we decided, 'Okay, we will write a grant proposal.'"

Clearly, it seems that in schools such as these, administrators succumbed to top-down pressure to apply for federal funding exerted by their superintendents. It was their job to make sure that schools in their jurisdiction appeared concerned about school improvement despite their underlying intentions for implementing a reform program. This is consistent with Meyer and Rowan (1977), who argue that organizations engage in certain activities for the sole purpose of generating legitimacy in the broader community, on which their survival depends. Independent of effectiveness, such actions can promote a perception that an organization is "appropriate, rational, and modern" (p. 344) even when the link between those actions to outcomes may be unclear or absent altogether. By challenging low-performing schools to pursue federal funding even if they did not intend to change, superintendents could claim that their districts' schools actively were taking measures to improve and, thus, satisfy public concerns regarding quality of schooling in the community.

Poising for Reform

Unlike the schools described earlier, a substantial number of schools expressed genuine interest in reform and viewed CSR funding as a meaningful opportunity for improvement. Schools began poising for reform by preparing grant proposals that entailed establishing goals for change, shopping for a comprehensive school reform model that fit the needs of the school, and demonstrating faculty support or buy-in. Each is discussed next.

Establishing Goals for Change

As part of the proposal, KDE required schools to identify and outline a detailed explanation of measurable goals for reform. Goals that are clear, identifiable, and attainable can reinforce worker commitment and lead to higher implementation of change (Brewer & DeLeon, 1983; Wagner & Hollenbeck, 1995). Typically, schools identified goals that reflected the components required for programs to be recognized as CSR models. For example, nearly every proposal stated goals pertaining to professional development and parental and community involvement. Not surprisingly, the overriding goal among most schools was to improve scores on CATS. Some schools stipulated rather lofty goals such as a 100% improvement rate on grade-level standards across all subjects, whereas others set more realistic, attainable goals such as a specific yearly increase in targeted content areas, particularly reading and math.

Levin (2006) notes that in the 1990s, borrowing from successful business practice, it was common for schools to establish visions, mission statements, and goals the entire school community could embrace. Schools often met this obligation by creating mission statements without giving much thought to how they would be fulfilled. Levin wrote, "The focus on vision was understood as a procedural demand in the cultures of these schools, where such demands were typically experienced in compliance with routines rather than commitment to a set of deeper changes" (p. 41). Consistent with Levin's observation, in this study, to meet the stipulation of the proposal for CSR, it is likely some schools simply established goals for change that aligned with the components required of the programs, much as they would create a wish list, without considering what action they would need to take to achieve those goals.

Besides these goals, in retrospect, some administrators admitted that they held a hidden agenda that entailed more opportunistic, practical goals such as acquiring money for the school to increase school resources and materials. For example, a principal of a rural middle school explained that he promised his staff new equipment if they were awarded a CSR grant. During the grant period, his school, along with many others, acquired new calculators, electric microscopes, globes and maps, new textbooks, and other supplies. As long ago as the 1970s, the RAND Change Agent Study on implementing and sustaining innovations in schools found that some school districts pursued federal grants to infuse their schools or districts with additional funding rather than for school improvement. Not surprisingly, researchers found that opportunistic projects were poorly implemented and terminated when funding expired (Berman & McLaughlin, 1978).

Shopping for Models

Once schools set goals, they began shopping for a CSR model that would best meet their needs for goal attainment and school improvement. Guides assisted them in making their choices, the most prominent of which was *An Educators' Guide to Schoolwide Reform* (Herman et al., 1999). Based on a review of research pertaining to 24 models, the guide included pertinent information and ratings so schools could compare and contrast each model based on various characteristics, such as the grade levels that the program targeted, its effects on student achievement, its cost, provider support, and so forth. Even so, a review of research involving more than 130 studies of student achievement conducted by the American Institutes for Research (AIR) found only 3 of the 24 schoolwide reform models listed in the *Educators' Guide* demonstrated strong evidence of raising student achievement (Herman et al., 1999). Further, few models in the guide specifically targeted the needs of middle-grade populations.

Besides the *Educators' Guide*, KDE developed and distributed its own listing of potential models. State workers contacted model providers to determine whether the companies represented viable choices based on their geographic focus or willingness to serve schools in the state. In that way, they reduced the options to a manageable number without imposing other criteria, such as quality or reputation. A KDE employee stated, "Even though a group of people working on the project questioned some of the programs as to whether they were really appropriate for our schools, my contention was that it was not our decision to make. If they met the general criteria, the decision was up to the school." KDE expanded its information base by assembling and sending teams to visit programs operating in other states with which it was not familiar. The employee recalled, "We managed to see quite a few programs and developed a nucleus of information that enabled us to field questions as schools inquired about various models."

Finally, KDE encouraged principals to assemble selection committees to examine the suitability of various reform models for meeting their schools' needs. Indeed, many principals formed teams comprised of administrators and concerned faculty members and sometimes parents or community representatives. Others appointed preexisting committees to function as a selection committee. Several organized teams of shoppers traveled to schools in nearby districts or neighboring states to observe them using models of interest. After selection teams researched the models, they made recommendations about their suitability. A teacher described her school's screening process, "We are on teams in the middle school, and one potential model was given to each team to investigate. We got on the Internet and telephoned people who were using that model, and then we met again as a faculty for each team to present their model. Then we voted."

Despite the democratic pattern promoted at the state level, several districts attempted to influence model selection in schools. In some cases, they succeeded. One administrator recalled, "We went to the information meetings. They gave us a book that listed out all the programs and all the choices. Even so, we were sort of told by the powers that be in our district, 'We want you to write for this particular program, and we want you to get this one.'" Similarly, in one or two schools, the process was also more closed than open. For example, a faculty member recalled his school's selection committee, "In reality, it may have been a committee of one, that being the principal."

Clearly, identifying a suitable reform model was not a quick or straightforward process. Most schools invested a great deal of time and money to sponsor selection teams to travel to various other sites in the broader geographic region to observe a model in action. Many faculty members, particularly those in small schools, recollected that the proposal process was extremely taxing on their time and resources. They found the process interesting but also distracting because of attending training meetings, shopping for models, preparing proposals, and demonstrating faculty buy-in.

In their examination of the input of seven SEAs early in the CSR movement, Lane and Gracia (2004) found that many states held model showcases to expose schools to the reform models available for implementation. However, they found this was not effective because marketing presentations by model providers tended to exaggerate the actual capabilities and strategies of their models. Thereafter, SEAs prompted schools to assess their needs, explore a range of models suited to those needs, and engage teachers in the model selection process. This study underscores the fact that KDE was ahead of the curve in supporting its schools in the initial stages of the reform adoption process, first by having state personnel become knowledgeable about the viable and available models and then holding information meetings (absent model providers) for potential school shoppers. In turn, they encouraged school administrators to send faculty teams on school visits to observe the models in action rather than base selection on marketing presentations. Ultimately, after choices were narrowed to one or two models, providers normally came to schools for presentations prior to any final decision by the school.

Buying In

Once schools decided on a particular reform model, they needed to muster support for it from the majority of their faculties. Federal guidelines required that programs have the support of school personnel before implementation (Cavell, 2002). Realizing the importance of staff buy-in, numerous model providers and states, including Kentucky, required a vote of support from at least 80% of the staff before a CSR model was introduced

(West, 1999). Most commonly, schools conducted a voting procedure to demonstrate faculty support.

The buy-in vote was a charged process in many schools. Faculties did not always vote unanimously for one program. Indeed, many times, teachers reported that the voting process in their schools was influenced by administrators or, in several schools, outright rigged. For example, the program facilitator in one large middle school admitted that the faculty was coerced to vote for their program. She said, "We asked them to fill out their ballot and then put their name on it. Some people felt that wasn't quite fair, that we shouldn't have had people sign their names." After some reflection she added, "I think that swayed some people to vote in a positive manner who otherwise wouldn't have. But to me, if you don't want to do something you should be a big enough person to say so." In a rural school, a group of teachers representing more than 20% of the school's small faculty reported they had voted against the model proposed by their selection committee but it was adopted anyway. Consequently, in these schools, the decision to change appears to have been imposed from either school or district administrators rather than emanating from the faculty.

These experiences of faculty buy-in suggest that though the notion is well intended and cited as important to successful program implementation (Graczewski, Ruffin, Shambaugh, & Therriault, 2007), in reality, voting may not provide an accurate indication of teachers' preferences or intentions. These findings are supported by Datnow's (2000) examination of hierarchical power relationships in school systems and CSR adoption in 22 elementary schools. She found the idea for model adoption commonly originated outside the school and the voting process was not a valid indication of genuine support and commitment for change among teachers. She concluded that the origination and direction of flow of the idea for CSR implementation influenced faculty commitment and the extent to which they adopted model changes.

Funding Announcements

Ultimately, with $2,347,527 from the federal CSR program in its first year of funding, KDE announced that 42 schools would be awarded three-year grants of $53,000 per year to implement CSR models. All schools, despite size, cost of model, or other criteria, uniformly received grants in the same amount. In keeping with the state's focus on middle-school improvement, nearly half the schools receiving grants served a middle-grade population. Early on, two schools were eliminated because of school reorganizations, leaving 18 of these 20 schools (across 11 districts) to receive CSR funding for three years beginning in 1999 and lasting through 2002.

The schools varied on a number of dimensions (See Table 2.1). Eight had kindergarten through Grade 8, two had Grades 7 and 8, and the remaining eight were traditional middle schools with Grades 6 through 8. Thirteen schools were in rural districts and five were in more populated

Table 2.1 Characteristics of 18 Reforming Schools

Model and School	District	School Size	Grade Configuration	Percentage Free/Red Cost Lunch	Percentage Minority	School Index (rounded to the nearest whole unit)
Core Knowledge						
School 1	A—Rural	<200	K–8	68.15	0.2	58
School 2	A—Rural	<200	K–8	60.55	0.0	52
School 3	A—Rural	<200	K–8	78.26	0.6	51
School 4	B—Town	>500	6–8	66.67	39.4	57
School 5	C—Rural	200–500	6–8	64.64	0.0	51
School 6	D—Rural	200–500	7–8	81.13	1.2	53
School 7	E—Rural	200–500	7–8	79.09	0.0	56
Success for All						
School 8	F—Rural	<200	K–8	90.38	0.3	49
School 9	F—Rural	<200	K–8	94.60	0.3	44
School 10	F—Rural	<200	K–8	93.16	0.0	55
School 11	G—Rural	200–500	K–8	56.98	1.0	54
School 12	I—Rural	<200	K–8	66.50	25.2	53
School 13	H—Urban	>500	6–8	65.24	24.8	52
National Writing Project						
School 14	H—Urban	>500	6–8	89.01	56.7	40
School 15	H—Urban	>500	6–8	81.50	52.9	39
America's Choice						
School 16	J—Rural	200–500	6–8	60.57	0.6	57
School 17	J—Rural	200–500	6–8	72.16	1.1	58
Community for Learning						
School 18	K—Town	200–500	6–8	36.62	6.2	63

Source: Kentucky Department of Education (1999).

towns or urban areas. Enrollments ranged from approximately 120 to nearly 900 students, and faculty sizes ranged from 14 to about 40 people. Schools in rural districts commonly had few or no minority students, whereas urban schools had concentrations up to 57%. Finally, students on free or reduced-cost lunch ranged from nearly 40% to 95%.

Implementing Models

At the time of initial CSR funding in 1999, the 18 schools implemented seven different whole-school reform models. However, for various reasons, two schools switched models between the first and the second year of funding, thus reducing the number of models to five. They were Core Knowledge (CK), Success for All (SFA), National Writing Project (NWP), America's Choice (AC), and Community for Learning (CFL). One reason for the apparent selectivity was the strong support that the KDE provided schools regarding model selection. The bar graph in Figure 2.1 illustrates the number of schools that adopted each reform model.

Figure 2.1 Reform Model Adoption

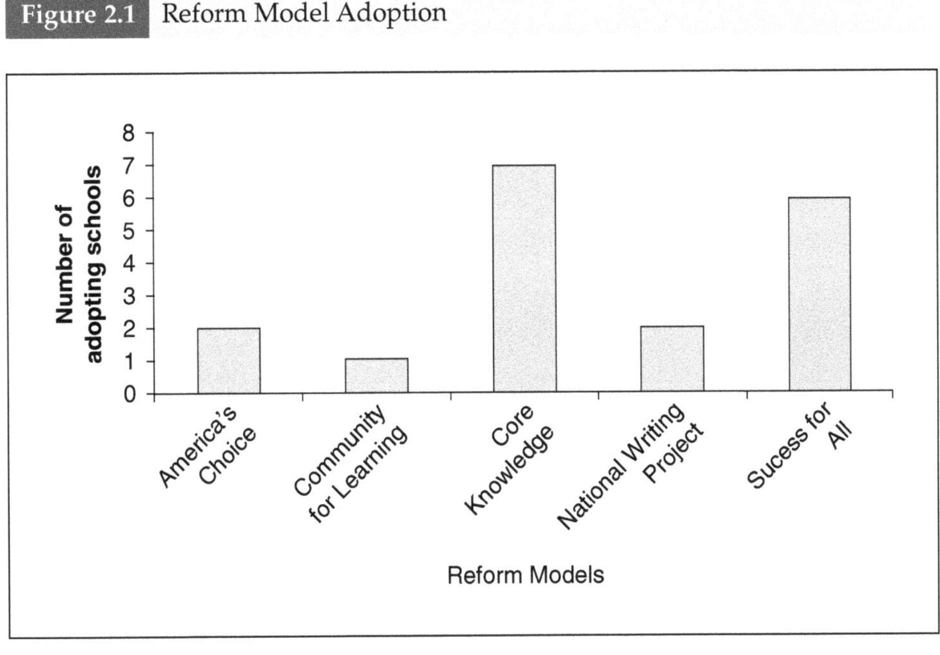

Source: Kentucky Department of Education.

Some of the prominent characteristics of the models are summarized in Table 2.2. As Table 2.2 indicates, the models varied by support provided by model developers, targeted grade levels, instructional features, promise of effectiveness, and cost. Other features of the reform models that were most salient to reforming schools are described next.

Table 2.2 Comparison of Schoolwide Reform Features, 1999

	Support Provided by Devolopers	Target Grade Levels	Main Features of Program	Evidence of Positive Effects on Achievement, 1998	First-Year Costs (in $1000s)
America's Choice	Strong	K–12	Standards and assessment, professional learning communities	No Research	$190
Community For Leaning	Strong	K–12	Individual and small group instruction, adaptive learning environments	Promising	$157
Core Knowledge	Promising	K–8	Sequenced curriculum, structured program for vocabulary and skills	Promising	$56
National Writing Project	N/A	N/A	N/A	N/A	N/A
Success for All	Strong	Prek-6	Prescribed curriculum in reading and math	Strong	$270

Adapted from Herman, R., Aladjam, D., McMahon, P., Masem, E., Muligan, I., Smith, O., et al. (1999). *An educators' guide to schoolwide reform.* Arlington, VA: Educational Research Service.

Core Knowledge (CK)

The greatest portion of schools, seven in all, chose to use CK. CK began in 1990 and by 1998 had been implemented in approximately 750 schools nationwide (Herman et al., 1999). CK was designed to address the needs of students ranging from kindergarten through eighth grade. According to *An Educators' Guide to Schoolwide Reform,* a prominent feature of the CK program is its focus on "cultural literacy" (Herman et al., 1999). Additionally, the program presents a core knowledge sequence which is a progressive guideline around which schools may organize and align their curriculum and offers strategies to develop vocabulary and skills to improve literacy. Even so, the program lacked a structured plan for implementation or any particular instructional strategies for teachers (Datnow, McHugh, Stringfield, & Hacker, 1998). CK was classified as "promising" in demonstrating evidence of positive effects of student learning (Herman et al., 1999). Further, the program was relatively inexpensive to purchase. For example, its first-year cost to schools in 1999 was roughly one-fifth that of higher-end programs, which, according to principals and selection teams, was impressive.

With only one exception, the schools in this study that chose CK were located in rural eastern Kentucky. Three were concentrated in one district. The aspect of the program that appealed to the majority of these schools was its focus on cultural literacy. Principals and other educators often commented that the program seemed like a good fit for their schools because they felt their children had little opportunity otherwise to gain cultural experiences beyond their immediate communities. They explained that because of the relative isolation of the rural areas where these schools were located, students rarely had the chance to go to movies, visit museums, or attend orchestral concerts. One school's facilitator noted that her school's band members had never seen stringed instruments.

A fundamental feature of the program, sequential curriculum, did not escape the attention of several principals. A principal of a middle school explained, "The CK representatives wanted us to follow a spiral curriculum that was not only vertical but also horizontal. That was its biggest asset, its selling point." He added, "I told the faculty, 'If this is the program you choose, we are going to make it fit. We'll mash every bit of the content from CK into our core content at the appropriate grade levels based on the implementation manual.'" The principal of a school in a nearby district echoed this. He said, "We wanted something that would enhance and reinforce the Kentucky's core content, and we thought alignment was the key. The one thing I was hoping for from CK was that it would be a tool to assist us in curriculum alignment that would integrate the whole middle school."

CK did not provide a structured implementation plan to users. Nor did it provide substantial professional development or guidance for teachers in terms of prepackaged instructional strategies for them to use in their classrooms (Datnow et al., 1998). It appears that its rank of *promising* in evidence of positive effects on student achievement along with its lack of structured implementation were not salient issues to the schools that chose CK when they were shopping for a model. Respondents reported that they were not particularly aware of these characteristics until after they had committed to using the model. It did, however, become of great concern to some schools later.

Success for All (SFA)

Another six schools identified SFA as the model they would implement with CSR funding. SFA was established in 1993 as a highly structured reading model targeting students in prekindergarten through Grade 5. By 1998, it had been implemented in more than 1,100 schools (Herman et al., 1999). The primary goal of SFA was "to ensure that all children learn to read" (Herman et al., p. 115). It also was designed so students could acquire basic skills in other subject areas, and build problem solving and crucial thinking skills (Cooper, Slavin, & Madden, 1998). It required schools to restructure their instructional schedules to allow for daily 90-minute reading periods for all students and additional individual tutoring for those unable to keep pace. The prescribed curriculum for reading time was highly structured and necessitated specific, detailed materials and resources and extensive training so that teachers could implement the strategies according to design. Another integral aspect of SFA tracked the success and progress of each student through regular assessments administered in eight-week cycles. Based on their performance on these tests, students were regrouped to maintain homogeneous classes during reading time. SFA was one of the most expensive models to implement in 1999. Despite its cost, partly because of what principals characterized as its "highly sophisticated and impressive" sales presentation, it appealed to many schools.

Five of the six schools using SFA in this study were in rural areas across the state. SFA encourages schools to participate in educational networks and to create partnerships to promote and support school reform efforts (Cooper et al., 1998). It suggests that schools in close geographic proximity form *clusters* for these purposes. Consistent with this recommendation, three schools were in one district where several other schools already used SFA through other funding sources.

SFA's theory of reading development targets beginning-level readers and their progression (Borman et al., 2005a). Because of this, all but one of the schools that had Grades 6 through 8 configurations shied away from the program during the selection process. Even upper-grade teachers in the kindergarten through eighth-grade schools frequently reported having reservations about the fit of the model to the needs of their students or to the instructional schedule. For example, the sixth-, seventh-, and eighth-grade teachers in one small school explained that they had researched SFA using the Internet when they were shopping for a reform model and were not convinced the model was suitable for their students. They were concerned that creating the required 90-minute daily reading period would harm student performance in other core classes. One teacher commented, "I recall thinking that SFA may meet the needs of the lower grades but is not as useful for the seventh and eighth graders. If we used our time for SFA reading then the kids wouldn't get enough time in other subjects such as science. And seventh grade is science-testing year." Concerns such as these caused some teachers to vote against the program. Rather than risk losing the opportunity to implement SFA in the lower grades, two schools quelled faculty apprehension by excusing teachers in Grades 7 and 8 from using the program. One urban middle school became a pilot school for the SFA middle-school program.

SFA appealed to schools that wanted to focus reform efforts on reading improvement and on raising test scores, especially in reading. An administrator in the urban middle school reported, "The whole thing was to get kids to learn to read and to like reading. That's a big issue, and we are always trying to think of things we can do toward that end." A teacher at the same school echoed this comment, "I would say we were looking for ways so kids would develop an appreciation for reading and to take them from one level to the next. We wanted to equip them with skills they could use on their own, like teaching them how to write correctly with meaningful sentences." An administrator in a small rural school reported, "Our goals in using SFA were to improve reading, CATS reading scores, and overall student achievement." Even though the program emphasizes reading, at least one school expected gains in other curricular areas that rely heavily on reading. The principal explained, "We hoped that by adopting the model and bringing up reading levels other good things would happen too." He went on to elaborate, "The local high school kept complaining that we were sending up ninth graders who couldn't read. They were falling far behind and couldn't participate in class because the reading in their science text was too high for them." He concluded by saying he hoped that SFA in his school would improve reading across the curriculum for all students.

America's Choice (AC)

Two schools located in the same rural district selected AC as the model they intended to implement. AC was introduced in schools in 1998 and evolved from the National Alliance for Restructuring Education (NARE), a program founded by the National Center on Education and the Economy, in 1989. Designed to meet the needs of students kindergarten through Grade 12, its goal was to enable all students to reach "high standards in the core subjects of English, language arts, mathematics, and science" (Herman et al., 1999, p. 18). By 1999, the program was implemented in about 40 schools, some of which were in Kentucky.

AC was developed on the premise that by providing schools with curriculum guidance, coaching assistance, and monitoring strategies, faculties could develop instructional practices that were more effective and, thereby, promote higher levels of student achievement. The success of the program depended in part on the talent and ability of in-school *coaches*. These were teachers identified from among the school faculty based on their interest and experience in the targeted content areas and who were willing to further develop their expertise through training offered by model providers to subsequently become peer coaches in their schools.

The principals of the two district middle schools that chose AC reported they deliberately did so together to enhance unity and continuity in their district. Both principals also found the model's emphasis on reading and writing impressive. Beyond that, one recalled that AC appealed to him because it seemed like it would provide the structure to keep the schools "focused and on course." Ultimately, the two faculties voted to select AC for these reasons and because model vendors led them to believe that AC was aligned with the Kentucky Core Content and would provide lesson plans to address that content.

National Writing Project (NWP)

Two large middle schools located in the same urban district chose to implement a local affiliate of the NWP. Although the NWP network had federal funding since 1991, it had been implemented in a limited number of schools as of 1999 and was not listed in the *Educators' Guide to Schoolwide Reform* (Herman et al., 1999). The mission of NWP is to improve student achievement and learning by improving the teaching of writing. Thus, the program is designed to help improve writing skills of students by providing a strong, ongoing component of professional development targeting literacy for teachers to enhance writing instruction. It does this by developing a network of teacher consultants in local schools and training them in professional development institutes held each summer. NWP also has program providers who typically are affiliated with local colleges or universities and work in each school providing professional development and inservice training for classroom teachers. They work closely with teacher consultants to support their efforts to disseminate NWP strategies to improve classroom instruction. Through summer institutes, NWP sites design and deliver customized inservice programs for local schools, districts, and higher-education institutions, and they provide a diverse array of continuing education and research opportunities for teachers at all levels. Unlike many other models, the program does not provide specific materials or a structured approach to teaching. Rather it advocates an open, dynamic approach to teaching writing based on effective professional training and networking for teachers. To that end, it encourages continuing communication between university faculty and teachers and sponsors advanced institutes, study groups, teacher publications, and other opportunities for teachers to explore literacy and develop as experts in the teaching of writing (National Writing Project, 1999).

Two schools in this study implemented NWP. The model provider was a teacher educator based at a nearby university and known for her expertise, effectiveness, conscientiousness, and sense of responsibility. Undoubtedly, this gave the program a hometown appeal to the schools that implemented NWP. One of the principals mentioned that during the selection process her faculty had considered two other models that also prioritized reading and literacy. However, neither was "exactly what they were looking for," particularly, targeting the middle-school level and having a strong component of professional development for teachers. She said, "I wanted all teachers to see themselves as reading and writing people, not just as a social studies teacher or whatever. I wanted them to focus on reading and writing because that is what the students were so low in." The other principal said, "Although I wasn't in this school when it made its selection, it is clear that the student body is deficient in reading and writing, and they need that across the curriculum, so it seems that NWP fits nicely here."

Community for Learning (CFL)

Finally, one school in a midsized district identified CFL as the program they wished to use during their CSR grant. CFL was founded by M. Wang in the 1960s and established in 1990 as a whole-school reform model. Despite its medium-ranged first-year costs, by 1999 it had been implemented in fewer than 100 schools nationwide. Designed to address all grade levels (K–12), its stated goal was "to improve students' academic achievement, behavior, attitudes, and to promote independent learning habits" (Herman et al., 1999, p. 43). It also encouraged success for students by linking schools with community institutions. Besides promoting collaborative relationships between the school and outside organizations, the program advocated an adaptive-learning-environments model for the classroom where teachers and specialists prescribe an individualized learning plan for each student and provide individual and group instruction accordingly.

It seems the one school in this study that chose to implement CFL did so in an entirely democratic process. In reflection, however, one faculty member admitted that she and others might have been swayed early on by promotional materials produced by the company. She said, "The team of faculty members assigned to explore CFL got a hold of a video from the company, and maybe because their presentation was so impressive, we thought we liked the program. It just seemed better than what any others had. That is why we chose it." Another faculty member suggested that the faculty's decision was based on more substantive criteria. She recalled that the prime reasons she supported the model were that it included an active parent-involvement component and *leveling* of instruction to meet the individual learning needs of each student. She said, "We thought it would be beneficial to students for instruction and assignments to be leveled."

Issues Related to Model Selection

Although dozens of models qualified for CSR status, Kentucky schools exercised apparent selectivity when adopting them, most likely because of KDE's strong guidance regarding model selection. Even so, much about some of the programs remained unknown because they were still scaling up or in early stages of broadscale implementation. As indicated in Chapter 1, federal guidelines stipulated that whole-school reform models must demonstrate 9 (and later 11) components to be recognized with CSR status. One component required research-based evidence of effectiveness to improve student achievement (Cavell, 2002). When schools in this study selected their respective models, SFA had the strongest evidence of effectiveness, AC showed promising evidence, and both CFL and CK were in greatest need of additional research. The NWP was not ranked (Borman et al., 2002). However, these ratings of effectiveness were based on relatively simplistic measures or otherwise understudied. The research on which the ratings were based commonly lacked rigor methodologically or was conducted by the model developers themselves, thus introducing researcher bias (Borman et al., 2002; Evans-Andris & Usui, 2001; Slavin, 2008). Moreover, the relationship between implementation challenges and fundamental differences in program design was misunderstood or neglected altogether. A recent publication by Rowan and Miller (2007) analyzed the effects of three CSR models based on their organizational strategies for promoting instructional change. They found that whether a program's underlying design exerted cultural, professional, or procedural control rendered different implementation outcomes in schools. Yet this typology wasn't recognized or clearly developed as the first CSR-funded cohort selected reform models for adoption.

Despite KDE's efforts to assist schools and encourage them to select models that would effectively address their schools' goals, it is likely that many selection teams didn't know enough about the models to ask the right questions. Consequently, these schools implemented models that might not be an effective or appropriate match for their needs. For example, some schools with goals of reading improvement chose models that only addressed reading peripherally. In one rural school, teachers said, "We were misinformed from the beginning. We were led to believe this was a kindergarten through eighth-grade program, but we found out otherwise once we had bought the model and the representatives came to the school for training." When schools were choosing models, only several were designed or otherwise well suited to middle schools. Thus, many schools with seventh and eighth grades adopted models that targeted

Grades kindergarten through 6. Reflecting back after three years of CSR, one superintendent observed, "I think the schools that showed the greatest progress were those that picked the model that fit them best." As her comment suggests, it seems that the *mismatching* of models in relation to the expressed needs or culture of schools likely affected program implementation and sustainability.

In their study of comprehensive school reform, Datnow and Stringfield (2000) found that some schools implemented reform models that were well matched to their needs, interest, and culture, whereas others adopted them without thought or attention to the fit of the model to their needs. Implementation and sustainability were less successful in schools whose model selection was not consistent with their needs and culture. They suggested that educators need to sharpen their consumer skills and develop a more mature process of critical inquiry to avoid making inappropriate decisions regarding model selection. Unlike the schools researched by Datnow and Stringfield (2000), most of the schools in this study participated in a careful, thoughtful, and guided selection process. Despite this, some still made inappropriate choices either because the evidence they based their decision on was misleading or their model providers could not "deliver" perhaps because of unforeseen challenges associated with scaling up and inability to meet the demands of a growing, national consumer base.

DISCUSSION OF THE STATE CONTEXT FOR SCHOOL REFORM

This chapter has provided an overview of the state infrastructure and context that shaped the reform experiences of low-performing schools. As the quote at the beginning of this chapter suggests, state personnel believed that because of the state's infrastructure and support, CSR represented a nearly failsafe means for school improvement. KDE provided ample information to schools about CSR and the programmatic options available to them and encouraged schools to apply for funding, but despite its efforts or the promise of CSR, more than half of Kentucky's low-performing schools chose not to pursue funding. Unlike other research where schools claimed ignorance about the reform process itself (Leopold et al., 2000), schools in this study intentionally declined the opportunity because of *cost-benefit* decisions related to perceived costs of time, resources, and effort that reform would require. Even so, some districts called out their schools and pressured them to pursue CSR grants to generate or sustain the appearance of legitimacy in the local community. This is consistent with an argument presented by Meyer and Rowan (1977) where *institutionalized rules* or expectations regarding organizational behavior emanating from the external environment may be unrelated to what is, in reality, efficient and effective. Conformity to such expectations allows the organization to appear rational and, thus, sustain legitimacy. Organizations must generate legitimacy to survive. In this study, it is doubtful that enthusiasm or support for change was ignited in instances where schools engaged in reform adoption in response to pressure to appear innovative.

KDE also shaped reform by imposing an adoption process that required schools to identify improvement goals, conduct fact-finding research to select a reform model that would address those goals, and demonstrate faculty support or buy-in for reform. The reform-adoption process organized schools for reform and gave educators a major role in determining the direction of improvement for their schools. Slavin (2004) argues that the voting process demonstrates emerging cohesion and a sense of mission among school staff. In our study, the voting process was not a valid indication of support for change in all schools. However, it appears that in schools where teachers and administrators alike were meaningfully involved in the adoption phase of CSR, both the shopping and voting processes contributed a sense of purpose and empowerment to participants. In 1998, when schools were shopping for models in the first round of federal funding, research on reform models was synthesized into consumer guides, but it is likely that model ratings and other information culled from these guides and other sources led some schools inadvertently to select models that were poorly suited to fit their goals, needs, organizational context, or workplace culture. Lane and Gracia (2004) note the importance of matching a school's needs and priorities for improvement with the appropriate model provider. Ultimately, the states in their study recommended a multistaged selection process entailing self-assessment, exploration of models, and faculty involvement in decision making. They found that such planning and involvement during the adoption phase resulted in higher model implementation. Despite the extent teachers engaged in fact finding and decision making, schools in this study were unaware of fundamental differences in reform models and their related outcomes when they made decisions regarding CSR model adoption.

Much about the models was unknown at that time. Rowan and Miller (2007) examined three CSR models to determine features that promote instructional change and discovered fundamental variations in model strategies based on systems of social control they exerted on users. These, in turn, produced different implementation outcomes. Cultural control promoted an adaptive approach to instructional improvement by encouraging teachers and teacher communities to explore and identify effective, appropriate instructional strategies and then use their discretion and autonomy in adapting and integrating those strategies in their classroom practices. The second type, professional control, relied on socialization to professional standards and expectations to gain compliance with strategies of instructional improvement. The third type, procedural control, imposed routine and scripted instructional guidelines for teachers. Rowan and Miller found that CSR models based on professional or procedural systems of control successfully prompted teachers to change instructional practices, whereas the model using cultural control was least effective.

This chapter introduces additional issues for consideration. First, schools were bound by a system of high-stakes accountability under KERA's testing system and later reinforced by No Child Left Behind (NCLB), which likely reduced the degree to which teachers were willing to change their instructional practices. This topic is discussed in Chapters 5 and 6. Second, the chapter calls into question whether decision makers and faculties thought about *changing for good*. Little evidence suggests that schools entered the change process with the intention of sustaining reform efforts beyond the defined three-year federal-funding period.

Over the three years of CSR funding, the 18 schools shared many similar experiences. Because of the state's infrastructure, the criteria it used to identify eligible schools, the way it shaped the proposal process, and the design of the CSR program, schools entered into reform on relatively equal footing. Even so, reflection on the experiences of schools also illuminates factors at each level of the organizational hierarchy including the district, the school leaders, and the faculty that took hold early on and led schools in different directions over time. This becomes particularly apparent when considering the sustainability of reform efforts. The first of these levels is the district. The district can help shape and reinforce infrastructure, identify and secure necessary resources, and generally motivate and recognize schools in their endeavors related to lasting improvement. The integral contribution of district support for the implementation and sustainability of reform efforts in schools is discussed in the chapter that follows.

$$3$$

Supporting Change
in Schools

*The district used to call all the shots, there were very few decisions for
anyone else to make, there was very little input. Now we are trying to
mushroom out, here and in schools, to let everybody have as much
input as they can on school improvement because if educated people feel
like they have some direction with the ship, then they have more
tendency to steer it in the right direction.*

—District superintendent

District support is critical to the success of schools as they attempt to
undertake and sustain reform efforts. Supportive districts promote a
vision for change and then actively assist local schools to fulfill that vision
by performing effective human resource development, identifying and
securing necessary resources, creating and reinforcing multiple channels
of communication, and helping schools assess and reflect on their practice
of teaching and learning. Further, districts that contribute to whole-system
capacity in and across schools create conditions where schools are more
likely to realize and sustain change (Fullan, 2005). Such districts demonstrate
strong leadership, effective patterns of information sharing, and mobilized
commitment at all levels. Through these and other strategies, districts may
recognize and empower schools in their endeavors related to lasting
improvement.

This chapter examines the ways districts contribute to their schools' ability to implement and prepare to sustain school reform efforts. It addresses these questions: How do districts support schools during their reform implementation period? To what extent do districts enhance the capacity of local schools? In what ways do districts increase the likelihood that schools will sustain reform strategies? In seeking answers, this chapter draws on the strategies and practices of two districts to highlight the nature and levels of support that distinguished them favorably from others. Specifically, while recognizing and reinforcing the abilities and respecting the autonomy of local schools, they provided support that promoted a culture of sustainable change.

Despite the contributions of districts as schools implement and then prepare to sustain change efforts, they do not always position themselves to offer effective support to schools. In the RAND Change Agent Study, Berman and McLaughlin (1978) noted that on the termination of federal funding, districts must make deliberate and explicit commitments to schools to assure program continuation. They identified four patterns of support emanating from the district that affected levels of implementation and sustainability of the program. Support was opportunistic, top-down, localized, or broad based. Of the four patterns, broad-based support most effectively promoted sustainable innovation in schools. It was characterized by buy-in, active staff involvement, budgetary allocations, and input from key personnel at all levels of the district and was most likely to lead to sustained reform efforts. Even so, findings revealed that few districts planned for the long-term sustainability of innovative programs for school improvement, even where the programs had been implemented successfully.

Recent research corroborates previous findings regarding the integral role of the district during school reform. Goertz (2005) examined district support for schools under No Child Left Behind (NCLB) and found that assistance to low-performing schools focused predominantly on technical capacity including school planning, curriculum adoption and alignment, and analyzing student performance data to monitor progress and for strategic purposes. Further, districts assigned staff to help schools in other ways such as writing school-improvement plans, recommending research-based improvement strategies, and providing guidance for budget and staffing allocations. Coburn and Russell (2008) add that reforming districts may structure professional learning communities and networking opportunities for educators to advance their instructional practice and growth. Finally, based on research in Chicago public elementary schools, Newmann, Smith, Allensworth, and Bryk (2001) found that districts effectively support school improvement efforts when they align policies to promote educational goals having a common instructional framework rather than impose policies that splinter or undermine school instructional program coherence.

Studies of comprehensive school reform (CSR) reveal a direct positive relationship between district support and program implementation (Datnow & Stringfield, 2000; Kirby, Berends, & Naftel, 2001; Taylor, 2005). Researchers typically have found that both urban and rural districts disseminated information about reform models and helped schools make selections early on in the reform process (Carlson & Buttram, 2004; Datnow & Stringfield, 2000). Further, supportive districts provided ongoing assistance throughout program implementation, specifically through leadership, securing resources necessary for reform, and buffering schools during periods of transition.

District support is also vital to program sustainability. For example, in their study of whole-school reform over four or more years, Kirby, Berends, and Naftel (2001) conducted exit interviews among schools that dropped their programs. Respondents most frequently cited lack of funding either for the program itself or related profession development and lack of district support as reasons for program discontinuation. Similarly, in a study involving nearly 400 schools, Taylor (2005) determined that schools were less likely to drop their whole-school reform programs on the termination of federal funding if their district provided support targeting professional development designed to promote the implementation of change. Interviews conducted in a subset of 24 of those schools identified the loss of district support as a primary reason leading schools to drop their reform programs. In another study of 13 reforming schools, Datnow (2005) found that changes in district leadership resulted in loss or reduction of district support for current reform programs, changes with instructional focus, and disruption in the coherence and stability of the overall reform effort. Such changes often are triggered by turnover among key personnel in the central office (Datnow, 2005; Datnow & Stringfield, 2000; Ross, 2001).

Although they varied by size, geographic location, and other dimensions, 2 of the 11 districts whose schools participated in this study stood head and shoulders above the others by their unwavering support of schools in the process of selecting, implementing, and sustaining CSR programs. Using different approaches, both succeeded in actively offering their schools support over the time encompassed by the study. The first district, Waterton County, is described in the following section.

Note: I have given pseudonyms to all district, school, and respondent names in this book to protect the confidentiality of participants.

WATERTON COUNTY

Three schools in this study were located in Waterton County, a rural county of approximately 32,000 residents in the southeastern part of the state.

As in other counties in the region, poverty and unemployment are widespread. In 2000, Waterton had a per capita personal income of less than $17,000 and an unemployment rate of nearly 9%. Further, 46% of adults lacked a high school diploma or its equivalent. More recently, development in tourism and a rekindled interest in coalmining and lumbering led to a growth spurt in the economic base. A small liberal arts college is located in the county and another in a neighboring county. Each offers a teacher education program and seemingly has a strong working relationship with the local school district.

When I first visited Waterton County in the fall of 2001, it had 11 schools serving more than 6,000 students, almost 80% of whom were eligible for free or reduced-price lunch. The district reflected a nearly all white population with little racial or ethnic diversity. It also was characterized by relatively high personnel turnover. Besides retirements, this likely was, in part, because of the absence of a teacher union and perpetual jockeying among educators to obtain school assignments closer to their homes. Finally, the district planned to open a new school in the next several years and move the seventh and eighth grades from the elementary schools into the new school. This in turn would reduce the size of several elementary schools dramatically, thus putting them at risk of closing.

Reforming Schools

Of the eight district schools with kindergarten through Grade 8, three were awarded funding through the CSR program. Each school was located in relatively isolated areas between 5 and 15 miles from the district office. Two had endured high turnover among principals in recent years. One principal was the school's fifth in four years. The other simply shrugged, saying, "I am one in a series," and explained that she had only been in her present school about two months, having started midyear. All three principals had extensive prior teaching experience. Two had strong family ties in the district and the third was from an adjacent district. They seemed knowledgeable about their school communities and realistic about challenges they faced. Each principal appeared confident, committed to improvement, and willing to work long hours to serve the school community.

The administrators concurred that although the initial impetus for reform through the CSR program was spawned by a former principal, since the actual start of program implementation three years earlier, the main source of support for change came from the district superintendent and central office. This was particularly important given the high turnover among principals during the funding period. Over the years of this study, it became clear that Waterton County supported school improvement by promoting a shared vision for reform, staffing in the central office, respecting the autonomy of schools, and offering expertise and encouragement for the sustainability of change.

District Staffing and Support Through Shared Vision

School support through district staffing began with the superintendent. Mr. Thomas was hired as superintendent in the late 1990s, coinciding with the year schools applied for CSR funding. He had a strong background in finance and business coupled with extensive experience as a classroom teacher and school administrator. When I met him, he was beginning his seventh year as superintendent. Similar to most educators in the district, both he and the assistant superintendent had lived and worked in the local area much of their lives.

Mr. Thomas described the district first by talking about its goals. He prefaced the conversation by stating, "We developed visions and goals together. We involved everyone throughout the district so that we can share those goals and talk about things we want for our district and kids in general." He then identified the district's goals: (a) to reach financial stability, (b) improve facilities, (c) reduce class size, (d) improve graduation rates, (e) lower dropout rates, and (f) install a middle school. It was understood that underlying all else, however, the goal was to increase student performance. Mr. Thomas's comments suggest that he led with a shared vision intending to promote broad-based support. He reiterated this by saying, "When you come together, you have a better understanding of what is going on."

Mr. Thomas supervised personnel holding more than 15 key positions in the central office. Referring to what he considered a relatively large staff, he explained, "I inherited some of it, but much of it is a result of eliminating some positions and creating others. For example, I created a position for a school improvement person." He later added, "My principals understand that my staff is a resource, and they are here to work. So there is tremendous support from the central office and it is purposeful, not accidental. Each person knows what their role is." Besides the more traditional positions that targeted curriculum, instruction, assessment, budgeting, federal programs, and facilities operations, district staff had demonstrated expertise and assumed responsibilities related to grant writing, public relations, and school improvement. Further, each staff member was assigned to function as a liaison to a district school.

The idea of matching liaisons with schools was attributed to the assistant superintendent and reportedly gained support throughout the district immediately. Each school was instructed to contact its liaison for information, questions, difficulties, and so forth. One liaison explained, "I have a pretty good relationship with my principals, and usually, I just pick up the phone and say, 'I am here if you need help.' I try to call them every day or so just to ask, 'Is there anything that you need?' Then, during the phone call we typically will chat about how things are going." Periodically, the assigned support staff rotated from one school to another depending on what its needs were. Mr. Thomas explained, "One of the things I did was change the school improvement coordinator to the two lowest-performing schools so that they have my best person. That may cause some talk among the liaisons, but I assign my personnel as schools' needs dictate."

The liaison arrangement, in effect, functioned as a two-way communication system between the central office and schools. It allowed information to flow both top-down and bottom-up. District liaisons became intimately familiar with their assigned schools, which positioned them to more effectively link school personnel with expertise and support on an individual, case-by-case basis. In turn, input and information flowing from schools via the liaison was pooled in the central office, thus enabling the district to be knowledgeable and effective in addressing the needs and concerns of schools more holistically.

Besides managing staff assignments and subsequent information flow, the superintendent, by his admission, worked to reduce the problem of turnover among principals and district staff that had plagued schools and undermined the district's attempts to improve schools. Mr. Thomas said, "Everyone wants stability with staff and the administrators. And the stability *is* reaching across the district." Indeed, over time, his efforts had a marked effect. One district employee observed, "He is calming; he is caring. That is his style. He is more personable than our previous superintendent." Further, there was no turnover among principals participating in this study from late fall, 2001, to the time the study ended, which was a dramatic improvement compared to previous years. Mr. Thomas explained, "My administrators are happy with their work, they are happy with the effort. We all share the same the goal, to improve, to make things better."

Finally, personnel in the central office were noticeably committed to school improvement. Under Mr. Thomas's leadership, they maintained a seemingly strong working relationship with the state department of education, with district schools, and toward one another. For example, they participated in and presented training sessions at the state level, established and engaged in active, positive communication patterns with their schools, and worked cooperatively with fellow staff members as circumstances demanded. Overall, they appeared both professionally and personally invested in the improvement of district schools, particularly those with grants for comprehensive reform. One liaison confided, "I have a feel for all three of these school communities. All these are my home. I grew up near one, my dad worked in another for 37 years, and my husband went to the third, where my children go now. These are my schools. They are educating our children, my children. So I have a personal stake in it. These grants have to succeed."

Traditionally, schools in rural areas have a strong sense of community (Kannapel & DeYoung, 1999), which may pose a challenge to districts as they attempt to unite schools for a common cause. In Waterton County, however, many employees across the entire district seemed to share this administrator's sentiments by expressing their underlying concern for all the children and their desire to offer them a high-quality education.

CSR and School Autonomy

The CSR program, by design, represented an opportunity for districts to jumpstart reform in struggling schools. For rural districts such as Waterton County, CSR funding represented a chance to bring programs to small schools that they otherwise could not afford. District administrators recognized this and acknowledged that the main appeal of the grants was their infusion of money for school improvement. For this reason, eligible schools were urged to apply for them. Mr. Thomas stated practically, "If you don't have funds, you tend not to start projects you can't afford, so we look for opportunities for funds to allow us to do things in instruction and instructional strategies." Another district employee agreed saying, "We couldn't have funded the initial expense of buying the reform program for even one school. We might be able to sustain those programs by taking from textbook money or professional development funds, but we never would be able to cover that initial first-year expense." This employee's statement suggests that he recognized the importance of funding for innovation and was contemplating the possibility of sustainability.

The district encouraged eligible schools to apply for funding but left it up to them to determine which reform program to implement. The federal programs director explained that district personnel lacked consensus regarding the programs schools should adopt. She commented, "As a matter of fact, there was another model that most of the central office people liked a little bit better, but we weren't really pushing it. We just kind of hoped they would like it a little better." In the selection process, for purposes of buy-in, it was important for schools to choose the program they perceived best suited their needs. Although several staff members suggested schools might have been overly influenced by the strong sales pitch delivered by representatives of the reform program they ultimately adopted, the district allowed schools to proceed in selecting the program they wanted, thus demonstrating respect for their autonomy.

Even so, the district, consistent with direction from the Kentucky Leadership Academy and reform program providers, urged schools to *cluster*, that is form a group whose shared identity was the use of a common reform program. From the onset of the reform period, rather than pitting schools against schools in the fierce competition of proposals and implementation, they worked in concert to develop and expand effective improvement strategies throughout the district. While honoring school autonomy, the district simultaneously encouraged schools with common interests to work as a cooperative unit, again, reinforcing the notion of a shared vision. Principals and central office staff agreed that they worked collaboratively as a district, lending guidance and encouragement to one another. They talked about it freely. I frequently heard comments similar to that of one administrator who said, "I think part of the process of improvement in this district is pulling together folks to support each other."

Principals recognized and appreciated the autonomy they were afforded in leading their schools during the change process. In describing the superintendent's level of involvement and interest in one reforming school, the principal explained, "His viewpoint, from what I can tell, is pretty much, 'if it works for you, it works for him.' His interest is that you progress and students succeed. If the reform program works, fine. If it doesn't, scratch it and find something that does. He isn't interested in forcing schools to do anything they don't see fit to do." A district staff member confirmed this attitude. Even after schools had used the same reform program for more than four years, she said, "If it is meeting their needs, great. And if not, let's look at their data and then look for something else."

District personnel also respected the autonomy of schools by permitting them to *test their wings* with little interference or negative repercussion. The superintendent explained, "I take a hands-off approach when things go well. But if they don't, I am there more often to get more involved with principals. Even so, I won't flat-out tell them what to do." The federal programs director related an episode that exemplified this stance. According to her, a local high school did not seek the district's input as it went about pursuing a CSR grant. She explained, "I stayed back and said, 'Here are my suggestions, if you don't want them, okay.'" The grant proposal was not funded. Afterward, the director cautiously approached the school, encouraged it to reapply, and reiterated her offer for further assistance. Ultimately, the school worked with the director and gained funding the following year. Importantly, this strategy upheld the integrity and autonomy of the school. Further, the district personnel's willingness to tolerate a degree of independence without retribution no doubt fostered a higher level of trust, cooperation, sense of empowerment, and innovation in the end.

Advocacy and Networking

Unlike most other districts that left schools to defend and protect their consumer interests, personnel in Waterton County advocated with and for the schools once they began implementing their common reform program. Explaining this as part of her job, the school improvement coordinator said, "We have been very demanding consumers. We have called the model providers and told them, 'we don't like this presenter,' 'we weren't satisfied with this presentation.' Or, we might say, 'we didn't feel like we got our money's worth. We want somebody else to come back.'" She concluded by saying, "The district and its schools are in this together." This proactive, assertive stance was rather unique among the 11 districts in this study. Despite multiple instances when school or district administrators indicated their dissatisfaction regarding service provision from reform program providers, active consumer advocacy appeared in only two or three other cases, and in each, it was initiated by the school, not the district. Through such actions, schools learned to be more vigilant in protecting and expanding effective improvement strategies as they worked with model providers throughout reform implementation.

In keeping with recommendations from model providers (Murphy & Datnow, 2003), a district coordinator reinforced the cooperative spirit among reforming schools by organizing and hosting a monthly meeting for their program facilitators. One facilitator described, "They are luncheon meetings, and we work as we eat. It gives us a chance to air our concerns, discuss what works and what's not working, develop strategies, and find solutions. That helps." The positive effects of the support group for reform were noticeable and frequently mentioned from school to school. It appeared that during these meetings participants established and reaffirmed a climate of rapport and trust and shared effective implementation practices that promised success. Further, a facilitator explained that key district administrators knew what each school was doing and transmitted promising ideas from one to the others. Importantly, over time, the support network became self-sustaining and helped schools maintain a proactive stance in their reform efforts.

Preparing to Sustain Reform

Because of strong district support through staffing, communication and networking, respect for autonomy, and a burgeoning shared vision for improvement and cooperation, schools were better poised to sustain their reform efforts. The district reinforced this orientation toward sustainability in several significant ways. First, it adopted and promoted the mindset that the schools were expected to sustain reform efforts. This was evidenced early on when the district employee quoted previously stressed the importance of gaining external funding to initiate school reform but speculated that it could be sustained through reallocation of internal resources. The superintendent explained his viewpoint, "Helping schools to sustain reform is critical. Allowing them to drift away from reform programs or switch to something else has been the trouble in this state and in this county in particular." Then he added, "There was a tendency at first when it didn't look like they were doing much, to switch programs. I said, 'let's stick with it,' knowing we would have to make some modifications. That is one thing I guard against, to keep that from occurring. A lot of

times, someone will say, 'let's try this,' and I will say, 'let's finish this.'"
Sustainability of reform efforts became a goal, district wide.

The district went to great lengths to support schools in their budgetary efforts to sustain reform as the termination of the funding period approached. Appropriate personnel helped the schools develop proposals for further funding to sustain their programs through a new federal initiative that would enable them to retain the reform programs they already had implemented. Personnel also provided expertise to help schools reallocate their present resources to budget for continued initiatives. One respondent recalled, "Oh boy! That was really hard work."

District personnel in Waterton County prompted schools to reflect on innovative practices. This strategy was employed as schools received feedback from the outside agency contracted to perform formative evaluations of reform implementation efforts. The agency would conduct the evaluation and then send its report directly to the principal. Unlike schools in most other districts that either shelved indefinitely or read and ignored these reports, one school administrator in Waterton County commented that her district liaison would review and help her school interpret the reports. She said, "We did it together. The staff and faculty met together after school with our district rep." The district also became more proficient in offering technical assistance as schools analyzed their test scores and identified factors related to school performance. About this, the district coordinator commented, "We may look at the data, but we don't always want to take the time to look at all those little nuances. That is a real challenge. Taking the time to implement what the data really tell us is even harder." Finally, related to this, district personnel continued to hold monthly meetings for information sharing, cooperative planning, and reflection on school progress. One district employee summed up their efforts by stating, "Helping schools stay focused on reform is a never-ending battle."

The district support system in Waterton County unified schools with a common, aligned vision for improvement, strong two-way flow of communication, and a structure for networking. It also provided advocacy, technical assistance, and so forth while empowering individual schools by respecting their autonomy and capabilities. Like the few districts noted by Berman and McLaughlin (1978) that offered schools broad-based support for lasting improvement, Waterton County appeared to promote and help its schools prepare for long-term sustainability of their reform programs. The following section describes a second district, Burkett County, that also was notably supportive of its reforming schools.

BURKETT COUNTY

In sharp contrast to the rural context that characterized the school system in Waterton County was the atmosphere defining the experiences of three schools in this study located in a large urban district. Burkett County, with a population of about 600,000, boasts the largest urban hub in the state. Its district serves roughly 90,000 students, in more than 130 schools, over 20 of which are middle schools. Reflective of the broader community, the school district has a minority population of about 37%. Nearly half of all students are eligible for free or reduced-cost lunch. Not surprisingly, a district as large and diverse as Burkett has many priorities, only one of which was the successful implementation of a CSR program.

Reforming Schools

The three district schools that participated in this study were middle schools with Grades 6, 7, and 8. Their student bodies had high minority populations, high percentages of special education students, and large numbers of English language learners. Compared to other district schools, they were characterized by high poverty and low performance. Two of them had significant principal turnover, which persisted in one school over the years of the study.

Support Through District Staffing

Unlike Waterton County, the first noticeable characteristic of Burkett County was the extensive bureaucratic organization of its central office. Burkett County's superintendent oversees three assistants, one for each school level. Dr. Roth, the assistant superintendent for middle schools, had transferred to this state to take this position in the mid 1990s. Through observation of her during school visits and speaking with her it became clear that, despite the size of the district, she was entirely familiar with the schools under her charge, including each of the three Burkett County schools in the study. She acknowledged this saying, "I visit my schools. That is what I do to find out what is going on in them, to nudge them, to encourage them. That is one part of my job, getting out and meeting with principals, visiting classrooms, and talking to people." Additionally, like other districts, Burkett County employed an array of specialists who worked from the central office to support district schools.

District Strategies for School Improvement

Burkett County is set up to provide general support for schools in need of improvement; although because of its urban location, sheer size organizationally, and the volume of students, it necessarily operates quite differently than smaller, more rural districts, such as Waterton County. The district offers numerous and varied opportunities for professional development for all faculty, administrators, and specialists throughout the year. Additionally, four full-day sessions are built into the academic calendar during which teachers and staff participate in common professional development. A district employee commented, "All schools have these professional development days, but I think if you have a grant for school reform, the thing to do is find how teachers can work together to learn improvement strategies promoted by that program. So having designated days for professional development is advantageous for reforming schools."

Besides professional development targeting faculty, the district recognizes that weaker or inexperienced principals may also benefit from leadership support and, thus, provides them mentoring. Dr. Roth explained, "Through my office and bringing in some retired principals, we actually place people to work alongside principals as mentors to give them guidance and help them become stronger." Two of the three Burkett County principals in this study received such support.

Burkett County also maintains a pool of instructional specialists or coaches to work with schools in need of improvement. They are district personnel but actually are assigned to work full-time at individual schools. In their effort to allocate the coaches effectively, Dr. Roth explained that there was more demand than supply, "We'll say, 'This school because of X, Y, and Z needs a full-time coach.' We only have 11 instructional coaches for the entire district, so some schools don't get one, but other schools will have one full-time." Later she added, "Some schools complain because others may get more help than they, but we don't see it that way. Teachers undergoing school improvement have to have a greater degree of support than more successful schools."

Beyond professional development, principal-mentors, and instructional coaches, district personnel developed two formal processes of support for schools in need of improvement involving *coaching* and *dialogue*. Coaching, a system of formative assessment, involves a three-member team visiting a school from fall until spring, for three to four hours on a weekly basis to observe in classrooms, and meet with the principal and the school's instructional leadership team. All three schools in this study were coaching schools. Dr. Roth explained the concept, "Some people use the word *monitoring* schools, I prefer *coaching* because that is more of what it really is. The team does walk-throughs, looks at documents, and employs observation rubrics. Those people come back and meet with me." She elaborated, "I follow up with the principal and instructional leadership team in the school so there is communication; we share data. Then we work closely with the principal and mentor. We say, 'here are our expectations, but we will help you get there.' Again, that is why I like the word coaching."

This district provides a second, more intense diagnostic and improvement strategy called *dialogue*, which essentially establishes a baseline assessment of schools in the beginning of the academic year to determine where they are and what they need to do over the year to improve. A dialogue team of 6 to 10 people spends one or two days in the school observing in classrooms using an observation tool, interviewing staff, students, and, occasionally, parents. It also examines key documents, such as the school portfolio, the consolidated plan, comprehensive plan, data, sample schedules, site-based decision-making council minutes, and so forth, to determine what is happening in the school. At the end of the second day, the dialogue team meets with the principal and her staff to make commendations and recommendations. The principal and staff follow up with short- and long-term steps because of the dialogue visit.

Support for School Reform

Through the federal programs coordinator, the district provided strong direction to schools in early adoption stages of the CSR program and helped identify and match the needs of the schools with appropriate service provision offered by a specific reform model. A teacher who had participated on the program selection team for her school explained, "When our school was shopping for a reform program, our principal was more interested in another program. The district's programs coordinator realized it wasn't well tailored to the needs of a middle-school population. She introduced us to the external model provider of a different model and, ultimately, we agreed to try it." The district administrator stated that besides trying to match reform programs with school needs she also tried to match programs to schools in conjunction with their leadership ability. Specifically, she directed schools having what she perceived to be weaker leaders to adopt more prescriptive programs and schools demonstrating stronger instructional leadership capacity to consider less prescriptive programs.

Regarding model selection, Dr. Roth emphasized her trust in principals to make decisions but also pointed out that if she didn't agree with the school's choice she would not hesitate to "go through the principal" to influence and redirect it. In fact, one school changed programs after the first year of implementation. Dr. Roth explained, "We got their test scores back and based on observing and visiting that school, I could see their program wasn't working. I talked to the principal about possibly looking at a new program. Ultimately, they dropped their reform model and picked up another one the following year." When asked about advocating for a school if program providers shirked their responsibility, an administrator said, "We would become proactive if necessary, but we've never really had that problem." In fact, I frequently observed model providers working in Burkett County schools during this study.

Preparing to Sustain Reform Through
Financial and Instructional Expertise

Burkett County assisted schools in their quest to sustain reform efforts as the expiration of federal funding was approaching by providing them financial and instructional expertise. Dr. Roth explained that all three schools in this study had been assigned a full-time instructional coach to continue working in the schools after the funding cycle ended. She said, "When the external people are gone, there has to be someone who is inside the building that can stay. With our resources, we make sure we give schools those people as part of the routine assignment of help." Beyond instructional assistance, the district worked with both schools that had chosen to continue their reform efforts to help adjust their budgets and redirect available money. It then supplemented those funds necessary to sustain the reform programs, on a scaled-back basis through a fourth year. Dr. Roth acknowledged, "Funding is essential to school reform. It results in giving people more time to work on things." She explained that there were special "district assistance funds" set aside for these purposes. She said, "School officials can make decisions on how they will use that extra 10 or 12 thousand, or whatever it is, for special development time for teachers in that building to have more support." Recognizing the integral role the district played by financially supporting her school's reform efforts, a facilitator reiterated, "If a school shows success, then you support that school's program with finances, you don't just drop it. You just can't do that and still expect the school to pick up on its own. You need to have that sustainability and a lot of times, it is achieved through money."

DISTRICT SUPPORT FOR SUSTAINING CHANGE IN OTHER SCHOOLS

Several other districts in the study shared at least some characteristics similar to those discussed earlier. Two different, isolated rural districts provided financial support to their schools as they sought ways to continue programs after their grants expired. The first district financially supported the school's explicit intention to sustain its reform program, whereas the second district allocated supplementary funds so the school could sustain reform efforts broadly rather than sustain its specific reform program. In that case, the principal explained that he and others realized the reform program they implemented with CSR funding had perhaps pointed them "in the *right* direction, but not the *only* direction." School personnel had begun the application process for funding from a different source to sustain its reform program, but on consultation with the district, they decided to withdraw it. The principal stated, "We went through the whole rollercoaster ride, we're not going to apply, we are going to apply, maybe we're not, we are, so the district just hung in there with us and supported us on it." He emphasized that when he finally reached the decision to redraw; the district concurred. The principal appreciated the trust in his decision-making capacity and the respect for the school's autonomy that his district demonstrated.

Other districts may have supported schools during reform adoption and implementation but simply did not attend to or appreciate their integral role in reform sustainability. In at least two districts, staffing changes in key administrative positions undermined the schools' efforts to sustain reform strategies beyond the life of the grant. For example, with district support, the middle school in Gray County appeared extremely successful in its reform efforts both in terms of program implementation and in other instructional and organizational ways. Like Waterton County, over the three years of CSR funding, it provided strategic expertise through district staffing and school administration, respected the autonomy of the school administration, and reinforced innovative instructional strategies introduced into its reforming school by disseminating them throughout other district schools. Right at the outset of the reform period, it hired a new principal who was innovative, highly motivated, charismatic, and presented himself as a capable leader. He was committed to improvement using the CSR program adopted prior to his arrival. The district did not interfere with his decisions and strategies. Moreover, the district reinforced the instructional coherence promoted by the reform program by aligning its schools' curriculum with the state core content across grades at all levels. Thus, with only slight modifications, the goals of the district, the school, and its reform program were consistent with each other. Additionally, the district allowed the school freedom to implement other strategies for instructional improvement, such as common planning time for faculty, which were recommended by reform model providers and others.

Over the three-year funding cycle, the school improved in numerous ways, not the least of which was remarkable gains on its index score in the state's assessment and accountability system. Because of his demonstrated skill and expertise in school improvement, the principal was transferred to another low-performing school when the funding cycle ended. His middle-school replacement came with high credentials and also seemed extremely capable but led in ways that sharply contrasted with the former principal. Most important, she described herself as fairly disinterested in trying to keep alive the reform strategies initiated earlier. Not surprisingly then, when I visited the school again one year after the second principal had taken the helm, there were few signs of the instructional strategies promoted over the previous three years. The former principal concurred with my observation saying, "Everything I did before I left that school was fine and dandy, but once I left, things dropped off. It shouldn't be that way. Over time when you allow that to happen, you may get by with having high test scores the first and maybe the second year, but sooner or later, the initiatives that made you strong are going to drop off or just flat level and never go anywhere."

A similar circumstance occurred in a nearby district, the main difference being that the shift in key personnel occurred in the central office rather than in the reforming school. When I returned to the district in the fourth year of the study, I found that it had hired a new federal programs director who did not seem interested in the program implemented earlier by three reforming schools. Instead, she promoted a new direction for improvement that undermined strategies initiated in those schools and dimmed their enthusiasm for change.

At least two districts offered passive cooperation to their reforming schools. They had encouraged their eligible schools to apply for funding to finance school change when they, in reality, had no understanding of what would be required of the district to support the schools. Consequently, they cooperated with the schools' principals when their intentions did not match the district policies. Otherwise, they offered little or no support to the schools throughout the grant period. The remaining several districts appeared too preoccupied with competing priorities, disinterested in the hard work of school improvement, or disenchanted with previous reform experiences and left schools to fend for themselves.

DISCUSSION OF DISTRICT SUPPORT
FOR SUSTAINING REFORM

This chapter has demonstrated the integral contribution of district support for the sustainability of reform in schools. Supportive districts offered effective technical assistance to schools beginning with the initial reform-adoption phase and beyond the expiration of CSR grants. Specifically, the districts encouraged and guided schools during model selection, advocated on their behalf if necessary, and offered them financial and technical expertise during and after the funding cycle. Further, in absence of systematic guidance from model providers on how to sustain improvement strategies, these two districts functioned as a bridge for schools by actively working with reforming schools to shore up their efforts to sustain reform practices. Although their strategies differed, both Waterton and Burkett Counties exhibited broad-based support (Berman & McLaughlin, 1978) of their schools in ways that were appropriate to district size. Burkett County's full-time, in-school assistance was consistent with research by Goertz (2005), who notes that district support for NCLB varied based on size and geographic location of districts. Larger districts were nearly three times more likely than smaller districts to provide schools with full-time, in-school staff support for instructional development or mentoring for principals.

Beyond technical support, Fullan (2005) maintains that capacity building is integral to school improvement and that the district should assume responsibility to help schools develop the capacity to function in effective, autonomous ways but in a common direction. To do this, the district must build a *coalition of leaders* at the school level. Further, the school's capacity is heightened and commitment for change is activated when districts engage schools in lateral capacity building, that is, when they routinely work collectively and plan collaboratively to shape the direction of change together.

Waterton County built capacity in a number of ways. It established and endorsed a vision for lasting improvement that became widespread and shared among educators across district schools. Intentional hiring practices and strategic placement of people in key positions promoted stability. A liaison system provided technical expertise for schools but, more important, established an effective system of communication between schools and the central office. This benefited schools and increased the organic capacity of the district in that administrators specializing in one area gained exposure to a broader host of school concerns and, consequently, became familiar with and competent in dealing with issues that previously may have fallen outside their area of expertise. District personnel also actively built capacity when they promoted clustering, encouraged critical reflection on practice and subsequent strategic planning, and established a forum where schools could network, share information, and enjoy group support.

Indeed, practices as these have been recognized in the literature as effective contributors to reform sustainability. Moffett (2000) claims that two-way information flow and communication is the *lifeblood* of successful reforms, and Slavin (2004) identifies support networking as key to the longevity of a reform program. Further, through these structured systems for information-sharing, facilitators codeveloped a *core* of expertise among themselves that likely promoted innovative behavior in schools. Coburn and Russell (2008) argue that communication and networking generate sources of social capital, a term used to describe the extent individuals derive intangible resources, support, and opportunities for social relationships (Coleman & Hoffer, 1987; Stanton-Salazar & Dornbusch, 1995). In that they increased access to expertise, enhanced the content of interactions, and built trust among participants, strategies practiced in these districts also tightened structural linkages in systems and, thus, built capacity.

Underscoring all support measures was Waterton County's respect for the autonomy and ability of schools to make decisions directing their course in the shared quest for improvement. In this rural district, the fierce competition and sense of independence traditionally held among the individual school communities was slowly eroding and becoming replaced with whole-system capacity marked by a spirit of empowerment, cooperation, and unity.

Carlson and Buttram (2004), Dewees (2000), Sherwood (1999) and others warn that issues of size, autonomy, complacency, and so forth may inhibit the ability or willingness of small rural schools to seek improvement. In their study of CSR implementation in five southwestern rural schools, Carlson and Buttram (2004) found that district involvement and support for reform was minor. Most commonly, superintendents were involved to some extent during the proposal process but relinquished responsibility for program implementation to school leadership. There were no data to suggest that districts contributed support for school improvement beyond the earliest stages of reform. Contrary to their findings, the evidence presented in this chapter reveals that Waterton County was committed to school improvement and deliberately established thoughtful and effective practices to build capacity in reforming schools and the district as a whole while respecting the integrity of the individual schools.

Burkett County also actively provided broad-based support to enhance the capacity of reforming schools. It offered a sound infrastructure through professional development, in-school staff assistance and modeling for novice or weak principals, and a means of assessing a school's performance and providing appropriate direction and recommendations for school improvement by a team of experienced educators through coaching and dialogue. Coburn and Russell (2008) recognize such strategies as important means to generate social capital.

At least two other districts that initially acted in supportive ways reduced or eliminated support of their reforming schools because of personnel changes. The hiring of a new school improvement director in one district and a new principal in another ultimately redirected how the districts approached school improvement altogether and left little support for the earlier reform initiatives. These findings are consistent with those of Datnow and Stringfield (2000), Murphy and Datnow (2003), Slavin (2004), and Ross (2001) who found that turnover in key administrative positions resulted in a new agenda and reduced district support for previous efforts.

Alternatively, about half of the remaining districts offered passive cooperation to their reforming schools, and the other half offered little or no support at all. They opportunistically encouraged eligible schools to seek funding for school change but left them to fend for themselves. These districts lacked appreciation for the importance of active support for schools during the funding period. Whether schools found support in sustaining reform efforts from their districts, principals and other key educators in some schools exhibited patterns of strong and capable leadership as they promoted reform efforts. The next chapter addresses the important contributions of leadership at the school level.

4

Promoting Distributed Leadership

We all have a job to do. Actually as the principal, if I am not able to give up a little bit, then I am not doing my job successfully because I can't do it all. I need to know about everything to some degree, but it is important to cultivate leadership among others and give them some freedom to do what they see fit. I trust them to make good judgment calls. . . . And I haven't had to eat any crow yet!

—Middle-school principal

Leadership for school reform is effective when it is distributed across administrators and faculties. Leadership may promote a carefully planned and well-managed change process, worker buy-in or commitment, and a supportive school climate, each of which may be critical for implementation and sustainability of organizational change (Datnow & Castellano, 2001; Evans-Andris, 1996; Kanter, 1983; Smylie & Denny, 1990). Historically, school leadership was bureaucratic, top-down, concentrated or centralized among few individuals, and focused on efficient management of schools. Studies almost exclusively targeted the roles and capabilities of top school administrators, especially the principal. In this present period of reform, far more responsibilities emerge than can be handled effectively by one individual. Schools require management of fiscal and human resources, but also demand leadership of instruction,

65

professional development, and so forth. Further, input from multiple sources having unique and complementary skills and talents may result in a richer, more effective change dynamic. As a result, research on leadership must broaden its focus to address the changing roles of the principal and teachers as they contribute to school improvement. Such leadership may be most effective when it is provided by the principal and distributed among teacher leaders.

Distributed leadership in schools is characterized by the recognition of expertise and opportunities for meaningful input in decision making among educators who may or may not hold formal leadership titles. It is a collective activity, marked by concertive action, as educators work together to pool their initiative and knowledge (Bennett, Wise, Woods & Harvey, 2003; Spillane, Halverson, & Diamond 2001). According to Spillane et al. (2001), distributed leadership is generated in the interactions of leaders, followers, and their situation. Because it promotes responsibility and encourages input at all levels, distributed leadership particularly is effective when schools take on the challenge of implementing and sustaining change.

This chapter examines leadership in reforming schools by considering the actions and contributions of principals, program facilitators, and faculty members as effective change agents. It asks the following: What leadership roles contribute to the mission of reforming schools? How does a leadership position become defined, structured, and delineated? To what extent are leadership functions shared and distributed? How does distributed leadership contribute to the likelihood of sustainability of school reform efforts? It finds that distributed leadership provides a useful framework to better understand why reform may be promoted, managed, and sustained in some schools and not in others.

LEADERSHIP FOR CHANGE

Leadership for change involves principals, program facilitators, and other teacher leaders. Principals are a fundamental source for leadership as schools engage in school reform. Leadership qualities most readily associated with the principal include defining, managing, supervising, and monitoring reform efforts in individual schools (Fullan, 1991; Leithwood, 1992). Sarason (1996) identifies principals as "gatekeepers of change" (p. 77) because their contribution during innovation is significant to its success.

Schools may also rely on in-school program coordinators or facilitators to actively promote and manage innovative behavior during periods of change. Program facilitators commonly identify appropriate instructional materials and resources, engage in modeling or instructional coaching, and generally offer advice and guidance to classroom teachers (Camburn,

Rowan, & Taylor, 2003; Datnow & Castellano, 2001; Evans-Andris, 1996; Mangin, 2007). Tushman (1977) notes that innovation demands that new roles perform cross boundary communication to link internal and external organizational information networks.

New models of leadership for school improvement focus less on contributions of individual leaders and more on collective, shared, social processes. School reform calls for a shift in notions about leadership from traditional hierarchical, centralized authority and its control over teachers to one that encourages collaboration between administrators and faculty, collegiality, and norms of mutual influence with shared decision making and problem solving. Smylie, Conley, and Marks (2002) argue that leadership performed across roles and stemming from both formal positions of authority and informal positions is conducive to more productive communication patterns in schools, group problem solving, innovative instructional practice, and capacity building among teachers. Such a model of distributed leadership represents a change in school culture by recognizing expert rather than formal hierarchical authority and is based on trust, collaboration, professional learning, and reciprocal accountability (Copland, 2003). It necessitates a fundamental restructuring of traditional positions, roles, power boundaries, and processes of leadership, yet this is not always a smooth process, as it may threaten status quo.

Distributed leadership is grounded in the interaction of school leaders, followers, and situations (Spillane, Halverson, & Diamond, 2001). In that respect, it is more than allocating tasks among formal and informal leaders. Consequently, an analysis of distributed leadership must seek the sources of leadership in actual practice rather than in formally described roles. The volume of formal positions alone does not suggest strong leadership or its effective distribution. Further, the influence of such leadership may be profound because multiple leaders having different areas of knowledge and expertise can work in collaborative, collective, and coordinated patterns to effect change in ways that are greater than the contribution of any one leader working independently (Spillane, Diamond, & Jita, 2000).

This holds implications regarding school leadership during reform. Although school reform creates a proliferation of new roles for teacher leaders (Camburn, Rowan, & Taylor, 2003), Little (2003) questions whether these roles attain long-term institutional support or contribute meaningfully to lasting change. Teacher leadership potentially can result in the development, reflection, and sustainability of innovative instructional strategies, but she observes, more often, it merely represents a reallocation of administrative responsibilities associated with implementing reform programs. However, in a study of comprehensive school reform (CSR), Smylie, Wenzel, and Fendt (2003) found that schools characterized by distributed leadership made the most progress. In those schools, tasks such as creating and sustaining a vision, engaging others, promoting instructional coherence, providing opportunities to develop knowledge and skills, and monitoring program implementation were performed in coordinated fashion by multiple actors.

This chapter begins by presenting leadership patterns in two reforming schools and highlights the integral contribution of the principal; the new role of the school facilitator, specifically, how it becomes structured and defined; and the involvement of other teacher leaders. It then identifies leadership functions required of reforming schools and their distribution among leaders. It considers tendencies toward sustainable change exhibited by schools and concludes by discussing effective patterns of school leadership and reform. The next sections describe leadership in Tipton Middle School and Greely Elementary.

DISTRIBUTED LEADERSHIP IN TIPTON MIDDLE SCHOOL

When I initially called Dr. Adams, the principal of Tipton Middle School, to discuss the school's potential involvement in this study, she referred me to her school's program facilitator saying, "I prefer that she be involved with such decisions." On the appointed day, I found the school in a run-down urban neighborhood. Even so, the steps leading to the front entrance of the large brick building dating from the 1920s were swept and decorated with pots of flowers. Inside, the halls were clean and orderly. Although it was the start of the school day, the front office was quiet. The school served nearly 700 students.

The Principal

When I arrived, Dr. Adams greeted me, invited me into her office, and began our conversation by stating she had been principal at Tipton for five years. Early on, she had appointed a small group of teachers as an advisory group. She explained, "I have always had a group of people to work with. When I got to this school, I asked the highly skilled educator (HSE), the technology person, and a resource person to form a group. I just felt like they all needed to be together and know each other and provide input."

Not unlike many other principals in this study, Dr. Adams' vision for Tipton was to increase student learning in reading and writing. She rationalized this by saying, "Everybody needed to focus on this because if students can't read the book how are they going to do the content?" This vision was promoted and shared throughout the school, especially among the faculty. Dr. Adams stated, "On the teacher level, everybody must take ownership that all kids need to read and write, no matter what content you are teaching."

The discussion turned to the school's experience with its CSR program. Dr. Adams explained in detail how her faculty, working together, identified and selected its program based on its consistency with the school's vision of improving performance, particularly in reading and writing. In working out the responsibilities various teachers would assume at the beginning of the reform process, the advisory group and others reviewed the school's consolidated plan, its improvement plan, and the reform model to determine how each document overlapped and who would oversee the various components. She said, "We just sat down and decided 'this is how we are going to divvy it out.' With this large faculty, I had so many people with diverse abilities and talents. " Later she laughingly continued, "They will probably tell you that I just told them, 'Here, you do this and let's meet back in two weeks.' But really, I knew the strengths of each person. Everybody has a piece of this reform, and it has worked out good." She maintained that the reform program the school ultimately adopted increased unity of the faculty. She noted, "I think we have a common language now among the adults in the building."

Dr. Adams seemed extremely knowledgeable about the reform program and progress the faculty had made toward schoolwide implementation. Besides attending training sessions alongside faculty, she said she tracked their progress by cross comparing their content lesson plans to examine their integration of instructional strategies promoted by the school's reform program, and their professional growth plans. Together with the program facilitator, she reviewed these, made suggestions, and returned them to teachers every six weeks. She laughed and said, "The first time we did this, teachers seemed surprised they got comments back. Now it is routine, and they expect it."

The Instructional Team

Dr. Adams looked at the clock and interrupted our conversation by stating the school's instructional support and planning team, of which she was a member, was meeting at 9:00 a.m. She led the way to the second floor and into a spacious room that served as the office for three of the four members of the instructional team. The meeting already was underway. Dr. Adams introduced me to the women. The first was Mrs. Shade, the school's reform facilitator who was also its Title I coordinator. She was in her fourth year at Tipton and, prior to this role, had been the school's highly skilled educator (HSE). The second woman was a full-time instructional coach on loan from the district. The external reform program provider also was present. Dr. Adams then directed me briefly to explain my project to the group. They collectively agreed the school would participate and invited me to stay for the remainder of the meeting.

For nearly an hour, we talked about many aspects of the reform program, Tipton's implementation experiences, and its progress, about which they seemed proud and satisfied. They attributed the school's success to careful planning, teacher leadership, professional growth, and a commonly shared focus on schoolwide reform. In fact, they explained that Dr. Adams had eliminated all other initiatives in the building that might distract teachers from focusing on the school's vision and its reform program. After that, they discussed plans for the school's next professional development day that would be devoted to faculty-led analysis, review, and discussion of the most recent performance scores on the Commonwealth Accountability Testing System (CATS) test and a report on the school's progress with reform implementation provided by the outside agency. Dr. Adams explained that ordinarily they took these reports with *a grain of salt,* as they often seemed out of context, unnecessarily negative, and unhelpful. Even so, she said she normally culled some aspects of the report that might be useful and distributed them for faculty review and consideration rather than burdening teachers with the report in its entirety.

Finally, the program provider left to model a seventh-grade science lesson for students and a small group of teachers in the library. She excused herself saying, "I try to present myself as a teacher in the classroom demonstrating lessons rather than just a program provider who comes in all perky after school when the teachers are already tired after a long day." The facilitator and another team member were on their way to a meeting of the school's leadership team, a group of 10 teachers who had committed to train their peers to use the reform program's strategies for their respective content areas. Dr. Adams described the teachers as "experienced, competent, and dedicated instructional support leaders" with whom she was "completely satisfied." Shortly after that, the meeting ended.

As this case demonstrates, the strength of reform efforts in Tipton Middle School rests in a pattern of leadership that began with the principal but was distributed to the facilitator, other teacher leaders, and a full-time district instructional coach. These key leaders planned together and then extended responsibility for various aspects of reform implementation to others throughout the school. The next section presents a school where leadership was expanding.

DEVELOPING DISTRIBUTED LEADERSHIP IN GREELY ELEMENTARY SCHOOL

I drove several hours to Greely, a once thriving mining community. The elementary school, serving about 300 kindergarten through Grade 8 students, was housed in a large, two-story, old building on the side of a hill overlooking the small, quiet town center. A high school sat farther up the hill behind Greely Elementary and a creek ran directly in front of it. As I passed through a cafeteria toward the office, small groups of mothers chatted as they waited for their children's dismissal.

The Principal

The principal, Ms. Ashley, was very friendly and eager to participate in the study. She had worked in Greely for more than 10 years. She had become principal four years ago after earning her principal certification with two other women in the district by commuting for several years to a university more than an hour away. Now, Ms. Ashley encouraged leadership development among other faculty. Six of the school's 20 teachers presently were pursuing administrative training to become principals. As if to justify the cadre of teacher leaders that was developing under her supervision, Ms. Ashley shrugged and said, "I love it here, but eventually, I am going to move on. I need more people than me to know what is going on and know what is important instructionally and businesswise."

Ms. Ashley seemed very knowledgeable and enthusiastic about the school's reform model. She said she actively promoted its concepts at the district level and had found central office to be supportive. She stated, "The superintendent's goal is that all children can learn, and we do whatever to make sure that happens. They generally support me in about anything I want to do that is related to that goal. They have always been willing to listen to me and so has the board of education." She also explained that the local school board rotated the location of its monthly meeting among the district schools and in anticipation of hosting the next meeting, she said, "We have a presentation ready to go that shows all we've been doing." Then she chuckled and added, "When they have a feel for what you're doing, they're more willing to give you support."

Reiterating the importance of the principal to demonstrate support for reform, Ms. Ashley mentioned she attended the national conference held by their model providers in the first year of program implementation. Since then, however, she encouraged faculty to attend in her place. She called this a *win-win* in that teachers gained professional development and opportunities for networking at the conference and, by increasing the number who attended the national training session, more teachers throughout the school shared responsibility for reform.

Ms. Ashley explained that she verbally promoted the use of the reform program among faculty members and observed lessons and monitored lesson plans for evidence that they were incorporating instructional strategies advocated by the program in their classroom teaching. Finally, she spoke of how she and Greely's program facilitator, Mrs. Christopher, worked together to promote the school's reform mission. After a while, Ms. Ashley realized Mrs. Christopher would be starting a break, and took me upstairs to meet her.

The Program Facilitator

Mrs. Christopher's fourth-grade students were filing out of their classroom when we arrived. We found her pulling reform program materials out of a filing cabinet to deliver to the seventh-grade math teacher. She was an older woman who had taught at Greely for 25 years. For my benefit, Mrs. Christopher began recounting her involvement as the program facilitator over the three-year grant period. She explained that the school had not identified a facilitator in the first year to reserve a portion of the grant money for materials and resources. However, implementation suffered so between the first and second year of the funding cycle, Ms. Ashley had asked her to serve as facilitator on a part-time basis. Ms. Ashley nodded and said, "She's been here so long she could walk into any room inside this building or beyond and people would listen and work with her. That was why she was the overwhelming choice for facilitator." Mrs. Christopher recalled that her late entry into the position caused her to have to catch up over that summer. Then, in the third year, the school needed her to teach nearly full-time again so presently she was facilitating for two periods per day, one of which was her planning period. She justified this by stating, "I don't give out hardly any effort now, the teachers don't need me as much; you know what I'm saying?"

Later that week, I had lunch in a large spacious classroom with the small group of upper-grade teachers. As they ate, they joked and teased with one another. There was much laughter but also more serious dialogue regarding class projects and student engagement in relation to their school's reform program. Several teachers had just arrived back from a national conference held by the program's sponsors, which sparked much conversation. As lunchtime ended, they agreed to continue the discussion during their common planning period later that day.

Greely Elementary demonstrated a pattern of distributing leadership that began with the principal and extended to a reform program facilitator. It seems that the principal was laying the groundwork for distributed leadership by cultivating a climate of trust and camaraderie among teachers and by supporting their efforts to obtain professional development in both gaining formal education and attending conferences related to the school's reform efforts. She also intentionally garnered cooperation for the school's reform efforts at the district level. The next two sections discuss leadership for reform among principals and facilitators.

PRINCIPAL LEADERSHIP FOR REFORM

As the two cases presented earlier suggest, principal leadership is integral to school reform efforts. Previous studies on CSR reveal that principal leadership and teachers' perception of principal leadership are critical indicators of levels of change in schools (Berends, Bodilly, & Kirby 2002a, 2002b). Principals monitored implementation progress, centered attention on school improvement, managed resources, and maintained a positive working relationship with the district office (Camburn, Rowan, & Taylor, 2003). Kirby, Berends, and Naftel (2001) found that principal leadership was the single most important predictor in model implementation in schools and among teachers individually. Further, schools in which teachers perceived there to be strong leadership stemming from principals had higher levels of implementation over time (Berends et al., 2002a).

The two principals in the schools earlier overtly promoted reform efforts during reform adoption and implementation. They intentionally became knowledgeable about the program their school adopted and participated in training sessions in their school and at regional or national conferences. Like Dr. Adams and Ms. Ashley, other principals effectively advocated reform implementation and marked progress together with their faculties by monitoring the work of teachers. They also encouraged faculty to participate in critical discussion about reform by synthesizing and sharing information contained in the periodic reviews issued by outside agencies, analyzing performance data based on CATS, and reflecting on instructional practice. Principals generated support for their school's reform efforts beyond their school. For example, when district support was not apparent, principals like Ms. Ashley deliberately garnered district cooperation for change. Further, they commonly reported they buffered their schools from outside scrutiny and criticism that inevitably accompanied negative reviews or declining test scores. It is likely Ms. Ashley preempted criticism at the district office by continually keeping it abreast of her school's reform efforts.

Principals' demonstration of support reflected the nature of leadership and extent to which it was distributed among others. Dr. Adams had already established a pattern of distributed leadership in her school. She worked in concert with a strong, stable team that shared a common vision, embraced innovation and improvement, and guided other faculty leaders, who, in turn, disseminated and modeled instructional strategies for their peers. Ms. Ashley was developing leaders in her school by encouraging motivated teachers to pursue administrative training, cultivating a climate of trust and rapport among faculty schoolwide, and supporting the work of her program facilitator. Both principals acted with high consideration of teachers as professionals and adult learners. Consistent with these findings, Copland (2003) detected that principals practicing distributed leadership exert less role-based authority and allow others to assume leadership responsibilities. Similar to the quotation at the start of this chapter, a principal has to willingly relinquish authority so that others may assume it.

One of the first tasks principals performed as their schools were awarded funding for reform was to assign someone to facilitate and coordinate the implementation process. The following section examines the ways in which the job of the program facilitator became defined and structured in reforming schools.

REFORM FACILITATION

Innovation in schools demands involvement beyond the principal and may require the creation of new positions. Recognizing their potential as leaders of change, CSR required that schools appoint a facilitator or "coach" to oversee and manage program implementation. However, schools commonly defined and configured these newly identified leadership positions differently.

Reform Facilitation and Administration

As in Tipton Middle School, principals in six schools selected program facilitators explicitly because of their demonstrated leadership qualities either at the school or district level. Recall, Mrs. Shade previously served her school as a HSE and presently oversaw its Title I program. In all but one school, these facilitators continued to maintain part-time involvement with other school or district programs such as curriculum development, Title I, technology, and so forth. These dual assignments complemented each other, and the facilitators readily balanced the time commitments of both sets of responsibilities. One facilitator of a large middle school explained, "I became our curriculum coordinator about seven years ago. Then we got the reform grant and they needed a facilitator. It is pretty hard to separate the curriculum coordinator from the program facilitator because they really go together so, the last three years, I have worked full-time in both those roles." Similarly, another school's facilitator also split her time working as the district's parent liaison. This arrangement seemed optimal because she worked both jobs from her school office and the nature of the district job complemented and enhanced reform facilitation. Like Ms. Shade at Tipton, facilitators holding other formal administrative duties typically shared workspace with individuals who filled complementary leadership positions such as the school's HSE, curriculum coordinator, or members of the school's leadership team. Faculty leaders viewed workspace sharing as beneficial as it increased their chance to discuss, plan together, and support one another.

Reform Facilitation and Teaching

Like Ms. Ashley at Greely, principals in nine schools selected senior faculty as program facilitators because of their deep roots, ranging from 17 to 26 years, in their schools. They often referred to these veterans as *master teachers*.

A principal reflected on the qualities of a teacher facilitator, "She's the kind of person anybody felt they could go to knowing she would do her best to help them. She isn't forceful, but she has a quiet dignity. People could trust her. They didn't mind her in their classroom knowing she had the best interest of students at heart." This principal and others perceived senior faculty suited for the job because of demonstrated excellence in teaching, command of faculty respect, or ability to get along with everyone. In several schools, this was important because of staff factions.

Rather than tapping teachers with seniority, two principals extended the opportunity for program facilitation to less experienced teachers who exhibited potential for leadership. A former teacher of special education explained that the assignment was a means to gain new skills and move into school leadership. She explained, "I became excited about the prospect of a new learning opportunity this job presented. I also felt I could lend some expertise and be successful in it." Another principal asked a second-year teacher with coaching experience to be the program facilitator. He explained he deliberately placed this young man in the position so he could develop meaningful skills and gain experiences relevant to a future administrative position.

Of the facilitators chosen because of teaching expertise or leadership potential, five divided their time between facilitation and more routine teaching assignments ranging from three to six periods per day. Balancing the constraints of this split arrangement was not easy; in fact, it was something like a juggling act. Recall that Mrs. Christopher was sandwiching time between her planning time and her next class to gather and deliver appropriate materials related to the school's reform model for another teacher when I met her. Rather than having a separate workspace like Mrs. Shade at Tipton and others who split facilitation with administrative assignments, the facilitators who continued to teach conducted work related to model facilitation from their classrooms, using their desks and cabinets to store paperwork and materials.

Teaching and facilitation represented separate sets of responsibilities that could not be fulfilled simultaneously. The immediate demands of teaching necessarily required Mrs. Christopher and the others to arrange facilitation around teaching obligations. Consequently, they snatched bits of time for facilitation during the school day but then sacrificed long hours after school and in the summer to facilitate and advance their schools' reform strategies. One principal hoped to protect his school's facilitator from teaching to avoid reducing her effectiveness as facilitator but regrettably found his budget would not permit this. He explained, "The one thing I did not want was a facilitator that I had to use in the classroom because you just can't handle everything that way."

As this principal alludes, the stability of the facilitator's job, particularly among those who taught part time, tended to vary yearly as it became more clearly defined, structured, and modified in the schools' contexts.

Principals commonly said they allocated time for facilitation in response to the fluctuating demand for teaching and related budgetary constraints rather than consideration of effective leadership for model implementation or sustainability. In fact, as a money-saving strategy, one principal doubled as the school's program facilitator for all three years of the grant period, and two schools used no facilitator in the third year. The principal of one of those schools explained, "The facilitator in my school isn't even part time. She's back to teaching and spends a couple hours each week working with the librarian making sure materials have been ordered or are in stock and asking teachers about what they might still need help with." Not surprisingly, the instability of the facilitator's job likely took a toll on the quality of leadership for reform. A principal acknowledged this saying, "Everything has been just kind of haphazard, and it hasn't worked well." A facilitator in another school shared a similar observation regarding the decreased time allotted for her job and admitted, "It has been very hard for me, and there's been a dramatic difference in model use among teachers." Undoubtedly recognizing the potential for compromising the quality of program implementation when work was divided between teaching and facilitation, the providers of Success for All (SFA) required that teachers relinquish other responsibilities to serve as full-time facilitators. Six of the individuals chosen because of teaching expertise or leadership potential worked as facilitators full-time in schools using SFA.

Boundary Maintenance and Work Overload

Role ambiguity may accompany new positions that are poorly defined or otherwise lack clarity (Datnow & Castellano, 2001; Evans-Andris, 1996; Smylie & Denny, 1990). In a study of teacher leadership, Smylie and Denny (1990) found the role and purpose of the teacher leader surrounded by misunderstanding. Some teacher leaders reported uncertainty about what they were expected to do in their job. They perceived that their classroom and leadership responsibilities were incompatible and experienced role conflict as they allocated time between them. Similarly, a study on leadership in six SFA schools by Datnow and Castellano (2001) revealed that new roles generated by CSR, such as reform facilitation, created challenges such as role ambiguity and work overload.

In this study, while championing their schools' reform efforts, facilitators who also taught or fulfilled other administrative duties frequently experienced job fragmentation. Because they assumed two sets of job responsibilities, they registered complaints such as, "I can't totally immerse myself in one job," and "I feel as though I'm constantly torn in two." Although full-time facilitators were better able to focus exclusively on the job of program implementation, they were not immune to such feelings. For example, a full-time facilitator explained she had been charged with overseeing school assessment, guiding the school's instructional leadership committee, and "anything else that needs to be done." She said, "My job has evolved into a lot of things. I also have become the literacy contact person, so when people from the district are here they ask 'Can I meet with you?' I don't think they really know my boundaries." Almost to herself she lamented, "Sometimes I would like to have back just the narrow focus of the classroom. I kind of miss that."

The ability of teacher leaders to cope with job fragmentation appeared to depend on how their roles became defined and their diligence in maintaining role boundaries in relation to the other roles that they were expected to fulfill. Boundary maintenance is the process of demarcating or negotiating occupational roles in the workplace. Despite how jobs are formally defined, Allen (2000) found that workers socially negotiate the content and limits of their jobs through micropolitical processes in daily interactions at the point of service delivery.

Boundary maintenance was a way for facilitators to protect themselves from stressful working conditions. Similar to the respondent earlier, another full-time facilitator seemed particularly aware of the need to maintain the boundaries of her position. She explained that the school's curriculum coordinator coincidentally retired when she became the reform facilitator and, because of this, the principal and faculty tried to draw her into other responsibilities. She intended to become more assertive in defining her boundaries the following year. She explained, "I have a myriad of duties. Although I'm really just supposed to be our facilitator, teachers keep coming to me about issues the coordinator handled. So my concern for next year as we continue to use this program is how much I'm going to be pulled into other duties. I won't stand for much of it."

In at least two cases, facilitators seemed unaware of the need for diligent boundary maintenance, and as a result, their jobs became defined by their principals. In the first instance, along with reform facilitation, the principal asked the woman to conduct a wide range of clerical and unrelated tasks. For example, once while I was in the school, she was busy planning a school dance and told me her principal asked her to attend it as a chaperone. Another time she was manning the front desk as the secretary was ill. In contrast, the expectations of the second principal seemed more consistent with the formally defined role of a reform facilitator. I observed the facilitator in that school usually working in classrooms with teachers and students. She told me, "Whatever my principal may ask me to do, it is always something having to do with program administration or otherwise directly related to classroom instruction." It appears that despite their talent and skills, these facilitators were passive rather than proactive in protecting the boundaries of their job responsibilities and allowed them by default to be defined by the principals' expectations.

In addition to job fragmentation, facilitators in this study occasionally found themselves the target of scrutiny and resentment from colleagues.

Unconvinced that reform implementation warranted full or nearly full-time facilitation, classroom teachers in some schools perceived facilitators to be shirking their "real" responsibilities as educators and made comments about them not having "enough work" or being "busy enough." One seventh-grade teacher alluded to this saying, "No one can see our facilitator working very much." Another teacher in the same school agreed, "There's a lot of nonteaching that goes on. I don't really know what she does with all her time." Similarly, a faculty member at a different school stated, "We're not really aware of what our facilitator's role is or what he is actually doing to facilitate anything." An administrator in a third school relayed his faculty's perception, "The teachers at this school think our facilitator is sitting in an office with a cushy job leaving them without the help or the support they need."

Job scrutiny occurred most frequently when facilitators lacked substantial teaching or administrative assignments and was particularly prevalent in smaller schools where the reduced teaching responsibilities of facilitators resulted in increased class sizes for classroom teachers. A principal in one small school admitted, "I am going to be candid with you. There is resentment. There are people here who resent that this facilitator is doing this program rather than teaching. She is doing her job, but it causes other folks to have to do more because they have more students. I have heard a lot of people voice these concerns."

Facilitators occasionally talked about adverse working conditions involving job scrutiny and attributed them to lack of understanding about the job. Aware that her faculty scrutinized her work the facilitator in one small school said, "It's always easier to walk in someone else's shoes. These teachers don't really understand everything that I'm responsible for. I think they think I don't have a lot to do. Maybe they see me in here talking right now while they've got a classroom full of kids and think we're just chatting about the weather." Another facilitator likened the climate surrounding her position to that of her former job as a special education teacher because of the paperwork she was burdened with, the resentment directed toward her, and the isolation she felt. Noting that teachers did not understand the nature of her job she stated, "It's a difficult role because you're sort of in no man's land. You're not a teacher; you're not an administrator; you're just there."

As they negotiated relationships with teachers and principals and established themselves as change agents, facilitators most successfully avoided or overcame scrutiny when they helped and assisted classroom teachers in overt, visible ways and engaged in work overload. For example, facilitators like Mrs. Christopher at Greely accommodated the demands of classroom teaching and reform facilitation, and she won the admiration of her peers by willingly working extended school days and sacrificing summer vacation. Another facilitator who taught four periods per day explained that her faculty no longer questioned her role as they did in earlier years of program implementation and, instead, seemed to worry about her heavy workload. She said, "Now teachers come and say 'How can I help?' It's amazing how we all help one another." In another school, a teacher observed, "Our facilitator goes beyond the call of duty to make the whole thing work. She's constantly getting out the word of our model and what we're trying to do with the program." Faculties commonly recognized and appreciated the efforts of facilitators whom they perceived to be working *extra* to help them and to promote their school's reform efforts.

It is clear that until new positions of leadership, such as the reform program facilitator, become defined and clarified, social dynamics imposed by classroom teachers may produce fragmentation, scrutiny, and social isolation of new teacher leaders. In this study, most facilitators preempted or reduced negative working conditions by proactively maintaining the boundaries of their jobs and willingly engaging in a vast array of tasks and responsibilities required of the position, even when this generated work overload. These are described in the following section.

NEGOTIATION OF TASKS AND RESPONSIBILITIES

Reform implementation generated numerous tasks, duties, and responsibilities. Although the obligations seemed consistent from school to school, the extent to which the principal, the facilitator, and other school leaders shared them varied.

Managerial Tasks

Program implementation, across all five reform models, involved routine managerial tasks such as overseeing budgets, ordering supplies, accessing and preparing materials for teachers, arranging for professional development, scheduling issues, and so forth. Facilitators completed most of these necessary tasks with minimal help from others, often describing them as clerical, mundane, time consuming, and distractive.

Some facilitators appeared particularly consumed by managerial tasks. For example, one program called for the periodic reassessment and regrouping of students based on their reading performance and required the review of parent response sheets to document home reading. Facilitators with seemingly disproportionate amounts of managerial tasks tended to be most apt to express concern about their workload. Referring to the paperwork involved with testing students and tracking parent response sheets, one full-time facilitator rolled her eyes and said, "That's all I ever get done." Another facilitator concurred. She said, "I'm packed down like a mule with paperwork." Similarly, a facilitator whose school recently had added the math component to the more traditional reading model complained that he simply was "stretched too thin."

Collaborative Duties

Besides managerial tasks, each reform program demanded more complex and challenging duties that involved working directly with classroom teachers. For example, program implementation required faculty training and periodic sessions for faculty new to the school, introducing new or modified implementation procedures, and designing opportunities for faculty collaboration. These might include providing teachers with resource information or guidance and substitute teaching while they observed in other reforming schools or model best practices in classrooms.

Program facilitators typically viewed collaborative duties as an integral part of their job and relished them. One facilitator explained, "I don't just roam around when I go in a classroom. I've done much collaboration. It makes the teachers feel more comfortable with the program." Another facilitator agreed saying, "I find this job to be overwhelming but exciting. Teachers are at ease with me in their classrooms helping as a resource and program adviser. I love doing it. It gives me a great sense of worth when I'm helping other teachers. Plus, I see the neatest things." Like these women, most facilitators perceived collaborative duties as a means of enhancing instructional capacity and described them as challenging, effective, and rewarding.

In schools where leadership was distributed or expanding, instructional collaboration was shared. Recall in Tipton Middle School, the program facilitator and the instructional team worked with other teacher leaders to plan, collaborate, and guide classroom improvement. They, in turn, disseminated, coached, and modeled reform strategies with other teachers. Even in schools such as Tipton, however, the facilitator usually coordinated the efforts of other teacher leaders.

Supervisory Responsibilities

Principals usually monitored and supervised faculty compliance with reform implementation. Both Dr. Adams at Tipton and Ms. Ashley at Greely monitored their faculty's progress in rather subtle, unobtrusive ways, through lesson plans and occasional classroom observations. Similarly, teachers in several schools reported having to highlight the integration of reform strategies in their lesson plans.

Nearly every facilitator or other faculty leader successfully avoided supervisory responsibilities even though they likely were most familiar with the teachers' progress toward the integration of reform strategies. They understood that teachers prefer critical feedback or evaluation coming from their superiors rather than those they perceive as their equals. Recognizing this, one facilitator clearly distinguished her role by saying, "In this school I monitor the *program,* but our principal monitors the *teachers.*" Another facilitator concurred, "Our principal monitors our teachers and makes his expectations about using the program known to them." Although she seemed familiar with teachers' classroom practices, she said she didn't do anything if she became aware of anyone not using the model. She explained, "That's an administrative problem. It's not mine." Similarly, a facilitator at a small school said he conferred regularly with the principal about the reform program but not about whether teachers were implementing it. He added, "It's not my job to 'watch dog' the faculty." One facilitator resisted her principal's request to monitor teachers. She emphatically said, "In no way did I want to become a threat to teachers. I just wanted to help them. So I waited and let a program representative come in to do that. I didn't want to do evaluation."

Only one facilitator, the young man who was being groomed for an administrative position, reported monitoring and evaluating faculty as part of his responsibilities. Although he didn't relish it, he indicated that the teachers in his school were accustomed to the procedures and seemed to accept it as part of his defined role. Even so, his principal enforced or managed faculty compliance.

Based on observations in one school district, Lytle (2002) found that facilitators practicing leadership styles characterized by norms of collegiality rather than authority might create a complex relationship between the facilitator and principal. However, in this study, most principals, despite their leadership practices, seemed to understand the preference of teacher leaders to avoid faculty supervision and assumed full responsibility for it. One principal voiced feelings shared by others, "I feel like I have to be careful to not put her in an evaluative role. That is my job, and I want to make sure the teachers see her as a facilitator, not someone judging their performance."

Networking

About half the principals, facilitators, and other teacher leaders in this study recognized the importance and advantages of networking and shared responsibility for it. Some attended national or regional conferences sponsored by their model providers or, like Ms. Ashley, encouraged other teachers to attend. At these events, participants met and traded important information about implementation strategies with educators beyond their district or state. A principal described these as energizing. She said, "First of all, it is great for networking. You get the chance to talk about education in a positive setting where everybody is relaxed. We get to talk to people across the United States who have implemented the same program." The state's department of education also sponsored a CSR grant information conference periodically that served, in part, as a forum where schools having success with reform programs could share their experiences to better prepare and inform newly identified applicants. Lytle (2002) noted that after his district implemented reform programs, teachers and principals participating in national and regional information networks for the first time became less parochial and more open to change. It is likely the educators in this study who participated in networks benefited in similar ways.

More devoted networkers communicated and spread the word about CSR horizontally with principals, facilitators, and colleagues in nearby schools. Recall in Chapter 3 that district personnel from Waterton County organized and held a monthly meeting for facilitators and other representatives from each school to network, learn about implementation strategies, effective planning and training techniques, and work together on developing instructional units for their schools' faculties. Besides technical aspects of school reform, these meetings provided group support as facilitators continued to define the parameters of their work. More than one facilitator remarked that the camaraderie they derived from these meetings helped combat a sense of isolation they sometimes felt in their job.

School leaders in several districts networked vertically. They visited with elementary "feeder" schools and high schools where their graduates would be heading to strengthen contacts and increase knowledge and familiarity about their reform program in the broader school community. They would communicate, share information and materials, and host faculty from other schools to observe the model in practice. For example, the facilitator at Tipton Middle School explained that presentations about the school's reform program to nearby feeder schools served a dual purpose of increasing the comfort level among the soon-to-be sixth graders as they prepared to transition to a new school, and of heightening interest in the reform program among elementary teachers, some of whom then reinforced similar strategies in their classrooms. Networking opportunities at the national, state, and local levels linked administrators, facilitators, and other teacher leaders to their external environments and armed them with meaningful information about resources and experiences to further improvement efforts.

Addressing Broader Changes

Leadership involves the ability to persuade individuals to consider innovative ideas and actions. Most facilitators and, in many cases, principals received extensive training ahead of their faculties on how to use and help others to use reform strategies. School leaders lacking such training tended to have been hired into their positions after initial program implementation. Whether individuals had been trained to use reform strategies, few facilitators reported having been trained on how to be leaders of change. Even so, clearly, many reform program facilitators, bolstered by support from their principals, were indeed just that.

In schools where leadership was distributed or expanding, the role of facilitator as a leader of change became more broadly defined and these individuals grasped the opportunity to address a wider scope of school reform efforts. One person described his vision of the ideal model facilitator, "This would be someone with extensive teaching experience and familiarity with the reform program so they could train and model with teachers, but most important, he or she should have autonomy and freedom to step out of role to do what's needed to get the job of school reform done." In keeping with this vision, facilitators, usually with administrators or other teacher leaders, structured and introduced common planning time for teachers, analyzed school performance data resulting from CATS, helped prepare planning documents such as the annual school improvement plan, and so forth. One principal relied on her school's facilitator to help integrate all of the school's programs. She explained, "He assumes other roles as needs dictate. Because we are engaged in *comprehensive* school reform, I think anything he gets involved with for the purpose of school improvement, even if it's not directly related to our reform model, is fair game."

The extent to which facilitators and others took on these broader responsibilities of school reform appeared to vary depending on their competency, their vision of what the job entailed, and the principal's willingness to distribute and support the leadership of others. One principal said, "From the start, I have preached that every person in this school can and must be a leader. Some area is your strength, and in that area, you must assume a leadership role so that the school can function holistically, as a total body. That gives everybody an opportunity to use their strengths and feel successful." Later she added, "I truly believe that over the course of this grant we have built a sense of empowerment among teachers. They feel more capable, and as a result, they are assuming leadership roles."

With few exceptions, facilitators and other teacher leaders indicated having positive rapport and strong enthusiastic support from their principal. Many attributed progress in reform implementation to the principal's support. One facilitator described, "Our model is strenuous, demanding, and teachers aren't ever going to love it. I depend on the support my principal gives me. I really appreciate it and think it helps me to do my job better." In another school, the principal praised the facilitator, to whom he had given broad responsibilities and the autonomy to fulfill them. He talked about her sweeping positive influence in the school saying, "I use her to accomplish many school changes because she knows what's going on in the building; she knows the reform program, and she is effective in getting information to me, the teachers, the parents, and the school community. She is organized and stays on top of things. She has been a joy to work with."

PREPARING TO SUSTAIN SCHOOL REFORM

The extent schools prepared to sustain reform efforts on termination of federal funding likely was linked to their patterns of leadership. Most models did not address the issue of sustainability after funding ended, whereas many principals saw this as a serious flaw and said they had given it considerable attention. Schools marked by distributed leadership, such as Tipton, seemed poised to rely on the capacity of their staff as they prepared to sustain their reform efforts. According to a teacher leader from that school, by the end of its third year of program implementation, the leadership team spanned all content areas but math and met regularly to discuss how to improve literacy schoolwide. In this school, where teachers helped teachers, a faculty member agreed saying, "We have leadership from various teachers many of whom were not appointed leaders. They were just innovative people who started this and that and came up with ideas and shared them with other people." As the school expanded leadership among faculty members, opportunities developed for more experienced teachers to acculturate and train new teachers to buy-in and use the program. The principal observed, "Teachers have taken on the role of *championing* the program." It appears that leadership distributed to teachers at Tipton Middle School was fundamental to successful sustainability of reform.

In other schools, it also seemed clear that the ability to sustain reform efforts beyond the three-year funding cycle would be related to the principal's leadership style and the degree to which capacity had been developed and fostered. For example, several principals already were planning for the following year and intended to continue promoting distributed leadership beyond its present state by spreading more responsibility and decision making to teacher leaders. Mrs. Christopher of Greely offered, "It takes strong leadership to get a program going to begin with." Then she added, "As time has gone on, our model has actually allowed leadership to grow, so now we have a school where leadership is much stronger and effective than before." A facilitator from another school with expanding leadership observed that their reform efforts had built school capacity. She stated, "All along, I've wanted to work myself out of a job. The idea was that enough people would believe in the reform model's instructional component and would have success with it that the rest of the staff would follow along. I really think that has happened."

As this respondent observed, sustainability seemed likely in schools that deliberately built capacity among faculty while simultaneously reducing time allocated to program facilitation by the third year of implementation. One principal remarked, "Our facilitator devotes very little time to this job—what time he gives is devoted to formative observations. After funding, that won't be necessary, but I think we'll be okay otherwise." Another principal who had encouraged the development of leadership skills among faculty concurred and said, "I think this faculty has culled and capitalized on our reform program to the point that they don't need to buy it to *do* it." Faculty agreed and anticipated they would be expected to sustain changes associated with the school's program.

LEADERSHIP AND THE CHALLENGE OF CHANGE IN OTHER SCHOOLS

In contrast to principals who relinquished authority and distributed the responsibilities of reform to others, some principals led their schools in ways more consistent with traditional hierarchical authority. They typically delegated assignments rather than sharing or extending leadership and worked parallel to instead of collaboratively with colleagues holding formal leadership titles. They commonly expected the program facilitator to assume full responsibility for CSR and took a hands-off approach. They did not cultivate a sense of shared ownership for reform among faculty. Because leadership capacity was concentrated with a few rather than distributed among many, reform endeavors in traditionally led schools often were vulnerable to administrative turnover.

As stated earlier, principals and facilitators regularly received more in-depth training about their schools' reform programs than did faculties, so they, in turn, could lead implementation effectively. For schools to have stable, continuous, trained leadership, principals commonly were asked to pledge to remain in their positions through the reform period. Even so, like low-performing schools elsewhere, half of the schools in this study had turnover among principals during their three-year reform-funding period. In fact, five schools endured a different principal *each* year and, in several instances, the change occurred midyear. Only two principals who *inherited* rather than actively selected a school's reform program reinforced and advanced their new schools' commitment to change. More commonly, incoming principals rode out the funding cycle and showed little interest in supporting the direction of the school's reform.

Although the pattern of turnover was not as intense as it was for principals, facilitators in four schools resigned their position early. This posed a challenge to schools, particularly when leadership was concentrated in one or two positions, as it tended to drain them of specific technical knowledge about how to administer, implement, and manage the school's reform program. Also, schools where authority and leadership were centralized had difficulty identifying talented, capable replacements. This problem was exacerbated in schools with small faculties. Principals, all from small rural schools, indicated the selection pool of personnel who were both qualified and interested in becoming a facilitator had been scarce at the beginning of reform and continued to be so. The principal of one such school described the problem of finding a promising alternate when her facilitator changed schools, "There is not a groundswell of leadership from any of the faculty in my school. I was hard pressed to find and persuade someone to do the job." Another commented, "It was not like somebody was begging for the job because they figured it was going to be tough." A newly appointed facilitator in a third school reinforced this observation as she described her recent assignment, "We lost two facilitators in the first two years of the grant, and I'm friendly with the principal. She leaned on me to do it." Even so, in cases such as these, principals typically did not attempt to resolve the situation by helping develop potential among teachers. Rather than developing leaders and expanding administrative capacity, these principals commonly resolved the circumstance by assuming much of workload themselves or letting reform fall by the wayside.

When leadership capacity was undermined by adverse conditions, particularly turnover, it is likely that reform implementation and its potential for sustainability suffered. Several schools anticipated difficulty in sustaining reform because of impending principal turnover. A principal who was departing one such school in the upcoming year explained that the school's continued use of its reform program would depend on her replacement's knowledge of CSR. She also added, "If the new principal here is not familiar with our model, I don't believe it will be sustained at all." Respondents from other such schools indicated that change efforts were linked to program funding and facilitation and anticipated that rather than being sustained they likely would diminish with the termination of those resources. One principal said, "After this year our facilitator will return to a more traditional Title I job. I hope the school will be able to retain what is positive about this model, but I doubt we will be able to without her assistance." Similarly, two other schools that had relied heavily on their facilitator rather than cultivating leadership among other faculty over the years of implementation expected problems with sustainability. The first principal said, "My faculty is telling me they can't do it without her. Their biggest concern is what we will do next year when we don't have her." The other admitted, "If our use of the program declines it won't be that we didn't support it but because our facilitator won't be giving them that hand they are used to."

Fink and Brayman (2006) argue that rapid succession in principal leadership reduces the departing principal's ability to create and leave a legacy, generates cynicism among faculty, and inhibits the ability of the newly arriving principal to be effective. They conclude that high turnover is detrimental to the school's culture and reduces the likelihood of long-term sustainable improvement. Copland (2003) defines sustainability as "embedding reform work into the culture of the school" and identifies turnover in leadership as "the most disabling factor" preventing schools from sustaining reform efforts (p. 393).

DISCUSSION OF DISTRIBUTED LEADERSHIP AND SUSTAINING REFORM

Strong, active leadership is vital to successful change (Evans, 1996; Fullan, 2005; Sarason, 1996). Leaders of change develop strategies, inspire people, and ultimately contribute significantly to a changing culture. This chapter provided information regarding leadership responsibilities and patterns of distribution among principals, program facilitators, and other teacher leaders when schools implemented whole-school reform models. It also considered how leadership arrangements contributed to schools' preparation for sustaining reform. It determined that strong organizational leadership, particularly when it was distributed, furthered the mission of reforming schools.

School reform commonly generates new change-agent positions. Schools implementing CSR programs created a reform facilitator position and configured it as full-time, part-time with other administrative responsibilities, or part-time with teaching. Facilitation coupled with other administrative duties was an efficient and relatively stable arrangement, unlike model facilitation coupled with classroom teaching where stability tended to ebb and flow depending on budgetary concerns and the demand for faculty lines in any given year. Because the reform work was often done in combination with other job responsibilities, many facilitators experienced a sense of job fragmentation. This especially was evidenced by facilitation coupled with teaching, perhaps because the two sets of responsibilities could not be performed simultaneously, whereas expectations of facilitation coupled with other administrative duties were complementary and the boundaries between them were relatively fluid. Many facilitators monitored and protected their job boundaries, but others risked having their work defined by others. Facilitators also engaged in work overload to combat scrutiny and win acceptance of classroom teachers.

These findings are supported by a qualitative study of leadership in 16 schools undergoing school reform in California in which Copland (2003) found that new leadership structures emerged in reforming schools that promoted involvement of educators besides the principal. Specifically, the coordinators' contributions to reform were critical. These were classroom teachers whose primary responsibility was redirected to focus on reform efforts. Because the new leadership arrangement was not yet defined or supported structurally, it often created role conflict and required negotiation of boundaries for tasks and authority. For example, Copland describes one person walking the fine line between her faculty role and quasi–administrative role. For the same reasons, Datnow and Castellano (2001) similarly found that tensions and ambiguities arose among teachers designated as reform facilitators.

This chapter also revealed that school reform required managerial tasks, instructional activities involving collaboration, supervisory responsibilities, networking, and, in some instances, broader reform-related efforts. Facilitators completed nearly all managerial tasks required of the programs, even those they perceived to be mundane, whereas principals supervised and monitored teachers. The fact that all teacher leaders uniformly declined supervising their peers is consistent with studies by Datnow and Castellano (2001), Evans-Andris (1996), Mangin (2007), Smylie and Denny (1990), and others who find that teacher leaders are reluctant to challenge the norms of equality, teacher autonomy, and the authority and power of school administrators. Consequently, they avoid actions that potentially would separate or alienate themselves from their colleagues. Noninterference with others' work is a common code among teachers (Evans, 1996).

Leadership involving instructional collaboration, networking, and broader reform efforts varied depending on the extent it was distributed. This is better understood in light of the work of Spillane, Camburn, and Pareja (2007), whose study involving more than 50 principals in one district revealed that leadership commonly involved principals, classroom teachers, professional staff, and administrators. Three patterns existed, including collaborative distribution where leaders coperformed leadership routines, collective distribution where leaders worked interdependently, and coordinated distribution where leadership routines were performed sequentially. Instructional and curricular activities were more likely to be shared than those that were administrative. Certainly, this scheme is instructive to understanding leadership patterns in this chapter.

Cultivating and distributing leadership among teacher leaders was useful for school improvement. It presented new opportunities for teachers to expand their professional capacity, participate in decision making, and contribute to their schools in other meaningful ways. Teacher leaders shared responsibility with principals for school reform and instructional improvement. Teacher leadership built capacity, which in turn prepared schools to advance their reform mission. Thus, the extent that schools implemented reform was influenced by patterns of distributed leadership. The first pattern was one of distributed leadership, where principals, facilitators, and other teacher leaders shared decision making and responsibility guiding comprehensive reform and contributed to the overall reform process. The second arrangement was found where distributed leadership was developing. In these schools, principals made a concerted effort to encourage knowledge sharing and extend decision making to teachers and to distribute responsibility for school reform. Finally, other schools exhibited a more traditional pattern where responsibility for leadership for all school activities, including CSR, remained concentrated with one or two individuals. Principals and facilitators delineated responsibilities and typically worked autonomously and parallel to each other rather than in an integrated or coordinated fashion. The reform efforts of these schools were threatened by administrative turnover.

The chapter reveals that distributed leadership is vital to the implementation of school reform. Further, reform efforts that were carefully planned, managed, and supported through distributed leadership showed promise of sustained school improvement. Alternatively, it appeared more difficult to prepare for sustainability in schools where capacity for leading change failed to spread beyond the principal or facilitator. Effective leadership builds capacity to support sustainable change (Fullan, 2001). It is likely that under strong, distributed leadership, teachers will embrace change and integrate components of reform into their daily work routines. This topic is addressed in the next chapter.

5

Gaining Teacher Commitment

As a faculty, we have committed to an improvement mentality. It is engrained in us now. We knew we needed to make a change because we thought we were getting there but we weren't. We were teaching the same old way, basic instruction geared to the middle of the class. Now, we are giving kids some phenomenal experiences in an excellent learning environment. We have adopted a common goal. We remind ourselves, "We can't sit back. We have to move forward." We all have a stake. We will not go back to the way it used to be.

—Classroom teacher

Teacher commitment is vital to the success of school reform, both in its implementation and likelihood of sustainability. Workers exhibiting high commitment tend to have workplace goals consistent with those of the organization (Hodson, 1991). Adding to this, Bogler and Somech (2004) note that commitment also is evidenced when workers agree to invest time, effort, involvement, and loyalty on behalf of the organization. During periods of school reform, teachers may demonstrate commitment by willingly and enthusiastically complying with goals and engaging in innovative strategies promoted by reform. However, in workplaces, such as schools where job autonomy is relatively high, there is no guarantee that workers will commit to change. Innovative reform strategies initially may spark teacher interest and enthusiasm, but as the realization of their permanence sinks in, it may be more difficult to sustain commitment to using them. Workers may withdraw compliance or willingness to change. A lack of commitment among teachers and administrators to adopt new practices and engage in reform can undermine its positive effects (Borman, Hewes, Overman, & Brown, 2002). In those cases, motivation or commitment to change may depend on organizational features to influence and shape behavior.

This chapter seeks to understand the importance of teacher commitment during school reform. It considers the degree to which teachers express their workplace autonomy in the change process and how schools go about structuring support for reform in ways that garner commitment from teachers. Strategies employed by schools in this study included involving teachers in collaborative opportunities through the effective use of common planning time, gaining teacher input for purposes of goal setting and decision making, and expanding and enhancing professional growth and opportunities to develop professional capacity. In these ways, schools successfully generated teacher commitment to improvement.

CONTROL OF TEACHERS VERSUS WORKPLACE AUTONOMY

The tension between gaining teacher commitment for reform versus undermining that commitment by overstepping workplace autonomy is rooted in a debate over the control of teachers' work (Rowan, 1990). Ingersoll (2003) explains that a classic organizational *disempowerment* perspective views teachers as deprofessionalized, disempowered, and uncommitted because of bureaucratic top-down supervisory control. From this perspective, teachers have little control or autonomy over their work. Under such circumstances, workers develop coping strategies ranging from compliance to resistance to create a sense of power and autonomy even when there is none (Hodson, 1991). Alternatively, according to a *disorganization* perspective, (Ingersoll, 2003), when workers have too much autonomy and influence, resulting from a *loosely coupled* (Weick, 1976) arrangement, the school is viewed as ineffective because it lacks appropriate or effective control over teacher behavior. Problems such as lack of commitment or compliance are resolved by tightening control and supervision over teachers. However, tighter supervisory control likely will increase resistance as workers attempt to protect their workplace concerns (as opposed to those of the organization) as a first priority (Hodson). Generating teacher commitment for reform challenges schools to strike a balance between exerting too much control versus not enough. Consideration of teacher autonomy enlightens this debate.

Teachers generally are perceived to have relatively high autonomy in their workplace and about how their work is done (Bidwell, 1965; Ingersoll,

2003; Lipsky, 1980; Lortie, 1975). They typically receive little direct administrative supervision, use discretion as they interact with students, and determine their action in their classrooms with little interference. Weick (1976) describes the power and control arrangements between teachers and administrators in schools as *loosely coupled*. Each of these two stable subgroupings maintains its own identity and exercises autonomy while acknowledging the weakly enforced connections to the other. During school reform, leaders of change likely derive a certain amount of consideration and compliance from teachers in demonstrating commitment to reform in exchange for tolerating a degree of autonomy and respecting their professional input in how that commitment may be expressed.

Indeed, job autonomy is positively related to commitment (Nir, 2002). It motivates workers to participate in shaping their workplace conditions (Lipsky, 1980). A key indicator of teacher autonomy is input in decision making. Using data primarily from three waves of the School and Staffing Survey (1987–1994) conducted by the National Center for Educational Statistics, Ingersoll (2003) found that teachers exerted the greatest control over academic decisions related to their classroom instruction, such as selection and presentation of objectives and concepts, grading and evaluation, homework, and classroom discipline. However, they had less input and influence over decisions that had effects beyond their classroom, such as those involving instructional programs, textbook selection, and overall curriculum. Even so, autonomy expressed through decision making contributes to teacher satisfaction and generates commitment.

Datnow, Hubbard, and Mehan (2002) discuss that teacher decision making and autonomy were important features of reform implementation when schools adopted comprehensive school reform (CSR) programs. Teachers made decisions about how to use reform strategies in ways that may have deviated from the strict guidelines of the programs but better accommodated the educational contexts in which they taught. By exerting autonomy and forming decisions, they socially constructed definitions of their schools' reform programs and shaped their behavior accordingly.

Professional communities, both informal and formal, offer teachers an important means to express and enhance workplace autonomy. They provide participants opportunities to network, solve problems, make meaning about instructional practice, and gain social capital by accessing new information and innovative ideas (Coburn, 2001; Coburn & Russell, 2008). They are particularly effective when they are integrative, which is where teachers across all experience levels engage in ongoing professional exchange and collaboration, value growth and development, prioritize norms of autonomy and professional empowerment over privacy and isolation, and collectively share responsibility for improvement and success (Johnson et al., 2004). In their study of early career teachers, Johnson et al. (2004) identified schools characterized by an integrative professional culture to be the most supportive and successful in retaining teachers.

Bidwell (2001) argues that, historically, increased bureaucratization reinforced educational stability and discouraged professional community- or culture-building among teachers. Presently, schools must acknowledge and capitalize on the capacity of teachers' collegial, integrative networks to produce innovative, effective practice.

In this study, almost everyone decided early on to try out the reform program selected by their school because they realized the potential for improvement or they respected and trusted their colleagues' recommendations about them. One seventh-grade teacher in an elementary school explained, "Some of the upper-grade teachers hesitated about implementing a reform model. But even though they had mixed feelings, I think because some faculty made the decision to go forward, most of us tried to give it a fair shot." In a large middle school the principal observed, "These teachers knew they needed improvement in writing and reading, and based on recommendations from other contacts whose opinion they valued, such as nearby university professors, they were willing to give CSR a chance." Despite their reasons, many teachers recalled feeling excited and "ready to change" as their schools embarked on the reform process.

In a few schools, commitment and support for change steadily increased as faculty began implementing their respective reform programs, but in most schools it varied over time. Schools' responses to periods of wavering faculty satisfaction and commitment to reform efforts distinguished some from others. Proactive schools showed initiative in garnering support and commitment among teachers, whereas other schools passively allowed faculty enthusiasm and corresponding program use to fade over time to the point that after three years it had vanished.

The following sections present the experiences of two medium-sized middle schools where teacher commitment to improvement appeared high by the third year of reform implementation. These schools positively reinforced their faculties' commitment to change by creating common planning time, promoting professional development, allowing mutual adaptation, and advocating on behalf of teachers when necessary.

FORESTVIEW MIDDLE SCHOOL

Forestview was one of three middle schools in a district of nearly 100,000 residents. Serving more than 400 students, it was the lowest performing school in its district and had been urged to apply for CSR funding when the opportunity arose. Eager to improve its standing among nearby schools, the faculty participated in the proposal process for comprehensive school reform and, ultimately, adopted a program geared on improving instructional methods mainly by using learning centers across all content areas.

On receiving CSR funding, Mrs. May, the principal, first appointed the curriculum coordinator as a full-time program facilitator and second, organized teachers into interdisciplinary teams. This coincided with the state department of education's promotion of common planning time. Hence, Forestview's teachers began common planning in interdisciplinary teams. Once the new organizational scheme took hold, faculty seemed pleased with it and maintained that over time it increased leadership skills and cooperation among them. The principal noticed this change too and attributed it in part to effective uses of common planning recommended by the school's reform program. She commented, "One of the greatest components they've taught us is how to develop and maintain the teaming process. Every day our teachers are talking to one another; they are planning with one another."

Recalling the school's earlier experience, one teacher said, "At the beginning, almost everybody worked *hard*. Some were brave and didn't do so much, and they got away with it, but we chickens worked our rear ends off. It was a lot of work." This comment implies that Forestview, like other schools, faced some reluctance and resistance among teachers to various aspects of the reform in the early stages. However, over time, faculty demonstrated commitment to school improvement by focusing on professional development, tailoring instructional strategies to fit their classroom needs, and taking measures to further develop and sustain newly learned practices over time.

Professional Development in Forestview

Forestview's reform program required that faculty reorganize their classrooms to create an environment where students could learn in small groups at their level and pace. The program facilitator observed, "It is different because teachers have been so used to lecturing and giving notes. But the work is more challenging." Although they favored the idea, teachers described the professional development or PD accompanying their reform program as ineffective. In the first year, it entailed a four-day training prior to the beginning of school, and in the second year, they were given workshop binders to accompany a shorter training. The facilitator stated, "Everybody got these," and held up a notebook for me to see. By the third year, almost everyone agreed that professional development had slacked off considerably. One teacher explained, "When we first started implementing our reform program, we got some professional development. Now we are to a point where everyone has developed an understanding of the program, and we are trying to do it in our subject areas. We still have some PD, but not as much as when we first started."

According to these educators, early training left them without sound guidance on how to approach and structure instruction in a new, unfamiliar way. The facilitator recalled, "After the first four-day training, we thought, 'Oh my gosh, we can't do that. How does it all go together?' It was really hard. It was frustrating. Some teachers cried and several older ones left after the first year. They thought it was awful." A teacher cynically explained, "It was just dumped in front of us that we were going to do this; we were given very few ideas, and I don't really think they had any. I think we came up with ideas for them to take to other places, but we didn't get the millions of dollars for it."

Voicing the sentiments of others, one teacher recalled she didn't like going to professional development sessions because they offered nothing that seemed applicable to her content area. She viewed them as irrelevant. This was a common complaint, particularly among teachers who taught outside the four core content areas, such as special education, music, physical education, and so forth. Even a math teacher stated, "They've helped with how to implement the model, but they really haven't given us ideas for our subject areas, well, not mine anyway. I have developed those on my own."

Despite their dissatisfaction with professional development offered by program providers, the school's principal and facilitator determined that skipping it was "not an option." Instead, these leaders began advocating for more relevant and effective training sessions. Further, the facilitator inquired about having providers tailor the program to better meet the needs of the school. Rather than complying with this request, providers responded by stressing the concept of model fidelity and insisting that faculty must use the whole program to get results. She recalled, "They told me, 'Every part of the program is *crucial* to success.'"

The facilitator went on to explain that on reflection and much discussion about the program, faculty members decided to do a certain amount of picking and choosing based on what they perceived to be working. She stated, "Ultimately, we came up with a lot of good ideas for ourselves mainly by trial and error. But it wasn't what they had given us." Faculty members confirmed this. A 15-year veteran teacher said, "Despite what the providers told us, we found out over time the good thing about this program is you can arrange it anyway you want. There is no set format. I guess it is like teaching. In general, you keep playing with it and refining it. I am still doing that to this day." Teachers concurred that because school leaders permitted them to modify or adapt the program to suit their needs the result was a program they could commit to.

Ultimately, most teachers demonstrated commitment to instructional strategies promoted by the reform program they had adopted. During any given session that we observed, roughly half the students worked in small groups while the others received more individualized direct instruction from the classroom teacher. Across classrooms, students typically appeared active, engaged with one another and the material, and well behaved as they explored and worked through instructional activities.

Indeed, many agreed that the school's reform program redirected the faculty's attention away from traditional notes and lectures toward innovative teaching. One teacher spoke for her colleagues by saying, "We've learned to use a variety of strategies with this reform program. You don't teach the same way every day; you are doing something different almost weekly. That is good because it keeps you fresh." Then she added, "Going through the same routine daily tends to get boring and causes you to lose enthusiasm. This program encourages variety, addresses individual learning needs, and gets you excited about your job."

Poising for Sustainability in Forestview

As the grant period was ending, educators began poising to sustain the instructional strategies and other improvement measures they had learned over the past several years. They asked that the program representatives return to the school one last time to provide guidance in making the transition from implementation to sustainability. Mrs. May recalled that they balked at her request. She stated, "The company wanted to just send us all this documentation that we could do ourselves and not come to see us. I said, 'No.'" When I contacted her several months later, she explained that with her insistence and backing from the district, program providers had returned to the school immediately prior to the grant's expiration and held training workshops, helped organize a faculty support team, and presented an informational session to the school's site-based decision-making council. The principal also requested that, for the near future, they inform the school of any new strategies related to ongoing model implementation and improvement.

Mrs. May was adamant that the school would continue using the instructional strategies and other aspects of its reform program. She reflected, "We changed the whole outlook on how our classrooms were run. We will continue. Because our grant is about over teachers were thinking it might go away, but I told them no because we had been so successful; we had really demonstrated widespread buy-in with it. We will continue." The school also prepared for sustainability by recognizing it would need to continue training and socializing new teachers according to expectations set forth by the reform program. Mrs. May explained that, at Forestview, this responsibility would fall to the program facilitator.

In sum, teacher commitment to reform at Forestview Middle School appeared high by the end of the third year of program implementation. During any given visit, one could observe numerous instances of innovative instructional strategies that appeared to reflect and uphold the integrity of the reform program's concepts, teachers involved in common planning, and active leaders who were engaged and informed. The school prepared to sustain teacher commitment for reform through the transition from implementation to long-term use by acquiring guidance from the program providers, designating the facilitator the point person for ongoing faculty training, and holding to its vision for school improvement over time. The next section describes teacher commitment in Littleton Middle School.

LITTLETON MIDDLE SCHOOL

Littleton Middle School sat on the outskirts of a small town in a rural district of more than 13,000 people. The school was the only middle school in the district and served slightly more than 400 students. Every time I walked in the front door of the school and noticed the posters advertising social or academic events or got caught up in the bustling traffic of teachers, students, parents, and visitors coming and going from the front office, I was reminded of its vibrancy.

Gaining Teacher Cooperation in Littleton

Teachers and administrators alike recognized the positive climate pervading this school, mainly, they explained, because it stood in sharp contrast to previous years. The current principal, Mr. Mackin, acknowledged, "Before I got here, the atmosphere wasn't conducive to education. The perception of the school wasn't very high in the community, and there wasn't a willingness to work. When I came, one of my goals was to turn that around, and I think I am succeeding." To increase faculty commitment, Mr. Mackin stated that he intentionally promoted ownership among teachers and gave them opportunities to assert professional autonomy whenever possible. Early on, he did this by entertaining the faculty's request to switch reform programs and by organizing them into planning teams by discipline.

Mr. Mackin had arrived at Littleton midwinter of the school's first year of CSR funding. He immediately realized the faculty was not satisfied with the reform program and wasn't using any part of it. He said, "Every time I talked to them, it was negative, negative, negative! But we weren't going to change just because they didn't like it." He began assessing the situation and recalled, "The first major problem was that teachers didn't feel they had any input when they decided on the model. Second, they didn't think they were getting anything for their money. Third, we sat down and the staff agreed they wanted to change." At that point, he explained he initiated the process of switching models by gaining approval from the state department of education and then contacting principals in regional schools to find out what programs they used and with what results. He encouraged his faculty to observe in those schools, and he did the same. They narrowed the choices, invited a company to present its program to the faculty, and ultimately voted unanimously to implement it. Finally, with permission from the central office, Mr. Mackin appointed a highly respected, competent district coordinator as a part-time program facilitator.

To promote a cooperative spirit among teachers, the school moved to departmentalization. Rather than organizing the faculty in pods by grade level that were somewhat self-contained, Mr. Mackin regrouped them by discipline and relocated them to different classrooms based on common subjects. In that way, teachers with common disciplines formed groups for planning and collaboration. A teacher explained, "Now, we have lunch together, we plan together, we select textbooks together. During common planning time, we talk about students and reform and what we are doing to contribute."

Indeed, one could readily detect a cooperative spirit across the school. In late morning, it was common to see vendors from the nearby town delivering food for small groups of teachers who had "ordered out" to have a working lunch. I saw teachers coteaching, helping one another carry out responsibilities, and the school holding events to reinforce both student and parent involvement. Cooperation among teachers extended beyond the school. For example, a math teacher and his class from the local high school periodically presented lessons at the middle school. A science teacher explained that he collaborated with colleagues in neighboring districts by sharing ideas, strategies, and projects.

In reality, since the principal and the new reform program arrived within six months of each other, it is difficult to determine whether increased teacher commitment was a result of strong principal leadership or the grant experience. Some teachers credited the principal for the improved atmosphere, whereas others attributed their new sense of unity and cooperation to their reform program. One said, "The number one thing our reform grant did was help everybody work together more." The program facilitator concurred saying, "I see teachers working more together. The school has purchased supplies that have long been needed with some of the funds it received through the CSR grant, and teachers are more excited about teaching." Another teacher agreed, "The school climate is the best. We work together like a family. We support one another. That makes for a smoother day-to-day running of the school." It is likely both leadership and the reform program worked in concert to produce more committed teachers.

The commitment for improvement among teachers carried over to their relationship with students. Mr. Mackin described teachers relating to kids on a middle-school level and interpreted this as an indication of an improved school climate marked by teacher commitment and student engagement. Students seemed respectful and mindful of their limits. For example, as I observed the start of one math class, the teacher greeted a student who had just returned to school after an illness. Then she introduced me to her students and began her lesson. Early on in the lesson, she sent a student to the office to get new markers for the dry erase board. He came back with the markers hidden in his pocket and told her with a grin on his face that the principal said for her to go buy some new markers of her own. She caught his joke and took it in good humor, but did not let it disrupt the class. She thanked him, resumed the lesson, and the attention of the group was hers. I repeatedly observed teachers, such as this one, who spoke directly to their students, were very personable with them, and treated them with great rapport and respect. Generally, students reciprocated this behavior.

Commitment for School Improvement in Littleton

Most teachers appeared good-natured, talented, and enthusiastic about teaching. I observed numerous lessons that were carefully planned, skillfully delivered, and engaging for students. Their instructional strategies aligned closely to the school's second reform model. A teacher suggested that this program kept them from stagnating. She said, "We were in a rut; everything was just being done the same old way. This program encouraged us to look at other ways of doing things and try new things. Sometimes, if you do something and it is not the best, but you are trying new things and you are engaged, then I think students are more engaged too." A math teacher commented on faculty commitment to reform. She said, "As a body, we are dedicated to try to improve. We knew we needed to improve. The first program we had did not work for us. I think it wasn't because we didn't try it. We did what we needed to do. We have continued doing what we need to do for the reform program we have now."

One day while I was at Littleton, program providers came to assess the school's progress in implementation. The facilitator showed me the massive amount of work she had done in preparation for these visitors, such as gathering together papers, faculty lesson plans, and student work for their examination. The visitors only stayed a short while and spent their time walking briskly through the halls glancing into classrooms. They did not review what the facilitator had prepared, saying they had seen enough to know the school was doing well. They left without offering any new recommendations or suggestions for improvement to the leadership team. The principal and facilitator later expressed their disappointed and said the visit didn't benefit their school in any way. Even so, they and several faculty members examined the materials themselves to ascertain progress. Then, based on that assessment, they planned future measures for furthering the school's improvement efforts. This case, like the one before it, reveals how a school responded to declining commitment for reform among teachers. The new principal first improved teacher cooperation, then worked to improve school climate, and finally, garnered commitment for broader school improvement.

TEACHER COMMITMENT TO REFORM

These two cases demonstrate how schools managed wavering attitudes among faculties in the early, difficult stages of reform in ways that generated a high level of teacher commitment over time. This support did not come automatically. The sustained commitment to change often resulted from deliberate efforts of the schools' change agents, including the principal, facilitator, and other teacher leaders, to ensure faculty support for reform. They did this through structuring common planning time for professional collaboration, increasing workplace autonomy by giving faculty voice, and empowering teachers by allowing program modifications.

Common Planning

First, both schools successfully initiated common planning time. Whether it was organized by discipline or was interdisciplinary, it encouraged teachers of all experience levels to work collaboratively, which further reduced isolation that traditionally characterizes the work of teachers. It increased information sharing and created opportunities for meaningful discussion and decision making about teaching and learning. It also generated greater cooperation and respect among faculty, which likely reinforced their sense of professional community and the schools' commitment to instructional improvement. Similarly, in other schools, highly committed faculties also used common planning time or team meetings for information sharing, reflection, positive communication, and community building.

One way that schools may generate teacher commitment to reform, including its sustainability, is through structured opportunities for professional dialogue and the development of professional communities. Fullan (2001) notes it is important to consider working relationships among teachers in the process of reform. He and others (Coburn, 2001; Coburn & Russell, 2008; Giles & Hargreaves, 2006; Johnson et al., 2004) maintain that collegiality, open communication, trust, and peer support promote professional learning communities and improved practice. Certainly, it seems that in schools such as Forestview and Littleton opportunities to work and plan together fostered collegiality, improved practice, and professional commitment.

Faculty Voice

Second, the leaders in both schools demonstrated a willingness to consider the *voice* of faculty and intervene on their behalf, if necessary, to reinforce their cooperation. In the early stages of program adoption, teachers in both schools sought professional development that had meaning to their work, particularly in their ongoing pursuit of improved practice. The leaders at Forestview contacted providers and insisted on more effective professional development and better service provision altogether. The principal at Littleton responded to the faculty's dissatisfaction with their first reform program by advocating that they change to one more compatible with the school's goals and the faculty's needs. Another principal who was new to her school explained she encouraged faculty input. She said, "Everybody here has a voice, and they are to use it. Everybody has a chance to say what should go into our planning."

Like Mrs. May at Forestview Middle School, several principals heeded the voice or input of teachers, particularly when they perceived it would improve reform implementation. This led a few principals to advocate for their faculties during the reform process. A rural middle school principal explained that program providers had presented an unimpressive training session at the start of the reform, which left the faculty deeply frustrated. He said he quickly mediated by complaining to them and scheduling an additional presentation. In another instance, a principal of a large middle school reported that her faculty was dissatisfied with professional development. She recalled, "It was good at the beginning, but after the first year, it was weak. They raised this as an issue for discussion that I then brought to the program representatives. But we were unhappy with their responses. They typically gave us fantasy textbook answers that didn't apply in the real world." She too registered complaint and scheduled additional training sessions. Other principals expressed their dissatisfaction with the inability of program providers to effectively field faculty concerns about implementation. Unlike them, however, the principals described earlier became consumer advocates for their schools.

Model Modification

Recall in Forestview, the leaders allowed faculty to tailor their reform program in ways they saw appropriate and effective. The facilitator in a different school made modifications herself. She explained, "I had to work to make this thing succeed. I revised the curriculum recommended by the reform program in the second year of funding. Those adjustments made it more consistent with what was to be taught based on the state's core content. Then people here were more willing to continue." Similarly, another facilitator concurred that teacher modification of program strategies was necessary for them to be effective. Emphatically she said, "You can't let the focus be on fidelity rather than good teaching. You have to make adjustments."

The issue of model fidelity versus model adaptation is debated in the literature (see Rowan & Miller, 2007). Often, reform model developers and providers argue that fidelity, meaning strict adherence to strategies, activities, and guidelines, is essential to derive positive effects from reform model implementation and warn that lack of fidelity can undermine positive results. On the other hand, 'mutual adaptation,' defined by Datnow, McHugh, Stringfield, and Hacker (1998) as "flexibility and negotiation between developers and teachers and a molding of the design to local contextual needs while still holding true to the goals and design of the innovation (p. 409)," is recognized by researchers as an inevitable feature of reform and acknowledges that change is mediated by the context in which it occurs. In a study of Core Knowledge in 12 schools, they found that because of mutual adaptation, program implementation varied from site to site but typically was shaped by users to better fit and address their schools' needs.

Over time, many teachers in this study engaged in mutual adaptation, which school leaders usually recognized and condoned. However, teachers who modified their programs ran the risk of becoming scapegoats in the event that their schools failed to make progress. For example, one teacher in a large middle school remarked, "The model has stayed the same, but our implementation of it has changed." She described that after the initial implementation of their reform model some teachers (including her) "eased up on the structure and strict strategies" and tailored it in ways that made it "more interesting" and "more relevant" to the needs of their classrooms. However, she said, "When our scores didn't go up we were blamed for our lack of fidelity to the model. So now, we've been reined in by our model facilitator. We comply just to appease her." Another teacher in the same school confirmed the lack of fidelity and explained that it was the only way teachers had agreed to continue using the reform program. In one small rural school a facilitator stated, "Teachers hate the reform model and are bored with it." "However," she added, "They remain committed simply because if we are doing it every day and we still get low test scores, then we can say, '*it* didn't work.'" These comments suggest that although the teachers' behavior presently appeared more consistent with the strategies promoted by the reform program, their commitment to it had lessened. Based on the experiences and attitudes presented here, it is likely that adaptation allows teachers to exert autonomy and professional decision making about practice. Hence, commitment is more apt to be gained when faculties can modify reform programs rather than abide by a policy of strict fidelity. Finally, through everything else, there was a relentless persistence among school leaders to promote their schools' vision for improvement. They were aware of improvement activities, familiar with innovative instructional strategies, and continued repeatedly to capitalize on chances to remind faculty that they were *changing for good*.

TEACHER COMMITMENT IN OTHER SCHOOLS

The faculties of several other schools also demonstrated high levels of commitment to reform, and it was common to observe innovative instructional strategies and effective use of instructional time. Many teachers used demanding curriculum and presented impressive classes marked by high student engagement. They worked collaboratively to plan for their classes or occasionally plan for shared instructional time where they would pair up and develop units that involved older and younger students together. Also, I observed *cross training* where teachers deliberately taught different subjects or grade levels to familiarize themselves with what was going on elsewhere in the school and among other teachers.

In Tipton Middle School, the principal continuously reminded me how hard working her teachers were and how, over the years of their reform program, the school had become a more vibrant learning community. She explained matter-of-factly that the program had given teachers and students something to rally around and identify with. It had given them a sense of commonality, unity, and shared focus.

Professional Development, Instructional Strategies, and Rapport

I observed teachers in Tipton cooperating and planning with one another and promoting strong rapport with students as well. For example, when I entered a social studies class in the early morning, the students already were completely engrossed in watching a daily news channel. Later, they worked in small groups on a writing assignment related to news events. The teacher visited each group, addressing many students personally with comments like, "How's your arm today?," "Are you feeling better?," or "Where's your folder?" and also gave them key words to discuss and asked them to anticipate what aspects of their responses might deserve further discussion in their groups. Throughout the session, he never took his attention off the students and constantly spoke with a calm and low tone. His presentation and the response of students suggested he had excellent rapport with them.

The next afternoon, I observed an English class, this time, presented by a teacher who after years of child rearing recently had returned to the classroom. The lesson focused on similes, metaphors, and poetry. The teacher read examples aloud in various poems and then gave the kids the opportunity to write their own. As they were transitioning, she reminded them first about the new concepts and second about rules for classroom behavior. While they wrote, she constantly roamed the room, reading, sometimes aloud, their work and always praising it. Students exhibited great respect for their teacher and one another. Intermittently, some wrote and others shared their writing. They laughed and made remarks like, "This doesn't make sense," "This is good!" or "Mrs. Michaels, read this one!" Several children also asked me to read their poems and comment on them.

Teachers at Tipton attributed their commitment to school improvement to the professional development they received from their reform program provider. One claimed, "Teachers know what she does is admirable and she can be trusted." Another teacher concurred saying, "Yes. No one minds staying for program training because we know it's going to be a great experience. She makes teachers believe they can create positive change." Commenting on the school's high faculty commitment the provider explained, "It's a challenge to motivate adults. I find that it's harder to work with adults than it is with children. But to maintain their motivation, I try to cultivate their interest and identify their talents so they will support the program." Like the faculty, the principal also recognized the high level of faculty commitment in her school and linked it to ability of the provider, the program facilitator, and to the distribution of leadership in the school.

This school's instructional strategies underscore the importance of growth and development in reinforcing the professionalism of teaching and increasing teacher commitment to school improvement. In a survey of 1,027 math and science teachers, Garet, Porter, Desimone, Birman, and Yoon (2001) found that professional development was most likely perceived as improving knowledge and skills and changing classroom practice when it focused on content, provided opportunities for active learning, and showed coherence with other learning activities. To have a greater chance of positively affecting practice, Darling-Hammond and McLaughlin (1995) advocate for professional development that is more considerate of teachers' time and more responsive to their needs and concerns. By holding it during the regular workday, it is more likely than traditional forms to make connections with classroom teaching and is easier to sustain over time. In their study, Garet et al. (2001) found that professional development was more effective if it was conducted in study groups rather than workshops; involved the collective participation of teachers from the same school, grade, or subject; and was reinforced over time. Examples of effective professional development strategies include mentoring, peer observation and coaching, ongoing seminars and courses of study tied to practice, collaborative work, interschool visitations, and so forth (Darling-Hammond & McLaughlin, 1995).

Lack of Commitment Among Individual Teachers

Despite commitment to reform in any given school, program implementation elicits different responses from individual teachers. Thus, even in cases where most faculty members appeared highly committed to school improvement, invariably, there were a few who remained disinterested, unengaged, or resistant. For example, in one school where I observed high teacher commitment marked by engaging lessons, a strong sense of professionalism, and an atmosphere filled with excitement and enthusiasm, I spent nearly an hour in a classroom where students read silently, did homework, or slept while the teacher busied herself by shuffling papers, reprimanding students, or grading. On the off chance that I had caught her on a bad day, I returned two more times over the next week but little had changed.

When I asked faculty and administrators about episodes involving resistant or unengaged teachers, such as the one just described, they sometimes offhandedly explained that in their opinion commitment to reform varied by age and that older teachers were more reluctant to commit to school reform. A younger teacher in one school stated, "Older teachers here seemed to just put up with having to accommodate the changes required of the program." The principal of another school concurred saying, "Older teachers here preferred not to change. The newer, younger teachers find the model helpful because of its structure, effectiveness, and the high expectations it asks teachers to buy-in to." A facilitator in a third school agreed and stated, "The program requires older teachers to make major changes and they resist," and he added, "Older teachers have more to change because they may have been teaching in another way for a longer time." These last comments imply that commitment may be tied to years of experience more than age. Even so, these explanations for resistance offered by these educators were not borne out in this study.

To the contrary, numerous older teachers in this study were committed to reform. As I discussed in Chapter 4, many of the reform facilitators were senior teachers. Further, I frequently observed classes taught by older teachers that were innovative, engaging, and embedded with strategies promoted by the school's reform program, such as the social studies teacher at Tipton. He was 66 years old. A science teacher in another large middle school offered her observations about reform behavior among a group of five older teachers who had retired the previous year. She stated, "Some of them were founding mothers of this school. They had been here that long. Those women, even the ones who did not agree with the program, were willing to do it because it was right; it was a program the school went for." Her comments suggest that when teachers' instructional strategies were not consistent with strategies of the reform model, they complied with the reform, thus prioritizing their commitment to the school's organizational goals for improvement over their practice.

A program provider also explained teachers' reform behavior in a way unrelated to age. She shared her observations, "You always have some teachers who are not as enthused as others even though they've been exposed to new ideas and tried them in PD and had access to the materials and opportunities to master them. Then, for whatever reason, things finally click and they're ready to integrate the changes into what they're doing." She went on to elaborate, "A teacher who always had been on the sidelines of reform finally asked me to come in and help her do a piece with her kids. She admitted, 'I am scared of this. I can do this part, but I don't know what to do after that.' Afterward, she was extremely grateful. I think she finally felt comfortable enough to say 'I am not getting it, and I know that other people do.'" These comments suggest that rather than resisting reform per se, teachers may resist integrating new practice when it pushes them beyond their comfort zone and elicits feelings of insecurity.

The presumption among respondents cited earlier that personal demographic characteristics such as age, gender, race, and so forth may affect teacher engagement or commitment to reform is contradicted by research. Based on a study of 71 CSR schools, Kirby, Berends, and Naftel (2001) found that teacher age, experience, and education did not significantly affect reform model implementation. Likewise, Berends's (2000) study involving a survey of principals and teachers in 130 reforming schools revealed that individual teacher background characteristics were not related to dependent measures while controlling for other factors. Teachers were more likely to support and commit to reform efforts based on indicators related to the quality of implementation such as resource adequacy and communication by design teams. Finally, a study by Rosenzweig, O'Brien, and Collins (2004) examining the effects of CSR models on teachers' instructional practice in 83 schools found that fewer than 40% of respondents noted change in their instructional practice related to their school's CSR model. These changers tended to be more experienced teachers. The remaining 60% of teachers, spanning all ages and levels of experience, reported no change in their instructional practice claiming they already used practices advocated by the models prior to implementation.

Garet et al. (2001) reinforce the observations presented earlier by arguing that even when teachers support school improvement, many are not prepared to implement new teaching practices because they "learned to teach using a model of teaching and learning that focuses heavily on memorizing facts, without also emphasizing deeper understanding of subject knowledge" (p. 915). This suggests teachers may resist change because of their training rather than their age, particularly if it advocates practice that is inconsistent with the way they learned to teach. This notion also is supported by Datnow, Hubbard, and Mehan (2002), who found teachers were more likely to practice reform strategies rather than resist them when they fit ideologically with what they considered to be good teaching.

LACK OF TEACHER COMMITMENT TO REFORM IN OTHER SCHOOLS

Unlike the schools described earlier where teacher commitment to change and improvement grew as time went on, more than a third of the schools in this study may have had high teacher commitment in the early stages of implementation but it leveled off and then declined over the three years of reform. In many schools, the lack of enthusiasm and commitment was because of ineffective service from program providers, whereas in others, it stemmed from organizational characteristics unrelated to the school's reform program.

Dissatisfaction With Programs and Providers

In schools where commitment declined, teachers commonly attributed it to the failure of program providers to deliver on their promises for materials and services made during negotiations with their schools. A facilitator explained, "We chose our program because the vendors led faculty to believe that it was aligned with Kentucky's curriculum and would provide lesson plans to address the Kentucky Core Content. Once we became familiar with it, we realized that just wasn't the case. We haven't seen a model lesson plan yet." The facilitator in a rural middle school indicated that commitment and motivation had declined in her school. She explained, "There has been a lack of teacher buy-in, especially as providers fell behind in delivering on promises. In our case, we were promised resources, materials, and training that never materialized, so teachers became disillusioned and disappointed." A teacher in that school added, "We were supposed to have a model classroom where we could observe exactly how things are done in terms of arranging the room, watching model lessons, and gaining mentoring from a master teacher. I haven't seen that implemented." Finally, a principal in third school shared similar observations, "Our faculty started out positive because they viewed reading improvement as so important, and it's what the program promised to do. But now they are dissatisfied because our providers have not given us training and materials appropriate for the middle-school level." She concluded, "At this point, we have a demoralized staff."

Teachers distinguished between training to learn how to implement program components versus professional development that would increase and enhance their capacity to teach. Only two of the five programs offered what faculty perceived to be professional development that actually enriched their content knowledge and/or delivery strategies. One teacher said, "We were looking for instructional methods accompanying this program that would be a level above the others. We wanted strategies that would convey truly high expectations and goals and would expose children to more than just basic curriculum. From what I saw, there was supposed to be a lot of things beyond curriculum alignment offered to us." In another school a facilitator complained, "The program our school uses is so scripted, you could teach a monkey to do it." Acknowledging that motivation and interest for implementation in her school was a problem, a principal of a small rural school explained that she blamed the program providers for only showing her teachers what to implement rather than how to implement. She said, "When a vendor sold us our program, they gave us training on how to teach their program. Anyone can read the manual and figure that out. But that was their idea of professional development." These comments suggest that some programs' training components lacked professional development.

Related to this was the competence of program trainers. Reflecting back on the three years of reform it seems that the frustration of several schools focused on ineffective program trainers. A teacher from a rural middle school explained that his school's faculty began to have misgivings after the initial training session. A second teacher concurred saying, "Actually, the training was like a sales pitch, but we had already bought the model so they should have provided us with something substantial rather than more promises." A principal in another school stated, "Here, teachers felt that the professional development was not effective. They thought the trainer didn't know any more than they already knew. They wanted someone with real, demonstrated expertise." The principal in a nearby school with the same program concurred. He said, "Training here was not effective. The trainers didn't understand the culture or individual circumstances of this school."

Consistent with educators in this section who described program training as an ineffective substitute for professional development, a study involving 26 schools using whole-school reform models across three states found that less than one-third of the teachers reported participating in effective professional development and collaboration. Laine (2004) looked at CSR implementation, professional development, and changes in classroom practice and found that professional development focused mainly on reform model implementation rather than meaningful professional learning.

Finally, some schools noticed a decline in quality of service provision over time because of a loss of interest, turnover in staffing, problems with scaling up, or other reasons. One program facilitator in a rural middle school said, "Support here has been awful. The first year was okay, but starting in the second year, all the external facilitators did while they were in our building was walk down the halls commenting on the bulletin boards." Reflecting on what she perceived to be the failing commitment of program providers over time, the principal of a small rural school said, "I think our providers had a wonderful product, but I am relating it to a car. You may have a wonderful car, but if you lose the service department, you don't really have anything." She continued, "It seems like the model providers had plans but couldn't develop them as fast as the model sold. They couldn't keep up with demand so, at least around here, the purchasing schools were let down altogether."

As the comments in this section suggest, support for implementation in these schools decreased over the three years because of the quality of service provision related to the reform programs. Teachers typically perceived training to be ineffective after the first year. They attributed this to either the incompetence or lack of interest among trainers, the content of program training rather than effective professional development, or failure of the program to provide useful materials and guidance. It seems they had certain expectations regarding what their reform program would provide that differed from what, in fact, was provided. It is not clear, however, if this gap reflected misunderstanding about what providers told them, overexuberant sales promotions, or difficulties that companies had in their attempts to scale up. No doubt, all three explanations contributed. Despite the reasons, unlike schools such as Forestview and Littleton, no one intervened on behalf of the faculty. Instead, administrators and faculties blamed providers and then became passive rather than actively taking measures to improve service.

Organizational Conditions Undermining Commitment

Ineffective model provision did not account for all instances of low commitment. Numerous organizational conditions emanating from schools themselves distracted teachers and undermined their commitment to reform. For example, recall from Chapter 2 that voting to demonstrate buy-in for reform did not accurately reflect faculty commitment. Specifically, about one-third of the faculties in this study expressed skepticism about the vote of support, indicating their principals had subtly coerced them into voting for the change. In several other schools, teachers confided that the results of the voting process might have been altered. These responses indicate a more general mistrust among some faculty of their administration. Conversely, requiring teachers to sign their votes suggests a lack of confidence in the faculty on the part of the administrator and likely is indicative of schools where faculty had no voice or meaningful input into decision making more generally. For these and other reasons, some faculties could not get beyond the weak leadership in their school. One teacher in a large middle school noted a "tremendous decline in faculty morale" because of ineffective administration and maintained that weak principal leadership had led to poor teacher commitment. She said, "There is lack of respect for administration. There is no backing on discipline, reform efforts, and many things. Commitment has gone down. I've been here 16 years and am considering transferring. I have no commitment anymore."

Undoubtedly related to weak leadership was high administrative turnover (discussed in Chapter 4), which also jeopardized commitment to change in some schools. Unlike Mr. Mackin at Littleton Middle School who intentionally set about building faculty commitment to reform, other incoming principals who lacked familiarity with or interest in learning about a school's reform efforts overall, or the particular program it had implemented, typically did not hold faculty accountable for progress in implementation. Referring to her school's third principal in three years, a teacher in one urban school said, "She doesn't require us to use our CSR model. It is not a priority anymore. It started to dwindle last year with our second principal, and this year it's been really bad. For example, we used to have 20 or more teachers that would come to CSR discussion meetings, and now, we may get six or seven." Another teacher concurred, "There was definitely a shift in priorities when this principal came. We don't ever even talk about our model in faculty meetings." The facilitator at that school lamented, "I know it's my job to make sure that I maintain a high level of motivation among faculty that will lead to quality of implementation. But it is very difficult here with such high turnover." Finally, exceedingly high principal turnover in one school created a coordinated culture among upper-grade teachers. One teacher explained that the absence of consistent leadership "left the door wide open" for teachers to do their own decision making. She said, "The upper-grade teachers have pretty much taken their own path." She went on to discuss that they had established their own norms and values that were not consistent with those of their school's reform program. The facilitator in that school recognized and aptly described the situation, "There have been times I've felt like I was on a battleship with an oar, and I was the only person trying to move the boat. This year, I think everybody's thrown an anchor out, and there's no way we're moving forward at all."

Other school conditions undermined teacher commitment. For example, some schools commonly showed a lack of respect for instructional time by interrupting it with unnecessary announcements over the intercom and allowing excessive downtime for snack or bathroom breaks and so forth. I also frequently observed classes marked by high numbers of infractions of classroom management and disciplinary codes that interrupted instructional time. Not surprisingly, these conditions often were accompanied by weak, unimaginative lessons where the teacher may provide a small amount of direct instruction and then do his or her own personal work at his or her desk while students did independent seatwork such as silent reading, drill sheets, or open-response questions with minimal teacher input or guidance.

Further, undue emphasis on the Commonwealth Accountability Testing System (CATS) created performance pressures that distracted teachers from reform efforts. One teacher expressed the experience of many by saying, "You know we are so heavy into prepping the kids for the test. A lot of people see this reform program as having nothing to do with the test and so there's a lot of discrepancy between the people who are gung ho on it and the people who aren't." Similarly, a facilitator in a large school commented, "Pressure from testing is a real downfall. The teachers here feel like they have to do so much assessment, they don't have time to teach."

Findings from a national study on CSR (Berends et al., 2002a, 2002b) suggest that in states with assessment and accountability systems, such as Kentucky, teacher commitment to reform implementation is lower. Similarly, Whitford and Jones (2000) note that high-stakes accountability in Kentucky schools undermined innovative instructional practices and dampened teacher morale. Finally, based on case studies in schools spanning three states, Datnow (2004) also finds that state accountability systems tend to be salient to teachers and distract them from the business of reform. In these studies, the presence of high-stakes testing conflicted with reform programs and compromised the effects of reform by presenting teachers with two competing goals (achievement and reform) rather than one.

Commitment to change was also undermined by pressures stemming from the simultaneous implementation of multiple improvement programs that lacked coherence or alignment with one another. Often, these programs vied for teacher attention. For example, other grant-writing episodes were costly in resource commitment, especially in smaller schools, and distracted educators from the business at hand. They simply wore or burned people out. One teacher expressed her concern, "It seems our school has so many programs." Another teacher nodded in agreement and added, "A lot of people consider it a burden to have all of what they perceive to be extra stuff on top of everything else that they have to do. They promised that this was going to be the touchstone to turn this school around. Has it been? I have no idea."

DISCUSSION OF TEACHER COMMITMENT AND SUSTAINING REFORM

This chapter began by describing the organizational debate over control versus autonomy in the workplace. A *disorganization perspective* argues that because of teacher autonomy and the loosely coupled link between teachers and administration, schools inadequately control teachers and cannot exact quality work from them. A *disempowerment perspective* argues that schools exert too much control thus reducing ingenuity, autonomy, and professionalism from teaching. On one hand, the lack of control and accountability leads to inefficiency and ineffectiveness and, in the case of school reform, accounts for the lack of commitment among teachers to school improvement and innovative instructional strategies. On the other hand, too much top-down control and accountability also results ineffi- ciency and ineffectiveness. Ingersoll (2003) notes that supporters of this latter view advocate enhancing teacher professionalization to increase control teachers have over their work. To generate teacher commitment for CSR, schools in this study fell closer to the side of the debate that advo- cates enhancing teacher professionalization.

To increase teacher commitment, successful schools promoted auton- omy and the professionalism of teachers. Both of the schools featured in this chapter organized teachers into integrative work groups for purposes of common planning, collaboration, and improving practice. It is likely that these groups became social networks for teachers that promoted col- legiality and also increased their social capital (Coburn & Russell, 2008). It is probable that teacher autonomy experienced through participation in these groups generated higher commitment for reform (Nir, 2002). Thus, in schools where teachers were empowered and allowed to express auton- omy, commitment, loyalty, and support for the school's goals also increased. Chapter 2 discussed how the state structured its application for CSR grants in a way that required meaningful decision-making input from teachers during program adoption. This chapter presented evidence sug- gesting that teachers also had important input into decision making regarding how they implemented their reform program and expressed autonomy, as they adjusted or adapted strategies to suit their instructional needs. Some schools, such as Forestview and Littleton, heeded teacher input and allowed them to exert discretion in determining what aspects of the program they would use and how they would use them. Rather than insisting on fidelity, strong, perceptive leaders willingly relinquished control over the reform process to empower teachers to modify and adapt reform strategies in ways that were meaningful and effective and allowed them to assume greater ownership for the responsibility of reform. They also advocated on behalf of teachers when they expressed dissatisfaction about the model or provision of service from model providers.

These findings are supported by those of Datnow and Castellano (2000). Based on their qualitative study of Success for All (SFA) in reforming schools, they produced a typology of teacher responses to reform ranging from strong support to those who vehemently opposed the program. They noted that despite recommendations against it, teachers in each group modified the program in ways that made it more consistent with their vision. Those who opposed the program made major departures from it to the point of even using different materials. The authors do not account for teachers who simply may have ignored the program altogether and taught without using any of its components. This passive behavior prevents a teacher from having to overtly challenge or defy authority and provides a way to exert workplace autonomy in a nonthreatening manner (Hodson, 1991).

It is likely that teacher commitment to reform was reinforced and expanded in schools where educators perceived their programs to be successful. The facilitator in one such school explained, "One of my biggest surprises is that so many more teachers are doing a better job. Some teachers have had real accolades, especially from our external facilitator who was bragging on them. And just seeing how their kids are progressing, they kind of come on board more and say, 'I need to follow the model more closely.'" Later she added, "I think when the teachers started seeing kids making progress, I mean, how could you be against the program? It's hard for anybody to talk it down." Teachers in that school noted students had become better writers and readers, and they had more positive feelings about themselves because of these successes. Alternatively, disappointments inevitably undermined faculty ongoing commitment to change. A principal described a pattern of declining commitment, "In the first year we had a very positive atmosphere in the classrooms. Last year it was less positive, and this year teachers have the least amount of commitment and enthusiasm because they are not seeing the effects of their hard work." The next chapter explores the nature of gains realized by schools and ongoing commitment to reform.

6

Celebrating Gains

*We benefited from having our reform program. We were very satisfied
with the experience. We got a bang for our buck; I can tell you that much.*

—Elementary school principal

In a decade of heightened reliance on assessment and accountability, an
increased tendency to determine the progress of schools by their
performance on standardized tests has overshadowed their success based
on other indicators. Researchers have tracked and evaluated the
effectiveness of school reform programs using similar measures. This
emphasis on high-stakes testing equates school quality with standardized
scores and assumes this is the best means of evaluating the effects of
school reform on educational performance. Consequently, improvement in
schools that is rooted in qualitative, contextual features such as quality,
climate, and so forth has been obscured.

Organizational effectiveness of schools commonly is measured using
what Ingersoll (2003) labels an *economic production* model that defines
success as the extent to which students learn academic knowledge and
represents a rational approach to schooling that prioritizes goals of effectiveness and efficiency. This model reinforces the use of assessment to
measure production or progress and as a bureaucratic or impersonal
means of controlling teachers. Pressure to demonstrate effectiveness
becomes equated with pressure to perform on accountability systems.

An alternative approach to organizational effectiveness defines the purpose of school in a broader way using a *societal* model (Ingersoll, 2003). This model considers social functions of schooling, such as socialization and acculturation of students. It holds that developing the social person including students' capacity to establish, engage in, and sustain positive relationships with their peers and adults is as important as developing their academic skills and talents. Such relationships among and between students and teachers commonly depict the climate of schools. School climate is an important indicator of successful educational performance. Drawing from the societal model, Desimone (2002) suggests that goals of reform should include improving student-teacher relationships and student engagement.

Applying a more encompassing definition of success, which in essence combines both the economic and societal views of schooling, Ingersoll (2003) argues that successful schools have high achievement and a positive social climate marked by well-behaved students; collegial committed staff; and a general sense of cooperation, communication, and community. Further, he notes that positive organizational climate is related to higher productivity. It promotes job satisfaction among employees and results in higher performance. In schools, positive climate may promote student academic achievement (Ingersoll, 2003).

Consistent with Ingersoll's expanded definition of successful schools, this chapter examines the outcomes of comprehensive school reform (CSR) models on test performance and on broader indicators of effectiveness. It also considers the influence of those outcomes on teacher commitment to reform. It poses three questions: (1) Did the CSR-funded models accelerate the rate of improvement in reforming schools over that of schools with no programs at all? (2) What was the nature of other gains schools may have realized because of their CSR experience? (3) What was the relationship between educators' perception of school improvement and their commitment to reform efforts? To answer these questions, it presents findings regarding gains on standardized test scores and perceptions of those patterns held by educators. It then discusses other tangible gains, changes in school culture, and spillover effects resulting from reform efforts.

COMPREHENSIVE SCHOOL REFORM AND SCHOOL PERFORMANCE

Over the last decade, research focusing on the relationship between whole-school reform and school improvement has produced mixed results. Studies conducted during the early scale-up stages of these reform programs found inconsistent or inconclusive evidence of effectiveness of these models on student or school performance (Herman et al., 1999; Wong & Meyer, 1998). For example, based on a three-year study of 163 schools participating in the scale-up phase of whole-school reform models sponsored by the New American Schools (NAS), a private nonprofit organization discussed in Chapter 1, about half the schools posted gains in math relative to their districts and fewer than half posted gains in reading (Berends, Bodilly, & Kirby, 2002a; Berends, Heilbrunn, McKelvey, & Sullivan, 1999; Kirby, Berends, & Naftel, 2001). Consistent with these findings were studies by Ross, Sanders, and Stringfield (1998) and Ross et al. (2001) that examined the effects of the restructuring effort of 25 elementary schools in Memphis, Tennessee. They found that student achievement increased significantly, particularly in math, after two years of implementation but failed to show significant gains in reading. Holdzkom (2002) also found that achievement gains occurred after two years of implementation.

Another body of research suggests that positive achievement outcomes are associated with intensity and number of years of reform program implementation. Studies examining the effects of Success for All (SFA) argue that SFA schools tended to improve at greater rates than the state average during the study period, and their performance continued to improve with each additional year of implementation (Borman & Hewes, 2002; Hurley, Chamberlain, Slavin, & Madden, 2001). More recently, however, when examined using a national randomized field trial, claims regarding the effects of SFA were more modest. After one year, the SFA students posted greater gains compared to non-SFA students in only one of four posttests (Borman et al., 2005a). After two years, findings were only slightly more promising (Borman et al., 2005b).

Recent studies continue to produce mixed results about the effects of CSR models on achievement. Research involving schools in an urban district compared three middle schools two years after implementing a CSR program called Different Ways of Knowing (DWoK) to three matched control schools. Findings revealed significant gains in the CSR schools on standardized tests in language arts, reading, and arts and humanities (Munoz, Ross, & McDonald, 2007). However, another study compared 12 elementary schools across urban and rural districts in different states using four different CSR models to 12 matched control schools on various measures of school improvement and student achievement using four individually administered reading tests. Using repeated measures analysis over three years, it found that reading scores were not significantly different from CSR schools to the control group although other findings were more favorable depending on methods of analysis and duration of implementation (Sterbinsky, Ross, & Redfield, 2006). Finally, May and Supovitz (2006) and May, Supovitz, and Perda (2004) tracked the effects of the CSR model America's Choice (AC) for up to five years in one school district. Using Bayesian hierarchical growth curve analysis, findings revealed that students in schools using AC showed greater gains in math and, to a less extent, in reading than students attending non-AC schools. Importantly, the study also indicated that by the fifth year, the effects of AC on math gains had diminished and the effects for reading were negative. Consistent with other studies, the gains were most pronounced among low-performing and minority students.

Taken together, research continues to show that the debate surrounding the issue of effectiveness of CSR programs remains unresolved. The remainder of this chapter examines the effects of the reform programs on goal achievement in this study's reforming schools.

Reform and Test Scores

As indicated in Chapter 2, when schools submitted their proposals for CSR grants they identified goals they expected to achieve by implementing a whole-school reform model. Recall that nearly all 18 schools had stated their primary goal for participating in the CSR program was to obtain higher achievement scores on the Commonwealth Accountability Testing System (CATS). Some schools, perhaps unrealistically, hoped for a 100% improvement rate across all subjects, whereas others set more attainable goals such as specific yearly increases in targeted content areas, particularly reading and math. In reality, the only indicator that schools used in evaluating whether they met their goal pertaining to increased performance was their CATS scores. The school index score and student scores (both individual and aggregated) on the Kentucky Core Content (KCC) tests were released each fall based on the previous spring's testing session. Schools compared newly released scores to earlier ones in hopes of seeing gains.

In actuality, raising test scores is a complicated matter. Besides any reform efforts at play in the school, researchers must account for factors that may affect school performance such organizational characteristics, teacher qualities, and student demographics. Further, recall that Kentucky's CATS index scores are a compilation of student achievement scores based on core content areas combined with nonacademic indicators such as attendance rates, retention rates, and so forth.

To determine the effects of the reform models on school performance, we measured "effects" first using the schools' CATS index scores and later using individual student scores from the KCC tests. Using the CATS scores, we anticipated that the 18 schools with CSR funding would outperform other low-performing schools that did not have a school improvement program during the same time. To test this assumption, we began with all 74 schools that had been identified by the Kentucky Department of Education as low performing in 1998 and thus eligible to apply for CSR funding and sorted the schools into three groups as follows: Group A was comprised of the 18 schools that were awarded CSR funding; Group B included the 13 schools that had applied for funding and did not receive it; Group C was the remaining 43 schools that were eligible to apply for CSR funding because of their low-performing status in 1998 but, for reasons discussed in Chapter 2, did not apply. Then we compared the 18 CSR-funded schools to the two other groups of schools.

As Figure 6.1 indicates, statistical analyses determined that, in fact, all three groups of schools showed improvement in academic achievement over the baseline (i.e., 1999) scores; that is, there was a time effect. Contrary to our expectation, the 18 schools having CSR models did not demonstrate higher achievement than those in Group B or C. In other words, the average CATS scores for the 18 CSR-funded schools were not higher than the average for the other two groups of schools. In fact, the average scores among the three groups of schools did not differ significantly from one another during the period 1998 through 2002. Also contrary to expectation, the analyses confirmed that the schools' rate of improvement did not differ by group. The overall conclusion was that all three groups of schools improved their achievement scores over the period 1998 through 2002, but CSR funding did not distinguish schools either by higher mean averages or by greater rate of improvement. Given that certain covariates had been identified in the literature, the analyses were repeated with the covariates for school configuration and poverty (indicated by the percentage of students eligible for free and reduced-cost lunch). These covariates made little difference in the results. See Figure 6.1.

Figure 6.1 CATS Scores by CSR Status

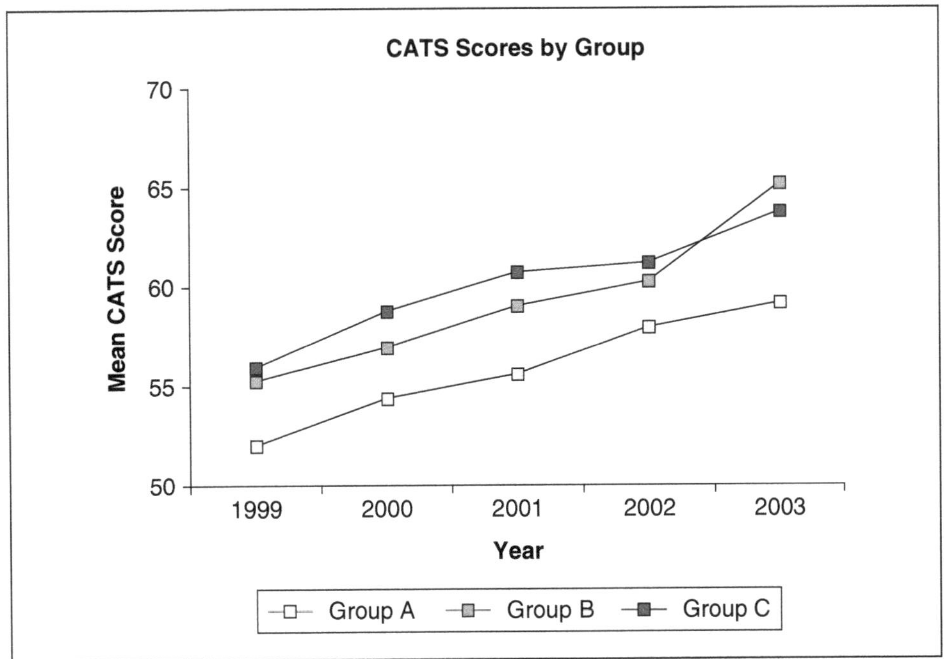

Perception of Gains and Commitment to Reform

Most often, schools erroneously assumed that during the years of grant funding the changes in CATS scores were caused by their reform program. Given the complexity of interpreting the results of CATS and because the mean CATS scores of all the schools in the sample, despite grant funding, increased over time, it is not surprising that educators often perceived there to be a positive relationship between their reform efforts and CATS scores even when there wasn't one. In those cases, teachers' commitment to their reform program was energized. For example, in one small kindergarten through Grade 8 school the principal and facilitator explained that there had been as much as a 32% increase in the number of students reading at grade level since program implementation, which they both attributed to the reform program. The principal stated, "Last year, it seemed like people were getting tired of the program. But when they realized our upward trend on test scores, that we went up about an average of eight points per year, they were like, 'Oh yes, it does work!' They got renewed and back on track." Similarly, a teacher from a large middle school described a link between the apparent effectiveness of his school's reform model and teacher commitment saying, "I feel like our commitment has gone up." He went on to explain that he had been new to the school in the fall of its second year of grant funding. He recalled that the faculty was skeptical about the reform program as they waited until CATS scores were announced to see if their scores had increased or declined. The announcement came in October and showed that the school had exceeded its performance goal, and it did so again the following year. The teacher concluded, "Enthusiasm has definitely gone up here because people feel like this is working. It makes you feel better about what you're doing when you're making progress. There are always some who may not like it because a lot of people struggle with change, but everyone thinks it is better now than it was two years ago." Clearly, in these two cases positive outcomes on test performance bolstered faculty morale and commitment.

Although it was difficult for administrators and teachers to conclude in reality whether the CSR experience negatively affected a school's CATS scores, it was certainly the case that teachers' regard for their reform programs declined if their school's test scores decreased. In nearly one-third of the schools in this study, there was a lack of measurable improvement on standardized test scores over the three years of reform implementation. In fact, more than one principal commented that their school's relative standing compared to other schools actually declined. This inevitably led to disappointment, which, in turn, undermined faculty commitment to change. Respondents in several schools said as much. For instance, the facilitator in a large kindergarten through Grade 8 school stated, "The teachers here hoped that by adapting a reform program they would see reading improve, test scores increase, and student achievement soar. What happened, though, was that despite an increase in the percentage of students reading at grade level, the improvement was not reflected in CATS tests; in fact, reading scores declined. That was a real blow." In another small school, the principal explained, "I believe our school was in desperate need of curriculum guidance. We looked to our CSR model to provide that." Then she added, "The faculty worked hard and was seeing the individual gains with students in the classroom. But when we got our test scores back, well, that was a letdown to everybody." A teacher in that school agreed, "I can't say we are not frustrated over our test scores. I think our kids really tried hard, and we did all kinds of things to try to motivate them. We thought they did real well."

Like teachers and administrators across all schools, these respondents indicated that their schools' faculties expected increases in standardized test scores because of the implementation of a reform model. However, they articulated a paradox that occurred in many schools. *Perceived* gains did not translate into increased test scores. Understandably, teachers and administrators found the discrepancy between perceived improvement and improvement indicated by CATS scores perplexing, and commonly, it dampened their spirit and support for change.

Two or three schools were hard put to find any redeeming value in their reform programs because of dismal CATS scores that did not improve over time. The facilitator of one such middle school lamented, "We've done it for so long and tried our very best, and yet the test scores went down. It is aggravating. We are frustrated and depressed." Similarly, the principal at a small rural school said that the school's commitment "plunged" when scores didn't improve over time like the model promised. She elaborated, "We kept asking, 'Why are our scores not going up?' The model providers would come in and say, 'It is usually after the third or fourth year, you will see that climb.' Here we are four years later, and we are still flat lining and in need of assistance. If our scores don't come up this year, we're facing being shut down or consolidated." Unlike others, one principal held out hope for school improvement. She continued to *believe* in her school's reform program because even though scores hadn't improved, she claimed she had seen its success in nearby schools. Referring to one she said, "I see Lakeland. They are just booming!"

Clearly, teachers' commitment to use reform programs reflected their schools' performance on CATS tests. Commitment and enthusiasm toward a reform program tended to increase when a school showed gains, whereas it tended to decrease if a school showed declines. This link between teachers' perceptions regarding the effectiveness of their reform model and school performance was somewhat understandable given the complexity of distinguishing between *real* gains resulting from reform efforts through CSR programs and gains attributable to other causes. Moreover, at least three additional issues tended to blur the ability of teachers and administrators to determine whether their schools were improving based on student performance. First, one reform program came with *its own* testing system to track student progress in schools, and in those schools, students took tests sanctioned by the reform program every six or eight weeks in addition to taking the annual state core content tests that corresponded to their grade level. Further, independent of their CSR model, nearly every school used a reading program where students individually read books at their reading levels and then took quizzes using a computerized testing program that monitored their progress. Using internally administered tests in addition to the CATS testing introduced the probability that students might show progress on one set of scores and not the other. The inconsistency or lack of correlation between CATS scores and other tests that schools might use to mark progress commonly generated confusion regarding the relationship between the reform programs and school or student performance based on CATS. For example, in one school two teachers claimed that CATS scores had gone up yearly since implementing its reform model, whereas their principal maintained, "Reading gains haven't been apparent on test scores."

Second, schools in Kentucky having kindergarten through Grade 8 are assigned two different school identification numbers, one for the primary grades and another for the middle grades. The schools earn two different CATS index scores that correspond to the school identification numbers. It was likely that the two "schools" inside one building would earn different CATS scores and possible that the patterns would be inconsistent with one another; in other words, in one building, a middle school's score could go down when the primary school's score went up or vice versa.

The confusion this arrangement could create became apparent to me when a principal and I inadvertently began reviewing graphs based on the *elementary* school's CATS scores, which had declined, rather than those from the *middle* grades, which had increased. The graphs were not labeled and so the mistake was easily made. In case I hadn't accounted for the two sets of scores for her kindergarten through Grade 8 school, she alerted me to be aware of the correct way to interpret the scores.

Third, educators had difficulty determining whether a group improved in a particular content area that corresponded to those emphasized by their reform model because of milepost testing. Recall Chapter 2 discussed Kentucky's assessment and accountability system and explained that the core content tests provide the basis for school index scores on CATS. However, students take different content tests depending on their grade level. For example, seventh graders are tested in reading, writing, and science, whereas eighth graders are tested in math, social studies, and humanities/practical living. If a middle school's reform program purported to address reading but only students in the seventh grade were tested in that subject area, it was difficult to assess whether the school was making progress in reading, particularly in Grades 6 and 8.

Although nearly all school administrators, teachers, and others tended to evaluate their reform programs based on increases or declines on annual CATS scores, at least one principal was more sophisticated in her interpretation of test scores and reform program effectiveness. She first explained that her school had shown gains in some content areas and not in others. Even so, she maintained that instructional strategies were improving, although test scores might not reflect this. Specifically, she was impressed with her school's improvements in climate and teacher initiative. In fact, in many schools, the dismay or disappointment of educators resulting from lack of meeting their goals related to gains on CATS scores was often offset by goal achievement or unexpected improvement in other areas. The following sections discuss additional areas of improvement that occurred in schools during their funding period.

TANGIBLE RESOURCES AND SUPPLIES

Besides hoping for gains in CATS scores, a second goal that many schools held for their CSR experience was to acquire tangible materials and resources. Interestingly, schools did not specify this goal in their initial grant proposals, but as Chapter 2 indicated, some principals verbally admitted in interviews that a hidden agenda was to use money acquired through the grant to increase school resources and materials. In fact, nearly all the schools did this. Schools spent a portion of their grant funds to purchase books, posters, microscopes, calculators, and a myriad of other supplies to satisfy specified requirements of the various reform programs and, in some cases, simply to acquire items the school wanted while it had the money to do so. Schools using less costly reform programs had more discretionary funds available, but even schools using programs that are more expensive managed to put aside some monies for new supplies. In an attempt to use funds to stockpile materials, a middle-school principal boldly discussed his plans for expenditures in the third year of implementation. He explained that teachers in his school would not be attending their reform model's national training conference that year. Instead, he was redirecting that money to purchase more supplies. He said, "Basically our money is being spent on getting children things to work with. I am buying materials that will last . . . more electronic microscopes, calculators, big-screen televisions, and such." Not surprisingly, teachers overwhelmingly seemed to appreciate this infusion of equipment and resources. A veteran teacher of 24 years in one school exclaimed, "We have more materials now than ever before thanks to that school improvement grant!" Other teachers echoed this observation. One said, "You give me more materials to work with, and I will be more productive. I am getting more materials. I am getting the students more involved. That is happening."

Discretionary funds generated by the reform grants served several functions. First, supplies purchased with grant money represented tangible gains for schools. In this way, they served as a positive reinforcement or reward in that teachers could acquire new books, posters, and equipment that they otherwise wouldn't have access to in exchange for adopting a school reform program. Further, they served as a subtle reminder to teachers to use their reform program's instructional strategies that the supplies accompanied. Finally, they also reinforced the autonomy of schools and teachers by enabling them to make decisions about budgeting and spending in ways that could serve their interests.

Recall the RAND Change Agent Study (Berman & McLaughlin, 1978) on implementing and sustaining federal programs in schools revealed that some school districts pursued federal grants primarily to acquire supplementary funding rather than to improve schools. The researchers determined that projects implemented for opportunistic reasons typically failed to show gains and were short lived. In this study, it appears that CSR funding provided most schools with discretionary funds allowing them to acquire supplies and materials. A small portion of schools, however, prioritized resource acquisition over reform implementation, and in those cases, it is reasonable to expect that preparation for program sustainability did not occur.

CONTRIBUTIONS TO SCHOOL CULTURE

As discussed at the beginning of this chapter, a societal view of schooling purports that school culture and climate are important aspects of school effectiveness. Climate is defined, measured, and used differently from study to study. Typically, early studies of CSR treated school climate as a causal variable affecting implementation. Even so, Lytle (2002) observed that faculties in his district's reforming schools developed a sense of collective responsibility for student performance, and parent involvement in school decision making improved. Only recently have researchers begun examining climate as an outcome or result of CSR programs. Ingersoll (2003) assessed climate by the degree of cooperation, cohesion, communication, community, and so forth exhibited by students with faculty, among teachers, and between teachers and administrators. Sterbinsky, Ross, and Redfield (2006) used a 49-item School Climate Inventory to measure school organizational climates and mark changes during the CSR implementation period. The inventory tapped seven dimensions of school climate including order, leadership, environment, involvement, instruction, expectations, and collaboration. Although there were variations by year and by urbanicity, the authors found that after three years, the climate increased more in CSR-funded schools than control schools on order, leadership, and expectations. The remainder of this section examines school climate and student engagement as they related to schools' reform efforts in this study.

School Climate

Besides possible progress measured by CATS scores or the acquisition of resources, another area where participants perceived they had realized gains over their funding period was school culture or climate. Although it was somewhat unexpected, teachers and administrators often commented that their school's climate had become more positive over the years of reform. Improvement in school climate was intangible and thus more subtle than the two sets of gains discussed earlier. Even so, it was evidenced in numerous ways. It was common to enter a school and find a warm, friendly environment where it seemed kids, teachers, custodians, and the principal treated one another (and visitors) with sincere regard, friendliness, and mutual respect. Each morning as I entered such schools adults would greet me and sometimes ask about my work, guards or others working the bus lines would smile and wave, and kids readily would approach me in the hallways as they would their teachers to chat or ask me if I needed their help in locating various parts of the building. A principal in a rural area confirmed these observations as they related to her school. She said, "I think we need to look at pictures of schools that are doing really good stuff that we can't assess. We are doing some outstanding things with kids, but it is not going to show up on a test score. We have a stranger like you come into our building and have 15 kids say hello. That is not something you assess, it is something you train and teach."

Students demonstrated consideration for their peers as well as adults. For example, I observed a science class where kids were reading and discussing parts of human anatomy. There were no crude remarks, giggles, or wisecracks that one might have expected. In another school, I listened while students took turns reading aloud from the text when one reader came on an unfamiliar word that he couldn't pronounce. Without looking up from her book, a girl nonchalantly helped him through the pronunciation and the group proceeded to finish the piece without comment, ridicule, or disruption. In several schools, students freely volunteered to assist students in wheelchairs navigate the hallways, carry books for students with injuries, or pick up items if someone accidentally dropped papers, books, lunches, or supplies.

Since this study began in the third year of program implementation, it did not determine whether informal indicators of school climate changed because of the CSR experience. Even so, a number of educators perceived a more positive climate and readily linked it to their reform efforts. For example, the facilitator in one small school said, "I saw the excitement in the way the teachers here approached the program. Sure, they felt fear, pressure, and frustration in the first year. But since then there's been improvement, and I think that's keeping that spark for change alive." A teacher in another school reflected, "Probably a lot of teachers just went along with the program at the beginning because they thought that was the thing to do. Once they saw what the model was about, they got into it.

I think they were more than enthusiastic when they saw what it did for the school." Principals noticed this as well. One explained that teacher commitment in her school had increased. She said, "I see teachers with the desire to fully be the kind that enjoys and loves their work and does it from that deep internal kind of commitment. For some, that wealth can be tapped into, and for others, it was there all along, it has just expanded. Then, we are still working with a few. But I think the commitment is stronger in this school than it was." These responses suggest that the commitment for change among some teachers may have increased over time based on the positive effects they perceived it held for themselves, their students, and their schools.

Another way reform programs seemed to affect school culture was in unifying faculties. In middle schools having Grades 6 through 8 or Grades 7 and 8, some reform programs provided faculties with a coherent curriculum, common instructional strategies, and so forth that could contribute to an atmosphere of commonality and unification among teachers. For example, teachers in a rural middle school detected that the reform program built consensus, camaraderie, and collaboration among the faculty. A teacher there explained that during their funding period the principal assigned teachers to committees to promote different aspects of program implementation. He ended by saying, "Those groups effectively kept teacher attention on the task of implementation and intentional teaching to the curriculum." Others also acknowledged that their school's reform model unified various aspects of the school's instructional program. One principal compared the present coherent instructional approach to the previous one, which he described as "so disjointed."

On the other hand, in some schools, particularly those having kindergarten through Grade 8, reform programs had a divisive effect. Upper-grade teachers balked at using strategies or materials that may have been designed for lower-grade students. The reform program exacerbated a split between the upper- and lower-grade teachers in the event that the upper grades were exempt from using the model and the lower-grade teachers perceived the model as a burden rather than as an opportunity. Educators noticed this. In one elementary school, a teacher said, "For a long time, the middle school and the primary have been separate entities even though we are in the same building. When we started the program, we all got trained and used it as a kindergarten through Grade 8 program because it was supposed to be a schoolwide effort." He continued, "Then it went down to a kindergarten through Grade 6. We stopped using it in the eighth and seventh grade." He explained that the school eliminated the program in upper grades because teachers perceived a lack of correlation between the reform program and core content, and it detracted time from other subjects. The program's absence in the upper grades subsequently served to further distinguish and divide the faculties of the two groups. Similarly, in another elementary school, the upper-grade teachers reminded me right away when I saw them after two years, "We don't do it [the reform program] anymore." One of them elaborated, "We take things from the program that we like best and incorporate them into our teaching. Otherwise, if we don't like it, we do our own thing. So it is not like we are stuck with it every day." Later, the school's facilitator recounted that the upper-grade teachers never had found the reform program useful or well suited to the needs of middle-school students, and that is why the principal ultimately exempted them from implementing it. The principal concurred saying, "Really, the program was only for kindergarten through Grade 6 to begin with, so we were stretching it to include seventh and eighth. Ultimately, it just didn't work well for the big kids. So we allowed those upper grades to just ease out of it."

Based on his study of the NAS schools, Berends (2000) found that because they were more complex organizations, larger secondary schools were more likely to resist organizational change. Further, larger schools were more bureaucratic rather than communitarian, resulting in a climate where teachers were less likely to collaborate around a common mission as envisioned by whole-school designs. In our study, it seems that the complexity of having elementary and middle-school teachers in the same building reduced the likelihood of all teachers rallying around a common reform program, particularly when its strategies did not target all levels from kindergarten through eighth grade.

Student Engagement

Another aspect of school culture is an atmosphere conducive to engaged learning or student engagement (Lee & Smith, 1993). In this study, the positive school climate carried over to students in that they appeared engaged most of the time. It was evidenced in schools and classrooms as students demonstrated interest, involvement, and pride in various functions and events. They often shared their enthusiasm with me. For example, one small school's choir gave me a personal performance of their holiday show, as I would not be able to attend the evening's event. I saw students in another school planning for "science night" where they would conduct poster presentations about projects related to their scientific research. The event was well attended and wildly popular among parents. In a different school, students proudly took me to their outdoor garden and others led me to the gymnasium to see their science fair exhibits. The entire area was filled with student entries. And as I rode the school bus with students in another district, they talked with me, compared homework assignments with one another, and pointed out their homes or homes of their friends along the way.

Teachers and administrators commonly attributed increased student engagement to their school improvement efforts. One facilitator remarked, "I feel like our teachers are doing more *hands-on*, which is going to engage children far more than *stand-and-deliver* type instruction." A teacher in that school explained that kids were exposed to more knowledge and experiences than before, which reminded me of the classes I had observed that day where students were dissecting frogs, using calculators, and participating in other engaging activities. Similarly, other teachers and principals said that because of reform strategies they felt they were reaching more students with individual learning needs. One principal said, "Our elementary test scores are not showing it, but I see growth in children. Even my own daughter who goes to this school struggles, but I am seeing so much growth in her. I see students and listen to them read. They have gone up so much. I am sold on our program. I see the success in the students. Our test scores are not showing it yet, but I think they will." In schools such as these, almost everyone agreed that students had become active learners.

Finally, some respondents judged student engagement to be greater based on indicators such as increased school attendance, more consistent homework completion, greater involvement in student leadership opportunities, and so forth. One principal said, "I feel like most definitely, our attendance rate are increasing, that is a positive to me because that means students are wanting to come to school." Another principal remarked, "The proof is in the pudding. Our [test] scores have gone up and this wouldn't happen unless students were engaged." Then she added, "Students like the reform program, there is student eagerness."

Most of the time, principals and other leaders viewed student engagement in ways that were consistent with classroom teachers. The following exchange, however, illustrates how respondents in the same school, on occasion, provided contradicting evidence. Clearly, the principal and classroom teachers used different indicators of student engagement, which led them to different perceptions. The principal said, "You see student engagement in the classroom now. That is a biggie; we work on that all the time. If you do a lot of the model's instructional strategies, you should have student engagement." Then she went on to describe hands-on activities that teachers practiced. However, a teacher in the same school painted a different picture explaining that students commonly came to class unprepared and had a sense of apathy about them. A second teacher concurred saying, "Student engagement here is in a continual decline. Students may appear engaged in the classroom because of artificial motivators such as detentions, pizza parties, and so forth that teachers might use. But really, the motivation is not there. But I don't think it necessarily has anything to do with our reform program." The contradictions in perspective regarding student engagement likely resulted from different orientations related to position and role. The principal's statements seemed to imply that the key to student engagement was through innovative teaching practices. Specifically, if teachers used hands-on activities then engagement of students would follow. On the other hand, the teachers seemed to mark engagement by students' demeanor and attitudes.

SPILLOVER EFFECTS FROM THE GRANT EXPERIENCE

In addition to the real and perceived effects from reform programs discussed earlier, many schools realized spillover effects from their grant experience. These were advantageous, sometimes rather unexpected, gains resulting from involvement in the reform.

Grant Savvy

A number of schools acknowledged becoming more grant savvy about setting goals for grants, identifying potential funding sources, writing grant proposals, and understanding the complexities and responsibilities of having a grant. Several districts or individual schools had already capitalized on these new skills and applied for grants for any number of purposes including programs targeting discipline, tutoring, computer integration, study skills, learning centers, and reading. A number of them had been awarded new grants. Some of these grants would enable schools to continue on their journey toward school improvement by paying for portions of a teacher's salary, providing money for equipment, excursions for students, or professional development at national locations for faculty. They also increased these schools' status and recognition.

Professional Growth

Numerous respondents indicated that they had grown professionally because of their reform experience. Several commented that they had gained confidence to become more proactive in finding and seizing opportunities for professional growth and improvement, particularly through regional and national seminars and conferences. A woman in her eighth year as principal acknowledged that she felt a "tremendous growth of professional self," and attributed it mostly to the grant experience. Similarly, a school's program facilitator was thrilled with the development of her own leadership capacity that the reform program experience tapped into. She said, "Five years ago, if you had told me I would be doing this at this point, I would have said, 'I could not, not at all.' The leadership role I took, that wasn't me before. I was more comfortable in my first-grade classroom where I'd been for 25 years. That is where I had intended to stay."

Catalyst for School Improvement

Educators commonly described their CSR experience as a catalyst for school improvement. One principal said, "CSR was good for us in that it caused us to look at ways to change what we were doing. It was the spark we needed to get things headed in the right direction. We knew that we had to change. The CSR grant was a great motivator." Echoing these sentiments, another school's facilitator and principal indicated that their reform model gave them goals and direction. The principal explained, "Our program gave our teachers a road map to say, for instance, fifth grade will read this and do this. It really gave us a focus I think." The facilitator agreed, "Our reform program also gave us unity and greater faculty commitment." Then she added, "We are like a comprehensive unit, and more teachers know one another's teaching. That is real important, not to be isolated with what you teach. We do a lot more of that now." One teacher in a small school summed up the sentiments of many others by saying, "A lot of the things about this school have taken a turn for the positive. I don't know if it is because of the grant experience, but yes, I think it is, and I am satisfied."

Community and Parental Involvement

Community and parental involvement may promote a more positive school culture. Further, in a study of eighth graders, Sui-Chu and Willms (1996) found that parent involvement was related to the child's school achievement. However, involvement as a volunteer in the school had only a modest effect, whereas involvement at home by discussing school activities and helping children plan their school programs had the strongest relationship to academic achievement.

In this study, community and parental involvement was one area where most schools did not improve. Although nearly all the CSR proposals had stipulated increased community and parental involvement as a goal in hopes of creating an alliance among teachers, administrators, community representatives, and parents, for most schools this did not happen. Some respondents explained that when the community becomes involved and parents invest in their children's academic careers, they share the school's responsibility of increasing student performance. They intended to mark progress by creating a greater number of school-community activities, increasing PTA memberships, promoting parent-child reading partnerships, and increasing attendance at parent-teacher conferences.

Although CSR programs were required to have a component designed to increase involvement in the community and among parents, most schools saw few gains in this area. Nearly all of them maintained this was "an exceedingly difficult area to change." One principal insisted, "With the exception of sporting events, the only way we can get people in here is to feed them. If we offer them food, like a chili supper, then they'll come." Indeed, contact with parents seemed routine in some schools, particularly kindergarten through Grade 8 schools. Most commonly, however, these interactions involved phone calls, school visits for discipline issues, or signing sheets testifying that their children had completed home reading. Nor were parent-teacher conferences particularly popular or well attended. Respondents in only two or three schools reported making important inroads into meaningful parent involvement because of their grant experience.

DISCUSSION OF THE EFFECTS OF REFORM AND SUSTAINABILITY

This chapter considers organizational effectiveness during school reform from a societal rather than an economic production model (Ingersoll, 2003). A societal perspective recognizes social conditions in schools will lead to a more productive climate for teaching and learning. It examined the effects of CSR programs on schools, particularly tangible gains as measured on CATS index scores and school materials, and then, more intangible, cultural gains such as school climate, student engagement, and spillover effects. It also considered the relationship between educators' perceptions of school improvement and their commitment to reform efforts.

Results from quantitative analyses showed that schools using CSR programs did not fare better in measurable gains on CATS index scores than other low-performing schools without such programs. Over a four-year span, beginning the year that schools received CSR grants (1999) through one year after CSR funding (2003), the CSR-funded schools improved but not at a rate that exceeded the improvement of other low-performing schools; that is, the gains on CATS index scores were not significantly related to CSR funding. Further detailed analysis examining student achievement across all low-performing schools also revealed that the impact of CSR was minor. Students in schools that had applied but did not receive CSR funding consistently scored higher than those in other comparison schools, whereas students in the CSR-funded schools performed the same or lower than those in comparison groups (see Evans-Andris & Usui, 2008, for further discussion). One explanation for this may be that when schools were denied CSR funding they were encouraged to seek support for implementation elsewhere. It may be that at least some of these schools implemented whole-school reform models without CSR funding, thus, masking the effects of the models on performance. Nevertheless, the findings reported here are consistent with quantitative results of numerous other CSR studies.

Despite the absence of a statistical causal relationship between school performance and CSR, teachers and school leaders commonly perceived a link between school reform models and test results for various reasons. These perceptions (accurate or not) tended to provide a basis for educators to celebrate gains or, conversely, to undermine enthusiasm for reform.

This chapter also demonstrated that CSR models were likely to have positive effects in schools that were obscured when improvement was based on test results alone. Schools realized other tangible gains in materials, supplies, and resources that they purchased with grant monies. Indicators of positive school climate, such as increased professional growth and deeper student engagement, also gave faculties cause to celebrate improvement.

Ingersoll (2003) notes that positive school climate is linked to higher performance. Further, Sterbinsky, Ross, and Redfield (2006) argue that participation in reform efforts increases when school climate is positive. Indeed, findings presented in this chapter depicted this pattern. Teacher commitment to reform was reinforced in schools that showed improvement either in tangible ways through perceived or real gains in test scores and acquisitions of new resources or in more qualitative ways such as improved school climate and student engagement. Finally, the CSR experience had spillover effects in many schools. For example, educators acquired new grant-writing expertise, sophistication in grant managing, or became assertive in seeking new grant monies, and they gained professional growth. This is consistent with Ingersoll's (2003) assertion that positive school climate should also be recognized for other types of qualitative gains. Spillover effects in schools often were entirely unintended consequences of the grant experience and represented pleasant, unexpected rewards for their efforts.

It is likely that the effectiveness of school improvement, both perceived and real, based on the tangible, quantitative indicators along with those that were more difficult to measure contributed to the likelihood that schools would embrace change as a more permanent, enduring feature of their workplace. The next chapter examines patterns of sustainability among reforming schools.

7

Changing for Good

At first, I don't know if I ever even thought about comprehensive school reform for the long term. It was just year to year. But now, I see it as an umbrella to pull together all the improvement efforts that we do.

—District administrator

A logical end point in the reform process is to consider the extent to which schools *change for good*, that is sustain improvement efforts over time. Chapter 1 noted that change in schools is sustained when it persists, endures over long periods, and has ongoing effects on classroom practices (Berman & McLaughlin, 1978; Datnow, 2005). Historically in education, few programs are sustained on a long-term basis, and improvement strategies adopted through reform typically do not become fully institutionalized as routine, standard practice.

Like the research on sustainability of other innovative programs in the educational arena, studies involving comprehensive school reform (CSR) reveal that fewer than one-third of schools continue a relationship with model providers after their funding period ends (Datnow & Stringfield, 2000; Evans-Andris & Usui, 2004b; Taylor, 2005). Early studies, particularly those based on quantitative methods, commonly measured sustainability by whether a school retained a formal relationship with a reform model. Not surprisingly, they determined that the sustainability of CSR depends on adequate funding (Berends, Bodilly, & Kirby, 2002a, 2002b; Kirby, Berends, & Naftel, 2001). In fact, Berends et al.

(2002a, 2002b) reported that lack of funding was the single most frequently cited reason contributing to a school's decision to drop a model. While these findings underscore the importance of funding in determining a school's ability to establish or retain a formal relationship with a model provider, funding may not be an accurate predictor of a school's reform behavior.

To more accurately assess and better understand the sustainabilty of improvement, schools in this study were revisited five years after they had adopted a CSR model. When they first began participating in this study as they were completing their last year of the three-year CSR funding cycle, they reflected back on the years of program implementation and projected forward to anticipate whether their schools would sustain reform program strategies. The previous chapters in this book capture the behaviors and the sentiments expressed by respondents in reforming schools regarding their experiences over those three years, particularly as they relate to state context, district support, distribution of leadership, faculty commitment, and gains attributed to the CSR models. This chapter provides information about the patterns of sustainability of behaviors and practices related to schools' experiences with the reform in the years after their CSR grants expired. It also considers the salient factors that contributed to school decision making regarding sustainability.

SUSTAINING COMPREHENSIVE SCHOOL REFORM

Taylor's (2005) report on whole-school reform models in nearly 400 schools revealed that within three years about one-third of the schools had discontinued a relationship with their reform model provider. Further, when schools were sorted based on reform trajectories by years of implementation, he found that 35% of schools institutionalized the change. Only 3 of 11 predictors of sustainability had significant effects on the likelihood of retaining or dropping a relationship with reform model providers. Teacher turnover was inversely related to sustainability, and middle school configuration and district-driven professional development intended to support strategies embedded in the reform program improved the likelihood of sustainability (Taylor, 2005).

Datnow and Stringfield (2000) reported on a small set of schools that were tracked qualitatively over eight years and noted that only three of eight continued to sustain school improvement strategies to the extent that they were fully institutionalized. More recently Datnow (2005) revisited the issue of sustainability, particularly in formal relationships between 13 schools and CSR model providers over time. Most schools terminated their programs because of changes in district policies, assessment performance pressures, loss of interest in the reform strategies, and so forth. Of the few schools that sustained a relationship with their model providers, two already were recognized as high performing, flagship schools in their district, and for that reason, they seized the ability to sustain their reform model while appeasing district mandates.

The findings of these and others studies demonstrate the challenge of assessing the continuing use or effects of innovative practices, perhaps because of the loosely coupled environment characterizing districts and schools where a decision at one level may have significant influence on behavior at another. For example, Datnow (2005) determined that district decisions to drop or change reform may be disregarded, at least in part, by schools. Likewise, a school may decide formally to terminate a reform program, but teachers may continue to use its instructional strategies in the classroom. Even so, in this latter scenario, Berman and McLaughlin (1978) warn that the continued use of innovative strategies by teachers is not enough to sustain project-related changes. Although their intentions to continue with school improvement efforts may be sincere, a number of circumstances may undermine them and create the possibility of redefining goals and priorities.

Recent findings of Giles and Hargreaves (2006) reinforce those of Berman and McLaughlin (1978) and others. Their study of reform programs in eight U.S. and Canadian high schools found that most innovations in schools don't last because additional funding requirements of the programs become impossible for schools to finance or because of *attrition of change*, which they define as changes in leadership, faculty, policy, or district support. Change or turnover at any one level may redirect the attention and efforts of practitioners to other issues. Although most studies on sustainability clearly indicate whether a school has continued a formal relationship with reform program providers, they are less informative about more subtle distinctions where schools have continued their reform efforts without program funding. For example, how and why do schools make these decisions?

By recontacting schools five years after they initially had adopted a reform program, this study readily determined whether they had retained a formal relationship with model providers. However, revisiting schools for the second period of observation and in-depth interviewing distinguished some schools from others based on the extent to which they demonstrated ongoing use of school improvement strategies. It revealed that on reflection, most schools in this study were strongly supportive of having had the CSR experience. Even so, they were almost evenly split between sustaining or dropping CSR-related improvement strategies. Specifically, two years after CSR grants ended, 10 schools were sustaining improvement efforts and 8 were not.

The following sections describe the patterns of sustainability that schools exhibited and the factors that were most salient to them as they made decisions about changing for good.

SUSTAINABILITY WITH FUNDING

Six schools sustained and funded a formal relationship with their reform program providers five years after program adoption. All three schools in Waterton County were in this group. When I returned to one of them, the principal greeted me by proudly announcing, "We have other funding now. . . . We were able to get another grant!" In fact, the school had committed to sustaining its reform program, initially by using Title I money to bridge over its first year without CSR funding and then by capitalizing on its newly acquired expertise of grant processes to seek and apply for additional external funds. Just that week, the school learned it had been awarded a coveted Reading First grant, which would allow it to continue using its reform model for several years. The principal acknowledged that, in actuality, Reading First grants targeted kindergarten through Grade 3 but explained that the school also intended to sustain its reform program in Grades 4 through 6 by using materials they already had obtained with CSR funding. This, along with a plan to contract with the model providers for fewer site visits because the school was in a *sustainability mode*, would scale back the expense of sustaining the program to an affordable amount. She reminded me that the district was still on track to open a new school in the upcoming year, which would eliminate Grades 7 and 8 from all the local elementary schools, including this one. Teachers echoed the intentions of the principal regarding program continuation. In conversation, several predicted that if I were to return to their school again in two or three years they would still be using their reform model. One teacher reiterated this saying, "At this point teachers just assume we will use this model. We don't really even question it anymore." Another agreed, "We know we're in it for the long haul."

From the vantage point of the school's leaders, after five years of reform, the district was still *paying attention*. According to them, the district reinforced its vision of school improvement by maintaining interest in their progress related to reform implementation and outcomes. Reiterating what she had told me two years earlier, this principal continued to have strong support from and rapport with the district. She said, "The district has been supportive by allowing us to keep using our reform program. It also recognizes that we have to make certain allowances, like reducing some of our professional development requirements. That way, it doesn't create a lot of added burden." She also noted, "This district provides such good information sources, you couldn't ask for better help."

Though this principal had taken her post at the school midway through its third year of reform implementation, she felt she finally had hit her stride as a principal leader. She said, "Quite honestly, when I came to this school there were real morale problems here, and I was so busy putting out little fires, I didn't have time to call the fire department. Now that our climate has improved, I have been able to broaden my focus on a few more things rather than just one or two issues. As I gain experience, I hope I can expand even more." Indeed, an improved climate was noticeable. Unlike in the past, teachers ate together, showed signs of working and planning collaboratively, and visited back and forth across the halls with one another in their spare time. They exhibited friendliness, compatibility, and an increased sense of confidence that I had not detected in earlier visits.

Not only had the principal broadened her scope of issues but also intended to continue expanding leadership by involving additional faculty members. She explained, "Leadership is one thing that requires me either to put off some duties or give them up to others. I need that time to get back in the classroom more and sit down with the teachers. Honestly, the facilitator has bridged that gap and will probably have to do it more, but I will need to pull other teachers in, which as of right now, I am looking at." Finally, the principal held high expectations for her school and intended to seize this new award as an opportunity to make a name for it. She emphasized that she hoped the school leaders and faculty would intensify their reform efforts "to turn small gains into big gains." As I departed from the school, she predicted, "Three years from now, we are going to be number one in the county."

Sustainability of the reform program was also underway in both of the other reforming schools in Waterton County. The principal in one explained that the district had shown her how to budget differently to finance additional years of program implementation. She said, "We are in our fifth year now. We take funding year by year." Like others discussed in Chapter 6 who enjoyed professional growth as a spillover effect from the grant experience, she commented, "I can't even begin to explain how much I've grown through this experience. I have a new view about leadership. Before, I felt like I knew what good instruction looked like, but this has opened my eyes to how inadequate that perception was." In fact, the school had expanded its reform program to include a math component, and based on classroom observations, implementation appeared to be flourishing. Consistent with the vision for school improvement that continued to emanate from the district, the principal reinforced the school's commitment to reform by trying to keep that vision alive. She confided, "To be honest with you, a couple of years ago, we had a few teachers who were like, 'well, the grant is over, we are going back to what we did before.' I am sorry; no, we are not. All children are receiving good instructional practices with this. If we go back to teachers doing their own thing, it is either hit or miss."

When I returned to the third Waterton County school, I learned that, two years earlier, it had put the decision of sustainability to a vote and the majority of the faculty voted to discontinue the reform program. This, no doubt, was at least partially because it was expecting to close after the new school opened. Despite the faculty's decision, the superintendent urged the school to continue the program possibly because he wanted to avoid treating one school differentially over others. Regardless, the school agreed to sustain the program with modifications and scaled back its use to the lower grades. This decision seemed to satisfy the superintendent and everyone else. The teachers in the lower grades, nearly all of whom were early career teachers, readily agreed to use the program. The more veteran teachers in the upper grades also were content with the arrangement. The principal explained, "The upper-grade teachers are now officially exempt from using our reform program for a host of reasons . . . mainly, teacher resistance and its ineffectiveness in the upper grades." While having lunch with the upper-grade faculty later that week, the math teacher said, "We like the way it works right now much better than when we were having to do all the reform program's stuff." The science teacher agreed saying, "We do sometimes use the materials, but we don't do it straight by the book." As a group, they agreed that their exemption had improved the climate in the upper grades and said they had set their sights on moving when the new school opened.

On returning to Burkett County, I found that one middle school had continued, with district funding, to sustain a formal relationship with its reform program. However, it had just discovered the district was finalizing plans to introduce a new homegrown literacy program that all schools would be required to implement. As the program facilitator described what she knew about the decision, she expressed concern and discouragement because she perceived it to be a literacy program different from the one the school presently used; the school would be required to use it, and the school would have to give up the reform program they had used over the last five years. She worried about the teachers and said, "Right now, a high majority would be real disappointed if we dropped the program because, at this point, we feel like we have finally worked through a lot of the kinks and this is a workable program for the types of kids we have."

Over time, rumors about this district-wide change clearly had generated anxiety, skepticism, and resentment among teachers and had begun undermining their commitment to the present reform program. One teacher expressed her concern, "I think people are wondering why they've been beating themselves over the head and trying to do this reform model and going to training and trying to keep up with it because we've heard that our district has a different program for us to implement whether we like it or not." Another teacher concurred and added, "All of a sudden, if you know that you are not going to be doing it next year, it takes a lot out of your sails about how much momentum you have."

In reality, the principal and facilitator explained that they were *in negotiations* with the district in an attempt to gain permission to continue using the whole-school reform model rather than switch to the district's new literacy program. Although the principal admitted she wasn't sure what would happen in the upcoming year, she tentatively declared, "From what I understand, hopefully we will be able to keep our program. If not, we will do it ourselves; we are not letting it go. We just have to sustain." This school hoped to be exempt from implementing the district's new plan, but if not, the principal implied they would somehow juggle both the district plan and their reform program simultaneously.

Like these schools, two schools in other districts also had continued using their reform programs with money that they pieced together with various budgeting strategies. However, the principals were reconsidering that decision for the upcoming (sixth) year, and the more we talked about it, the more certain it seemed they would drop their models and discontinue the related strategies. Both schools were in districts described as cooperative but not overly supportive or involved, so in that respect, neither principal anticipated that their district would care particularly about their decision one way or the other. Their explanations for dropping their models were similar. They both said their schools had exhausted their respective programs by implementing them as fully as possible, but the faculties had become disillusioned primarily because of lack of strong results in school performance. Second, both their schools had experienced higher than expected teacher turnover that they attributed partly to burnout from using the program. Finally, the expense of maintaining the reform program was becoming burdensome. One of the principals said, "The momentum of the program has really plunged. The implementation level is not very strong at this point, not from the trainers, not from the facilitators, not from the teachers. It is increasingly difficult to sustain it." Neither of these principals resented or begrudged the CSR experience; on the contrary, they were grateful their schools had been given the chance to improve. However, because neither perceived that improvement had occurred, they thought it was a good time to cut their losses and move on. In fact, one of the schools was currently shopping for a different program. The principal confided, "We fully intend to stop the current program after this year and purchase a new one in the upcoming year if funding is available." He reflected, "I think we kind of maxed out our potential with the program now, and it is time to look for something else to give us another boost."

Of the six schools in this section that had sustained a formal relationship with their model providers through five years, two schools in Waterton County planned to continue reforming indefinitely. Two others, one in Waterton and one in Burkett, seemed likely to drop their models in the upcoming year because of actions initiated at the district level. The remaining two schools in different areas of the state had become disillusioned with their reform programs and indicated they would drop their models and corresponding reform strategies after the fifth year.

Despite the support that Burkett County extended to its reforming schools over the last five years, it was not clear how much longer the school would be able to sustain its reform model given the district's new reading initiative, which they perceived to be inconsistent with their reform program. In her study of CSR implementation and sustainability, Datnow (2005) found that 13 schools in one large district responded differently to new district mandates, but only the district's one high-performing, flagship school sustained its previous reform program intact in the face of pressure to use new initiatives. As this finding suggests, such independent behavior is unusual for most schools, and more commonly, they would succumb to district mandates for new school improvement measures. In fact, I discovered in the fall of the next school year that the school had complied with the district's directive and switched over to the new initiative. While interviewing at the district office, the assistant superintendent for middle schools, Dr. Roth, explained, "I sat down with the principal, and we talked about it. She and her instructional colleagues, including the highly skilled educator (HSE), met with their teachers, and I think we resolved the issue pretty well. They bought into the district program."

COMMITMENT TO SUSTAINABILITY WITHOUT FUNDING

Three schools had discontinued their relationship with model providers after the grant period ended, largely because of issues with funding. Even so, they appeared committed to sustaining reform strategies.

Forestview Middle School

When I returned to Forestview five years after the initial implementation of their reform program, the principal, Ms. May, readily claimed the school was successfully sustaining its commitment to reform and estimated that about 85% of the faculty continued using the instructional strategies proposed by the model. She claimed, "You can go into any classroom on any given day and continue to see elements of it. Our teachers still make prescription sheets for kids. They still do center work that provides individualized, diverse instruction." In fact, several days of classroom observations substantiated her claim. Teachers across all core content areas along with classes such as physical education used instructional strategies promoted by the school's reform program.

When talking with teachers during this return visit, most of them described the school as being in a period of routinization or sustainability. One teacher said, "I don't hear a lot of teacher comment about the program anymore but that is because it has become routine. You don't talk about it because it is something you know that you do. It goes without saying." Another teacher commented that sustaining the reform was easier than implementing it. She elaborated, "You use your most energy at the beginning because that's when change is hardest and when the most work is done. Once you get into the flow of it, not as much energy is required. That doesn't mean you are not still doing a lot, but everything goes smoother. It is much easier to do because you feel more comfortable with what you are doing."

Ms. May acknowledged, however, that sustainability didn't occur automatically. She reminded me of the measures she and others had taken to ensure the model's survival in the school. Since I had last seen her, she continued to reinforce the school's vision for improvement and did not hesitate to contact reform model providers when the school needed clarification or guidance on various instructional strategies. She also retained assistance of the school's facilitator, particularly in training and socializing new teachers to use the reform strategies the school had adopted five years earlier. She explained, "Our facilitator takes new teachers under her wing and works with them. Usually, she tries to get the initial part of the training done as soon as possible, before school starts in those first few days when we are here doing inservice. She meets with them and goes through the whole program. Then she provides a lot of follow-up." Referring to the school's most recent new teacher she continued, "He is paired up with some mentors who will help him. He goes to see them on his planning time, to check out their teaching styles, and to see what they are doing in grouping and leveling."

Finally, the principal predicted the school would continue to sustain its reform efforts indefinitely because of their successes with it. She said, "At first teachers were like 'when are we not going to have to do this?' I told them we are always going to do it because this is where we got our success. It is beneficial to us. Our kids learn differently now; they take a lot of responsibility for their projects and things that they do in the classroom. It was good, and we are going to continue."

Tipton Middle School

Tipton Middle School was another school that sustained its reform strategies without additional external funding. When I returned to the school, I found that its improvement efforts continued to be strong. Members of the instructional team remained intact, and the system of *teachers training teachers* with reform-based instructional practices appeared to be thriving. I saw extensive evidence of model-based strategies in each of the classes I observed over the days I was there. Enthusiasm for professional growth remained high. One teacher summed up the sentiments of many when she said, "I think I am at a point that I am refining what I find. I try to incorporate new strategies and take some old strategies and make them even better. I am always learning new strategies with this reform model. I have new goals every year, and each year I teach something new."

Since the expiration of its grant cycle, assistance from the external program provider had been scaled back dramatically, but the school still paid her to come in on a monthly basis. She worked with teachers and students during the day and held training sessions after school. As one teacher described, "She usually starts off the session with some kind of craft lesson or minilesson for faculty and then talks about what she has seen in the school and how she sees the changes in the students' performance in the year. Then she will also meet with us one on one from time to time." According to this teacher, the faculty still looked to the provider for guidance and motivation even though they were capable of moving ahead independently as a group now. The model facilitator acknowledged this saying, "The training sessions that I hold now are almost completely teacher led. I don't have to do anything." A teacher concurred saying, "Teachers have bought into it. It has become part of our curriculum." Another way the school reinforced its commitment to sustaining its reform program was by holding a *super-sub* day once a month where teachers were released from classroom teaching to have in-school professional development. They used the release time to observe in other classes or model for teachers who observed them. Alternatively, they spent time analyzing student work. On those days, the former program facilitator, who continued to hold a formal administrative role, was available for anyone who wanted guidance or input during his or her planning period.

Because of these efforts, several teachers predicted that the school would likely continue to sustain strategies promoted by its reform model indefinitely. One said, "Even though the facilitator's time has been cut back tremendously in this school, we have others here who will share their expertise or work with other teachers. We have a lot of teachers who know the model's strategies." A third teacher explained, "I don't see us as dependent on our program provider as much as we were before because there are a lot of people who know those skills now and work with their partner teacher if they are new and share those ideas." Further, newly emerging teacher leaders began assuming responsibility for functions previously performed by the model facilitator. For example, sixth-grade teachers had taken over the function of vertical alignment by visiting fifth grades in local feeder schools.

The former program facilitator explained, "We encourage people to share successful instructional strategies in large group meetings or during common planning time. This is beneficial to everyone, especially new people who weren't here in the first three years [of reform]. Also, we analyze student work throughout the year to determine where we go from here." Additionally, they modeled lessons, developed a binder containing what they had found to be the most important and effective instructional strategies related to the model, and continued to provide substitutes once a month to allow teachers to observe and model for one another. The facilitator commented that this was likely responsible for model sustainability.

As Tipton was in Burkett County, it faced having to comply with the new district initiative. However, in contrast to the school described in the previous section, educators in Tipton did not perceive that the initiative would conflict with or jeopardize the focus of the reform program that they already used.

Greely Elementary School

When I returned to Greely Elementary School, I found both Ms. Ashley, the principal, and Mrs. Christopher, the former reform facilitator, still working there. The principal was quick to tell me that in the two years since I had seen her, the school had been awarded three new grants enabling them to offer specific innovative services and programs to students. Additionally, the new monies had allowed teachers to gain further professional development both locally and at national conferences.

Further, although it no longer financed the CSR program it had implemented, like Forestview, there was ample evidence that leaders and teachers continued to use many of the strategies promoted by the program. In fact, Mrs. Christopher described ongoing implementation to be strong. She said, "The books and materials have been bought. We know how to find everything we need for implementation even now." She also said that the principal still emphasized the reform model's strategies whenever she could. For example, there was normally some mention of information stemming from the reform program in the daily announcements coming from the principal's office, the principal continued to check lesson plans for evidence of program implementation in instruction, and she repeatedly reminded them of the need to use program strategies at faculty meetings. Several teachers confirmed Mrs. Christopher's contention. I observed evidence of instructional strategies in classroom teaching and by reviewing homework assignments. Further, one teacher explained that a committee continued to work on aligning the core content and curriculum mapping, and teachers continued to look for opportunities to do interdisciplinary teaching. One said, "I think that most of us rally around it, especially in the primary grades."

The school climate remained remarkably positive at Greely. For example, the upper-grade teachers I was most familiar with still helped one another and worked together, sometimes by team teaching or conferencing to coordinate lessons across content areas. They still sought advice and assistance from one another. They still joked and enjoyed one another's company as they ate lunch together. And some were still taking coursework and commuting together in hopes of soon attaining their administrator certification.

The principal talked about changes that had occurred in the school since CSR funding ended. It was almost as if she was reminiscing about the good old days. She said, "I believe student engagement was higher when the reform model was here. Students were really focused on getting specific content knowledge. There were things they could go home and tell their parents about, things the parents might not have known." Then she added, "I think the engagement of students is not as high anymore. Now, we just have to get *the test* out of the way." In fact, she expressed concern about the emphasis on testing that seemed to be pervasive. She said, "Our kids are becoming better test takers without the experience or foundation of learning to fall back on. When they get to the higher level where they have to explain their answers, they need that base knowledge; they don't have a single reference about what to write about."

However, over the days I was at Greely, I began to detect *cracks in the armor* of the school's ability to sustain reform strategies independent of model providers. For example, it seemed that the tight linkage between the principal and the former program facilitator was weakening, particularly as it related to sustainability of the reform model. Mrs. Christopher no longer had the title of program facilitator, and she had relaxed her efforts toward implementation. She mentioned that in the past, when they had CSR funding, she would train new teachers to use the school's reform model, but now, because she was not the facilitator, she *thought* that Ms. Ashley showed new teachers about the reform-related units, curriculum, and accompanying strategies. She also said that in the case of interns or student teachers she *presumed* that their resource teacher would inform them about the reform strategies. The principal believed that teacher turnover was the main culprit in undermining the use of specific instructional strategies promoted by the reform program the school had implemented. She said, "Turnover has hurt us, especially when it is key implementers." Then she added, "What has happened to us is when they replace teachers in positions, sometimes we get teachers who have not been trained in our reform's strategies. They generally are 14- or 15-year veterans who don't want to make the changes that need to be done." Although this may be accurate, it is also plausible that the new teachers didn't change because they were unfamiliar with the expectations and instructional strategies of the previous reform program, and the school no longer designated someone to facilitate training.

In retrospect, Ms. Ashley said she and other faculty members at her school were very satisfied with their reform experience. They perceived they had attained high levels of implementation and attributed gains on the school's Commonwealth Accountability Testing System (CATS) index score and student engagement to the reform model. The principal was taking deliberate measures to try to sustain reform strategies without funding. Although they had terminated their formal relationship with model providers two years earlier because of the expiration of the CSR grant, the principal said she had recently approached the district school board about putting in a pitch at the next district board meeting to reinvigorate the use of the reform model to regain ground they had lost over the last two years.

Each of the three schools in this section had dropped a formal relationship with their model providers when their CSR funding period expired. Only one of the schools had found a way to finance the services of the model provider and school facilitator on a dramatically reduced schedule. Even so, all three had continued using strategies promoted by their respective reform programs. The first two schools seemed completely satisfied with their new reform status. The third school, Greely, was more cautious about the risk of losing ground rather than ongoing improvement and hoped to curb it by reinstating the model they had dropped two years earlier.

SUSTAINED MOMENTUM FOR IMPROVEMENT AND INNOVATION

Littleton provides an example of a school that dropped its reform model and related strategies that accompanied it when the grant period expired but sustained strong momentum for improvement and innovation that the CSR experience had sparked. When I returned to the school, the principal Mr. Mackin remained at his post but the former program facilitator had returned to a full-time job at the district. At least a portion of her job was still devoted to parent liaison. The decision to drop the model seemed to have been based largely on lack of funding. They could not come up with the funds to retain the program facilitator. Indeed, she had contributed such a huge part to the school's leadership that it created something of a hole when she left. Recall that this school had switched models after the first year so they were just gaining full momentum for implementing their program when funding expired. Loss of funding translated into loss of the program facilitator and teachers described that, in her absence, they had difficulty picking up the slack in lesson planning, ordering materials, and using instructional strategies promoted by the program. One said, "Since she left, more burden has fallen to the teachers' shoulders. We weren't ready for it yet." Another said, "It was like stopping in the middle of a movie." The program facilitator continued to work closely with the school in her capacity as parent liaison at the district level, but she no longer performed any responsibilities associated with program facilitation. When asked about the potentially detrimental effect of her departure on the ability of the school to sustain its reform efforts she said, "I am not tooting my own horn, but I think every school would benefit from having a facilitator to devote time to the job that I did. That would be an ideal situation for every school to have." Despite little evidence of teachers trying to sustain reform-related practices, other indicators suggested that enthusiasm for ongoing improvement was high. For example, the school climate continued to seem very positive. Nearly everyone mentioned this. The former program facilitator echoed the comments of many by saying, "I think the school climate is better in that teachers work together more as a family, and basically, they are more supportive of one another. I think the day-to-day running of the school is smoother." Recognizing the progress in this area the principal admitted, "I guess it would be that we are running a tighter ship."

The principal also continued to stay on course with his intentions to distribute leadership among faculty. He said he had had some success with this effort but was moving slowly to avoid overwhelming those teachers who were still somewhat inexperienced. He was using his new teacher leaders as "channels of information" but not necessarily "trainers of faculty" as the former program facilitator had been. He hoped that might come later.

NO SUSTAINABILITY

Like the school described in the introduction of this book, on returning to the remaining eight schools five years after the initial CSR funding, few, if any, showed signs of sustaining aspects of their reform programs. All of the schools had terminated their reform efforts two years earlier, when their grant funds had expired. Four of these schools attributed their decision to drop reform to characteristics about the reform program itself. Often they articulated their low satisfaction by complaining that the program had been ineffective in adequately addressing the needs of the school or its students, its structure was overly rigid and stifled creativity, or the school had not perceived gains such as increases in test scores after using the model for the specified term of the grant. Many of the educators from these schools already had expressed these dissatisfactions in the third year of implementation. Then, they perceived their external model providers had not delivered on promises made to the schools early on, which, in turn, undermined their commitment to implementation. These promises commonly involved service support, compatibility of the reform program with Kentucky's Core Content (KCC) or effectiveness in test gains. Mainly, the most salient feature about the programs that caused these schools to drop their model was the lack of strong gains on CATS scores.

In one of these schools, however, the pervasive attitude toward school reform was that they would do it again but not necessarily with the same model. It seems that the educators there still believed in the notion of CSR but had become more scrutinizing, selective consumers because of their reform experience. The former program facilitator stated, "We thought our model was good at the time we selected it, but now, I don't think it went deep enough in its reform efforts. It didn't provide enough support to teachers, and it didn't emphasize classroom strategies or instructional methods." The principal concurred. She said, "The model was static. It didn't change, improve, or grow over the three years, so why would we want to purchase it again or continue using it?" The principal said she had hoped the reform program would integrate the curriculum and render higher performance levels, but the model had failed the school in both of those respects. Finally, she also explained that the program had fallen out of favor with district personnel, perhaps, because of some of the problems she had just described. Teachers in that school confirmed they were still willing to try "almost anything for improvement," and for the present, at least the sentiment among almost everyone, seemed to be one of cautious optimism that new opportunities for improvement would present themselves at some point in the not-too-distant future.

Unlike the schools mentioned earlier, the remaining four schools decided to drop reform efforts because of changing circumstances rooted in the school or district. All four schools had high principal turnover. Two were also "victims" of district decisions to introduce initiatives that disrupted the consistency between the districts' perspectives on improvement and CSR. Schools undergoing organizational changes such as these typically were characterized by low engagement, low teacher commitment, and a deteriorating climate. Teachers in one school said as much. One commented, "It [lack of sustainability] is probably partly because of the end of funding, but it is mostly the leadership thing. We were doing great with that CSR grant when our former principal was up here, and we intended on still doing it in the years after the grant." However, under a new principal's administration, several teachers complained there was "absolutely no accountability any longer for using the reform program." They agreed that reform efforts related to the school's CSR grant ended with the departure of their previous principal after the third year of implementation and funding. Most of the educators in these schools that had dropped their models two years earlier seemed satisfied and relieved to have returned to a more normal existence, that is, life without the pressure and burden of whole-school reform. In reference to one such school, a district administrator confirmed this suspicion by saying, "Because of that school's principal turnover, we didn't focus on the reform model. That was a waste of whatever thousands of dollars; it didn't help student achievement."

DISCUSSION OF PATTERNS OF REFORM SUSTAINABILITY

This chapter examined the issue of the sustainability of whole-school reform once CSR-funding expires. Berends, Bodilly, and Kirby (2002a; 2002b) and others have found that lack of funding is a strong predictor of a school's decision to drop a CSR model; the findings presented in this chapter show that funding may determine a school's propensity to establish or retain a formal relationship with a model provider in the first three years, but it is not an accurate predictor of a school's reform behavior after CSR-funding expiration. A third of the schools in this study sustained reform efforts either by finding other sources for funding or by developing budgeting strategies to retain their reform programs for subsequent years of implementation.

It is likely four of the six schools that continued to sustain a formal relationship with model providers over five years would drop their model at that year's end. Decisions at the district level resulted in one school closing and another school dropping its reform model in exchange for a different, newer initiative. The two other schools planned to drop the formal relationships they had with their model providers and stop using the corresponding reform strategies. Their decision to discontinue using a program and related strategies was not because of funding but because the burden of the schools' reform efforts more broadly (including funding) was not outweighed by significant tangible results, particularly in school performance and student achievement. The decision of these last two schools described is broader but consistent with Datnow's (2005) study of sustainability of CSR in 13 schools using Success for All. It revealed that schools with declining test scores found it increasing difficult to justify their reform efforts. After five years, those schools established test preparation as a highest priority and dropped the model.

Four additional schools terminated their reform program relationships after the three-year CSR period because of funding issues but informally continued sustaining innovative improvement strategies learned through their CSR experience or continued to improve in other ways. The vision for improvement was clear and commitment for reform was high in those schools. They had built capacity for both leadership and instruction, and they intended to continue their present reform mode indefinitely. Despite their capacity to sustain improvement, they received virtually no assistance from model providers in making the transition to their new status.

Theoretically, at the end of the three-year grant period, model providers have a common practice of systematically and gradually withdrawing professional development and technical assistance from schools so they can become self-sustaining (Taylor, 2005). In practice, the experiences of the schools in this study suggest otherwise. According to the respondents, reform model providers did not attempt to prepare schools to disengage from the formal relationship or transition from program implementation to sustainability. As the end of funding approached, signaling the termination of many school and provider relationships, program providers delivered no preparatory guidelines, formal or otherwise, suggesting how schools should approach sustainability independent of a formal, funded relationship. In contrast to any possible planned strategy of withdrawal by providers, schools whose providers did not visit regularly or failed to deliver the goods in the third year left their clients feeling ignored, overlooked, forgotten, or shunned.

The remaining eight schools dropped their models on the expiration of funding from their grant period. Those droppers were about evenly split in basing their decisions on reasons having to do with the school or district versus problems or weaknesses rooted in the models, such as lack of effectiveness (real or perceived), growing disillusionment among users with the reform strategies, or a disparity between strategies promoted by model in relation to the needs of the school.

Slavin (2004) suggests that schools may halt innovative efforts or, in the case of CSR, drop models for a number of reasons including personnel turnover, burnout among users, change in policy, loss of funding, and other reasons rooted in the school or district. He does not account for the possibility of schools dropping models for reasons involving the reform models themselves. This seems much like a *blame-the-victim* orientation in that it places the burden of success on the schools rather than holding model providers accountable for their products. In fact, more recently, Slavin (2008) acknowledges that to increase implementation levels and program effectiveness, reform strategies must be modified, within reason, to better suit the context where they are implemented.

Finally, findings presented in this chapter raise an important issue regarding the effect of time on sustainability. CSR grants, by design, spanned three years anticipating that models would need a sustained three- to five-year implementation period to realize gains in student achievement and school improvement. Berends (2000) found that commonly school performance actually declined in the early years of CSR and then began to increase noticeably after the fourth year of implementation. This pattern is substantiated by Borman, Hewes, Overman, and Brown (2002) and Zhang, Shkolnik, and Fashola (2005) who found gains in student achievement relative to comparison schools after controlling for intensity and duration of implementation (three to five years). On the other hand, after tracking the effects of a whole-school reform model over time in one school district, May, Supovitz (2006) and May, Supovitz, and Perda (2004) found that math gains diminished and effects on reading reversed from positive to negative. The findings of these studies have important implications for schools that continued to engage in formal relationships with model providers to attain higher test scores.

Half the schools in this study that implemented for fewer than four years dropped their reform efforts largely because of lack of evidence that it was working. Based on the studies in the preceding paragraph, it may be that an accelerated rate of improvement in those schools would have been forthcoming. On the other hand, at least two schools had continued a formal relationship with their model providers through five years of implementation and still did not see strong results. Their objective decision to terminate their relationship with model providers and move on was similar to findings in Datnow's (2005) study. Consistent with her research, it appeared that the five-year mark was a critical juncture when schools assessed their performance status in relation to their reform efforts and decided either to continue to sustain or to terminate reform.

When considering the experiences and outcomes of the schools that sustained their models or related innovative practices in contrast to the other eight schools that did not, it appears that integral components of sustainability may include district support; strong, stable, and distributed leadership; teacher commitment; and perceived goal achievement. Clearly, these work in concert with one another, and I will continue to explore the relationship of these components to sustainability in Chapter 8.

8

Reforming Reform

The significance of this reform was its comprehensive effort. That correlated very well with what this state had been doing for the previous two or three years with the whole notion of a comprehensive plan of school improvement. Prior to that, significant amounts of money went to districts and individual schools, but each source of money kind of established its own little program and very few were significant in making great change. Another piece about this reform was the kinds of programs it put forth. They were "proven," they had a track record with data, and they had success rates. A third thing was the cohesiveness of it, the pulling together of the school staff to identify and decide on how to address the problem because, in too many instances, the solution was something that was given to the schools as opposed to being elected by the schools.

—State education administrator

There is a culture of continuous improvement here now that everybody recognizes because we have been using these strategies for so long. I just think it has become part of the culture of the school. It would be a hard thing for it to just disappear immediately. I think without being supported and fed it could trickle down and fizzle out, but as long as we nurture it, I think it won't disappear.

—Former reform program facilitator

When schools initiate reform efforts, the thought of changing for good is commonly the furthest thing from their minds. Countless reform initiatives introduced in recent decades have had negligible effects on school improvement, particularly improvement that moves schools away from traditional practice to become learning organizations or communities where practice is coherently integrated around goals for effective teaching and learning. Failed reforms burden schools financially and represent enormous costs of human effort and resources. Further, poorly integrated or inadequately supported reforms undermine school climates by generating frustration and cynicism among practitioners. Understanding factors that shape the process and permanence of change will contribute to more thoughtful and effective reform practices in schools.

Sustainability of school reform is change that persists, endures over time, and has an ongoing, lasting effect on classroom practices (Berman & McLaughlin, 1978; Datnow, 2005; Fullan, 2005). When change achieves both classroom assimilation and system incorporation, it becomes established or institutionalized (Berman & McLaughlin, 1978; Datnow, 2005). Although the literature on effective school reform is growing and shows promise, the studies have not sufficiently addressed the issue of sustainability in-depth. Findings often have been limited by how the term is defined and measured. The research on sustaining educational reform suggests that conceptually, sustainability should be considered in ways that go beyond the formal continuation of a project to consider qualitatively the persistence over time of some or all aspects of reform-related changes. Yet what factors promote such lasting change in schools?

With this question in mind, this chapter offers a review of key findings presented in this book about school reform and sustainability. Using the experiences of 18 schools that sought improvement by adopting externally developed reform models with funding through the federal comprehensive school reform (CSR) program as an example, it reviews schools' selection and adoption of reform models in 1999 and follows them through to their decisions and practice involving the sustainability of reform five years later. It summarizes the patterns of reform sustainability that schools exhibited two years after their federal funding expired and then presents a conceptual model for sustainability that accounts for the schools' experiences. Finally, the chapter offers recommendations to strengthen the effectiveness of the implementation and sustainability of school-improvement strategies.

The first quotation at the beginning of this chapter suggests that educational policymakers, decision makers, and practitioners assumed the CSR program held great potential for schools because it was supported by federal funding; it promoted carefully planned, field-tested, or research-based strategies for improvement; and the process of reform selection and adoption, implementation, and sustainability gave choice and voice to users, that is, it required the involvement and input from teachers from the outset. Underlying all else, it represented a coherent, integrated approach to change, a feature that was absent in previous reform periods. Despite the potential effectiveness for school improvement that whole-school reform models may have held, schools targeted for funding through the CSR program posed unique challenges because they typically served high concentrations of students living in poverty and at risk of failing or dropping out, were low performing based on their state accountability index scores, and often lacked the organizational capacity necessary to implement and capitalize on improvement strategies.

This book determined that reform was influenced by external conditions emanating from the state context by the way it structured the reform proposal and adoption processes. The state's infrastructure supported low-performing schools by providing them highly skilled educators (HSEs), additional resources, and so forth but, on the other hand, added the burden of high-stakes testing. Consistent with Lane and Gracia (2004), this study showed that support of state educational agencies is important in shaping the process of change in districts and schools. The state's involvement in the CSR process effectively structured the identification of eligible schools in a way that allowed districts and schools the autonomy to determine whether they would engage in the reform. State personnel became knowledgeable and informed about reform models to provide schools with current information about the viable choices. Finally, the initial proposal procedure designed by the state organized schools for reform by requiring them to identify and prioritize reform goals, participate in model shopping, and engage teachers in meaningful decision making, as they narrowed their choices and voted to adopt reform models. Beyond that, the state continued to keep in contact with reforming schools by using them as a source for practical information to guide and advise later cohorts as they contemplated the possibility of reform themselves. Leopold, Childers, and Hawley-Rowe (2000) found that some schools declined the opportunity to participate in reform by claiming ignorance about the reform process or reform models. On the other hand, Kentucky provided sufficient information for all schools to be knowledgeable about the reform process and models, but many declined to participate because they perceived that the benefits offered by CSR did not outweigh the costs of participation.

Active district support was integral for reforming schools because it built capacity in and across schools. Exceptional district-support practices were broad based and included promoting and sustaining a shared vision of improvement that focused on alignment and coherency, providing technical expertise and in-school support staff, respecting school autonomy, generating effective communication channels, structuring opportunities for networking and information sharing, advocating for schools, and so forth. These findings are consistent with others where districts offered technical support (Goertz, 2005) and networking opportunities for educators to collaborate, gain social capital, advance innovative practice, and grow professionally (Coburn & Russell, 2008). Districts that demonstrated active support or, to a lesser extent, passive cooperation rather than no support promoted a higher likelihood of schools sustaining reform efforts.

In schools, leadership, particularly that which spanned and was distributed across educators, was effective in the reform process. Principals held an instrumental role by establishing an environment that was conducive to collaborative faculty input in leading change. Like many other reforms introduced in schools, whole-school reform models created the need for a new school leadership position, the program facilitator. Schools configured this position as a full-time assignment or part-time coupled with either administrative or teaching responsibilities. Consistent with other research (Datnow & Castellano, 2001; Smylie, Conley, & Marks, 2002) this book revealed that a new teacher leader position (such as the reform facilitator) might be surrounded by job fragmentation and instability in the configuration of their assignments from year to year. Reform facilitators also were likely to experience misunderstanding and resentment. It goes beyond other research by finding this was particularly the case when facilitators held few responsibilities associated more commonly with faculty positions such as teaching or administration. However, facilitators could reduce the negative aspects of their jobs when they practiced boundary maintenance or engaged in work overload.

The work of implementing reform involved managerial tasks, collaborative instructional duties, supervisory responsibilities, networking, and addressing broader reform efforts. Typically, facilitators completed managerial tasks and principals supervised progress. Otherwise, in schools having some variation of distributed leadership, teacher leaders shared the responsibilities of reform. The likelihood of sustainability seemed most promising in schools where leadership was distributed or in schools where principals were making a concerted effort to build capacity by distributing and laying the foundation for shared leadership.

Strong, distributed leadership or leadership that was expanding to include informal leaders was effective in garnering and sustaining teacher commitment to reform over time. Conditions in reforming schools were consistent with those identified by Ingersoll (2003) and others who note the fragile balance between respecting and denying workers autonomy. School leaders who empowered teachers were rewarded with innovation and commitment to reform. Such schools respected the professional autonomy of teachers, solicited and attended to their input into decision making, and valued their ability to adapt model reform strategies in ways that enhanced their effectiveness in the school context. These schools also provided structured networking and information sharing opportunities and generally promoted the professional empowerment of teachers in multiple ways. In turn, teachers in these schools became highly committed to school improvement and willing to implement innovative instructional strategies that they perceived to be effective.

On the other hand, schools that reinforced traditional norms of bureaucratic control over teachers, had weak leadership, or failed to appreciate the professional capacity of teachers were marked with low buy-in for reform, poor use of instructional time, and an unwillingness to exert effort to improve practice. The book revealed that schools must actively promote and positively reinforce teacher commitment during periods of reform or it will fade over time. Faculty members withheld commitment to reform when they became dissatisfied with programs and providers or when organizational conditions such as principal turnover, failure to protect or prioritize instructional time, or unrealistic pressure to perform on state tests undermined rather than reinforced their efforts.

Consistent with Ingersoll's (2003) *economic production* model of school success, schools typically measured the effectiveness of whole-school reform programs by their gains on standardized tests and state accountability index scores. Evidence revealed that based on their state accountability index scores, CSR-funded schools, as a group, did not benefit from having a reform program. Although school scores increased over time, according to quantitative analyses, they did not outperform others because of their reform status, a finding that is consistent with many other studies of CSR. Even so, schools commonly and erroneously perceived their gains in performance to be linked to their CSR efforts, and their commitment to their programs was either reinforced or undermined accordingly. Consequently, increased performance scores commonly reinforced improvement efforts, whereas flat or declining scores affected teacher commitment to reform in a negative direction.

Educators' ability to clearly understand performance gains or lack thereof was blurred by factors that previously have not been identified in the literature. First, they inadvertently but frequently failed to distinguish the results from state accountability tests with results from internally administered tests that were linked to reform models or other improvement programs adopted by their schools. Second, schools having kindergarten through Grade 8 were assigned two different state index scores (one for the elementary grades and another for the middle grades) that often showed inconsistent patterns of gain or loss. Third, the practice of milepost testing prohibited schools from tracking the gains of individual students from one year to the next and, thus, obscured the ability of schools to make sound judgment regarding their improvement resulting from their reform programs.

Previous studies examining the success of CSR models almost universally apply measures consistent with an economic production model rather than one that is more societal. Findings in this book underscore the importance of a *societal* model of school success (Desimone, 2002; Ingersoll, 2003) that values the social functions of schools that promote positive socialization and acculturation of students. The societal model is characterized by positive social climate, collegial committed faculty, positive relationships between faculty and students and students with one another, and student engagement. Independent of test results were qualitative improvements in schools related to social indicators. Educators perceived gains in tangible resources and contributions to school culture, particularly increases in school climate and student engagement. Finally, schools also enjoyed spillover effects from the reform experience, such as grant expertise and professional growth, that previously have not been documented in the reform literature. Educators were inclined to commit to ongoing school improvement efforts when they perceived that the school was improving because of their hard work. As a result, gains, both real and perceived, were a contributing factor to sustainability.

PATTERNS OF SUSTAINABILITY

The book identified four outcomes regarding the sustainability of school reform efforts using CSR. Table 8.1 summarizes four patterns of reform sustainability in the 18 schools discussed in this book.

Table 8.1   Patterns of Reform Sustainability in 18 Schools

After Three Years	After Five Years	Projection for Sixth Year
Sustained models with funding (6)		
Waterton County School	Yes	Yes, new grant funds (spillover)
Waterton County School	Yes	Yes, funds reallocation (district support)
Waterton County School	Yes	No, district decision to close school
Burkett County School	Yes	No, new district initiative
2 schools in other districts	Yes	No, perceived lack of gains
Sustained strategies without funding (3)		
Forestview Middle School	Yes	Yes
Tipton Middle School (in Burkett County)	Yes	Yes
Greely Elementary School	Yes	Yes
Sustained momentum for improvement (1)		
Littleton Middle School	Yes	Yes
No sustainability (8)		
Schools in other districts dropped models and strategies	N/A	N/A

After three years of model implementation, six schools sustained a formal relationship with a model provider, three schools sustained their program's reform strategies without funding, one school continued its quest for school improvement that had been sparked by the CSR experience, and the remaining eight schools dropped their models along with the reform strategies associated with them when CSR funding expired. However, they were evenly split on more underlying causes of dropping reform efforts that likely had to do with lack of organizational capacity (characterized by high turnover, weak leadership, lack of commitment, and so forth) or lack of capacity of the reform model including related services from model providers.

Five years after model adoption, two schools of the six funded-sustainers intended to go forward in sustaining their formal relationship with a model provider. One of these schools had received new funding through a different grant, and the other expected to continue funding its program through internal budgeting allocations. Having built on whole-school capacity spawned by district cooperation, leadership, commitment, and perceived gains, the three schools that earlier had sustained their programs' reform strategies without funding all showed indications of reform continuation. In fact, one of these schools was actively seeking new funding to reinstate a formal relationship with its former model provider. Finally, the last reforming school continued to demonstrate momentum for improvement without model practices. It too was actively searching for ways, including further funding, to sustain its momentum.

Two of the four schools that dropped their formal relationship after five years, did so because of changes in district policy that interrupted their sustained use of CSR. The two remaining schools dropped their models because of disillusionment mainly from lack of gains, burnout, and the cost of funding the model at the expense of other initiatives. The patterns described here warrant a broader definition of sustainability that recognizes schools' unwavering interest in improvement.

The book reveals that nearly one-third of 18 schools that began implementing reform programs in 1999 sustained them either through formally funded relationships with model providers or through informal institutionalization of reform strategies acquired through the reform experience. One additional school intended to continue striving for school improvement independent of its reform model. The models represented among the five schools that planned to sustain related reform practices into the sixth year (either with funding or without funding) included Success for All (2), Community for Learning (1), National Writing Project (1), and Core Knowledge (1). That roughly 33% of the schools sustained reform over time, mirrors other qualitative findings (Datnow, 2005) and is also consistent with national, large-scale, quantitative studies examining a broader range of whole-school reform models (Berends, Bodilly, & Kirby 2002a, 2002b; Taylor, 2005). That patterns of reform sustainability cut across different reform programs and reflect the experiences of reforming schools nationwide suggests that sustainability may have less to do with model characteristics than the structural, organizational context in which reform occurs. An organizational model for sustaining change is detailed next.

A MODEL FOR SUSTAINING CHANGE

The experiences of schools presented in this book provide support for the perspective that change relies on capacity building at all levels to be sustained. In determining the conditions and strategies necessary to effectively sustain reform in schools, Smith and O'Day (1991) argued that reform must coherently and systemically address weaknesses and discontinuities in the overarching educational system. This points to the need for a supportive state infrastructure to set the stage for reform sustainability and extend consistently from the state to the local level. Fullan (2005), MacIver and Farley-Ripple (2008), and others observe that sustaining reform also requires that the district further support and reinforce it through a communicative environment, adequate resources, and so forth. Reform that builds whole-school capacity (Fullan, 2005); has strong, distributed leadership (Smylie Conley, & Marks, 2002; Spillane, Diamond, & Jita, 2000); respects the professional culture of teachers (Ingersoll, 2003); and recognizes school improvement in multidimensional ways underscores the importance of change that is coherent, comprehensive, and well integrated. Reform such as CSR involved stakeholders throughout the entire educational arena including the state, the district, reform program providers, school leadership, and classroom teachers. Continuous and sustainable improvement in schools occurred when a vision for change was shared and the capacity to implement and sustain it was fostered through the whole system. These arguments combined with the findings presented in this book indicate that sustainability of school reform is related to and dependent on five key factors identified next.

State Infrastructure

Schools that sustain reform measures derive support from the infrastructure and context for change established by the state education agency. State infrastructure provides capacity-building mechanisms, such as HSEs and assistance teams who provide technical advice and reinforce school improvement efforts. The state establishes a knowledge base about the reform programs that is invaluable in guiding schools to narrow the focus of their reform efforts to those that are compatible with other state initiatives. It also shapes reform adoption in a way that moves much of the decision making to the local level. While providing structured support, it prompts schools to establish coherent unifying goals for change and coordinate efforts between teachers and school administrators.

District Support

Schools attribute success in continuing reform largely to strong encouragement and effective broad-based support from their district to use reform-related instructional strategies. District personnel establish a vision for change that guides schools in their reform efforts. They also assist schools in identifying external funding sources for reform and offer technical support for grant writing, budgeting matters, and so forth. The district builds lateral capacity across schools by extending opportunities for networking and information sharing. In this book, all six schools that initially continued using their models with alternative funding, for example, reported strong, active district support or passive cooperation. Similarly, the schools that dropped their model but kept on track with reform efforts were located in cooperative districts.

In contrast to districts that are highly active in their ongoing support of reforming schools are districts that offer minimal or no support to schools. Recall that seven of the eight schools that dropped their models altogether after three years were in districts that did not seem interested in seeing a sustained relationship between the school and model implementation. Districts tended not to recognize the accomplishments of these schools in relation to their reform implementation efforts and, sometimes, pushed the schools to take on new initiatives and strategies that were outside the scope of what they knew because of the CSR experience. The eighth school was located in an active, supportive district but was plagued with high administrative turnover to the extent that it undermined any improvement efforts shown by the school.

Leadership

Leadership that is stable and distributed is a critical component of reform sustainability. Principals view their role early on in the whole-school reform process to include active demonstration of support to the schools' overall commitment to change. They gain recognition as effective and supportive of teachers' efforts and share leadership functions with them. To sustain reform strategies for school improvement, the principal and teacher leaders support and complement each other's work, hold respect for and positive rapport with each other, and successfully negotiate tasks and responsibilities necessary for ongoing reform. Moreover, both principals and teacher leaders work collaboratively with and engage other faculty in their efforts for reform. They perceive these duties as a means of enhancing instructional capacity and describe them as challenging, effective, and rewarding. Distributed or expanding leadership is critical to the sustainability of strategies for school improvement. The support, familiarity, involvement, and long-term vision of these leaders contribute to model implementation and the likelihood of its sustainability.

All the schools in this study that sustained their model with funding, sustained reform strategies without a model relationship, or sustained momentum for school improvement were backed by strong and coordinated school leadership that was distributed or expanding to include others. In contrast, schools that did not attempt to sustain their reform program or measures of school improvement typically were plagued by instability or related problems with school leadership. Principals in these schools commonly took a hands-off approach early on in the reform process and left the job of implementation entirely to their facilitator. In cases where leadership was not distributed or expanding, capacity or initiative for leadership was not developed among others and made these schools particularly vulnerable to the devastating effects of high turnover or weak leadership.

Teacher Commitment

Teacher commitment is a key component of reform sustainability. In part, teacher commitment is a response to effective leadership that resists the power to control teachers and instead garners cooperation by promoting their autonomy and decision-making capacity. This especially is evident as teachers attempt to adapt reform strategies to better address their unique workplace conditions. Teacher commitment also is a result of intentional efforts to facilitate and enhance opportunities for empowerment through collaboration, professional development, and high-quality learning experiences. As with school leadership, all the schools in this study that sustained their reform model with funding or exhibited other forms of sustainability were backed by strong teacher commitment. In sustaining schools, there might be individual teachers who chose to exercise their autonomy in independent, uncommitted ways, but overall, when the majority of a faculty showed commitment to the organization and to the reform, the school was able to sustain continuous improvement.

School Improvement

Reform efforts that produce observable gains are likely to be sustained. Gains are defined as improvements in assessment and accountability measures and include qualitative, societal improvements that are linked to workplace satisfaction and conditions that promote teaching and learning. If gains are difficult to discern, educators may substitute *perceptions* of gains for concrete evidence. The line between real gains on tests that are caused by reform programs and gains that are perceived to be caused by reform programs is difficult to determine. When real or perceived gains are not forthcoming, users look to other tangible gains, such as additional resources and materials that result from reform funding. They also come to appreciate gains or improvements defined more broadly to include school culture, school climate, and student engagement. In this study, unintended spillover also increased perceptions of CSR as a positive experience. Real or perceived gains generate and reinforce enthusiasm and commitment to reform and its sustainability.

The strength of this model lies in its organizational foundation. The model involves the state educational system in its entirety, including the state infrastructure and context, the district, and the school's contributions from administrative and faculty leadership and from the teaching core. Leadership at all three levels that actively recognizes, respects, and supports the work of others helps move the system toward a common goal of lasting improvement. Fullan (2005) argues that reform sustainability relies on such system-wide, organizational capacity building.

Ingersoll (2003) articulated a tension in school systems that focus on controlling the work of teachers. Power relations in schools traditionally have centered on administrative control versus teacher autonomy (Bidwell, 1965; Weick, 1976). Autonomy is fundamental to work and commonly is expressed through decision making about how work will be performed. Teachers historically have made decisions about their classroom instructional practices involving pedagogy, homework, classroom management, and so forth but have had little input in schoolwide decisions regarding how work is done (Ingersoll, 2003). The notion of schools as *learning organizations* empowers teachers and encourages their input to information sharing, social networks, and professional community building. Through these means, teachers can establish trust and respect of colleagues and administrators, increase their social capital, and build strong ties that reinforce innovative behavior and commitment to the school and reform (Coburn & Russell, 2008; Giles & Hargreaves, 2006).

This model suggests that in a supportive state and district climate, effective leadership that is distributed to teachers and encourages meaningful participation in decision making and professional community building will increase teacher commitment. Teacher commitment is also reinforced by noticeable signs of school improvement. This calls for an expanded definition of school improvement that recognizes societal, cultural gains in schools, such as improved climate, student engagement, and community involvement. This, in turn, increases the likelihood of reform sustainability. The second quotation at the beginning of this chapter suggests that ongoing improvement becomes part of the school culture but it must be *nurtured* to persist. This model that builds organizational capacity identifies ways to nurture ongoing school improvement.

WHAT HAPPENED TO CSR?

As indicated in Chapter 1, the CSR program was authorized as Title I, Part F of the Elementary and Secondary Education Act, in 2002. CSR became an important component of the No Child Left Behind Act (NCLB), as it represented funds to support more integrated, coherent improvement strategies for schools designed to help children reach proficiency. Congress appropriated funds to support whole-school reform for eligible schools until 2006. After that, funding was directed to a Center for Comprehensive School Reform and Improvement to support the work of schools and districts. Whole-school reform models continue to operate in many schools across the United States and remain a viable choice for school improvement even though federal funding no longer supports the adoption and implementation of school reform models through the CSR program. A review of model effectiveness was conducted recently using rigorous standards (Kidron & Darwin, 2007) that involved four of the five models represented in this study. Based on evidence for positive effects on overall student achievement, Success for All was downgraded to *moderately strong*; America's Choice, Core Knowledge, and National Writing Project, a model not rated in the 1999 Educators' Guide, showed *moderate evidence*; and Community for Learning no longer existed.

In theory, the CSR project represented strong national policy intended to reinforce a coherent, integrated, systemic reform movement and improve equality of educational opportunity. In practice, however, research continues to reveal that, depending on a host of factors, the effects of whole-school reform programs are mixed. Consistent with findings from other research, the quantitative analyses conducted for this project suggest that the schools funded in the first round of CSR awards did not outperform other similar schools that lacked CSR funding. Despite the lack of strong quantitative outcomes of these school reform models, positive changes occurred in schools. However, because they are more difficult to quantify they have gone largely unexplained in the literature. The qualitative findings from our study suggest that many positive changes and improvements occurred in a majority of the schools because of their reform efforts.

This raises an important issue for further consideration. Namely, national policies should focus on developing new ways of thinking about student performance and school improvement. Instead, NCLB and other related policies have heightened the emphasis on traditional assessment and accountability systems. These continue to exert school improvement performance pressures associated with high-stakes accountability, which reduce the degree to which teachers are willing to change their instructional practices. For example, Bodilly, Keltner, Purnell, Reichardt, and Ikemoto (1998) found that incompatibility of accountability and assessment systems and CSR models created conflict between what was being learned and what was being tested. Further, Berends et al. (2002a, 2002b) and Datnow (2004) found that performance pressures associated with high-stakes testing encouraged educators to focus on basic skills and test performance rather than engage in innovative instructional strategies promoted by reform models. As a result, schools in states having high-stakes testing showed lower levels of reform implementation. Thus, the extent to which low-performing schools in this study could afford to engage in a reform program that might promise growth in the longer term rather than gains in the short term likely dissuaded educators from implementing or sustaining programs that didn't produce immediate pay offs. The fact that the reform affected schools in this study in many positive ways that were not easily measured suggests the need to develop new student performance assessments and school improvement indicators that reflect and reward these gains. Other recommendations emanating from this study are detailed next.

RECOMMENDATIONS FOR EDUCATORS

The findings presented in this book have important implications for the effective implementation and sustainability of school improvement at four levels in the educational system including the state, the district, the local school, and the reform providers. To help schools *change for good* I have prepared a set of guidelines for each.

At the State Level

Through a preliminary screening process, a state education agency (SEA) becomes aware of information regarding capacity, success with scaling-up, and effectiveness that it can then pass on to schools. Kentucky's SEA did a commendable job of screening reform models to determine the most viable options for schools. However, it held to a philosophy of minimal interference to respect the autonomy of schools and avoid influencing their model adoption decisions in any way. Unlike schools, a SEA is in a position to be more knowledgeable, see the broader picture, and be a positive source of information for schools as they make adoption decisions.

- SEAs should share potentially relevant information regarding reform programs and improvement strategies with schools to increase their ability to make more-informed decisions when choosing reform options.

Related to this, SEAs may not prevent schools from making poor choices based on a reform model's effectiveness or other characteristics, but they are in a position as they examine school proposals and award grants for reform to be more proactive in evaluating the match between the goals and needs of schools and the key services and strategies of reform programs.

- SEAs should more closely monitor grant proposals and external reform provision in ways that increase the likelihood that schools will select reform options that will meet their needs.

Kentucky's SEA structured the application process in a way that elicited the greatest amount of participation among educators at the local level, which undoubtedly increased their involvement and investment in the reform adoption process. Beyond that point, however, the state missed opportunities to support schools. There was a stark absence of in-state conferences or meetings among faculties with similar concerns or interests. For example, one respondent reported that their school was the only school in Kentucky to be using a certain model; when in fact, there were six more schools in our study alone using the same model.

- SEAs should facilitate and structure networking or channels of communication among schools with similar reform interests so that they might learn from and support one another throughout implementation and beyond.

Severe organizational weaknesses, such as unsupportive, disinterested district offices or high turnover among principals, may prevent schools from deriving even minimal advantages from the reform experience. In fact, in this study, the lack of capacity and subsequent failure to gain benefit through CSR reinforced the negative perception that surrounded at least four schools. Certainly, schools such as these are in need of improvement, but reform efforts should prioritize building organizational capacity.

- SEAs should adjust their screening mechanisms when determining school eligibility requirements to anticipate which low-performing schools are most able to benefit from organizational reinforcement before undertaking other school improvement measures and address this issue accordingly.

Given the limited availability of data and the analytic expertise at the school level, many schools do not make appropriate determinations regarding the causal relationships between school improvement efforts through reform implementation and gains.

- SEAs should assist and educate districts and schools in drawing and interpreting correlations between reform and outcomes using valid and reliable measures.

Finally, schools may experience many benefits that fall outside the range of gains that are quantified and tracked by the state assessment and accountability system that are strongly linked to improved performance and academic outcomes.

- SEAs should develop more comprehensive performance measures that acknowledge social improvement in schools along with academic improvement.

At the District Level

Districts that show active support or passive cooperation most successfully provide schools with the assistance they need to implement and sustain reform efforts. In this study, districts that showed minimal attention to their schools were least successful in providing schools important assistance and support.

- Districts in conjunction with local schools should initiate and promote a shared vision of improvement and then actively implement effective strategies that develop and expand their technical and instructional capacity to fulfill that vision.

Schools that were pressured to apply for grants and got them usually did not have sufficient buy-in to support implementation. Schools that were pressured to apply for grants and did not receive them often resisted the intrusion of the district into their affairs and resented the time and resources grant proposal preparation detracted from other more meaningful and relevant activities.

- After having informed and collaborative conversations with schools, districts should respect their autonomy to participate or decline reform opportunities without repercussion.

In this study, only one or two districts created formally structured opportunities for persons from reforming schools to network, share information and expertise, and support one another's common interests and concerns. The tactic was highly effective and successful in building social capital and expertise at both the school and district levels.

- Districts should develop structured opportunities for information sharing and networking for purposes of school improvement and then help facilitate those opportunities in ways that respect and recognize the skills and talents of the participant base.

Some schools in this study sustained their reform model or strategies for longer than five years. Schools need and benefit from support throughout the life cycle of reform rather than only at the beginning stages. Schools also may need assistance with consumer advocacy regarding service provision related to their reform model.

- Districts should be willing and ready to provide different types of support to schools depending on the stage of reform they are in.

The end of a grant funding cycle is one critical juncture for dropping reform efforts. A second period of attrition in this study emerged two years later, after five years of model adoption. Although attrition was often related to funding or model characteristics, the decision to drop a model was also related to other issues, including decisions at the district level that had trickle-down effects at the school level.

- Districts should distinguish between organizational and structural reasons for dropping reform versus issues embedded in the reform program and provide support accordingly. Further, rather than allowing reform sustainability to be dictated primarily by funding, districts should help schools make informed determinations regarding the sustainability or the point at which they will draw the line and break from the relationship, strategies, or guidance provided by an outside agency when it appears that gains are not forthcoming.

At the School Level

Schools that strive for lasting improvement are organized around a coherent vision for effective change. In these schools, principals build capacity by developing and distributing leadership and respecting the autonomy and voice of teachers. Faculty demonstrates commitment for continuous improvement and celebrates gains and successes resulting from reform efforts.

In this study, there were several instances where the voting or adoption process in schools was coerced. Teachers likely knew their school lacked organizational capacity to successfully support reform efforts, but despite that, they were coerced into following through with model adoption.

- School leaders should allow reform adoption processes to proceed in an informed but unfettered manner. Specifically, teacher support for reform should be valid and willingly given.
- Consistent with the vision for change at the district level, principals should support and promote that vision in the school. They should also continue to look for ways to develop and distribute leadership by meaningfully engaging others.
- Given the vital role of the program facilitator as a change agent, principals should take care to make thoughtful decisions pertaining to hiring, placement, and job configuration of program facilitators; hold realistic expectations of their responsibilities; and support them as they do their job. Candidates should be carefully selected based on previous educational experiences along with their technical, interpersonal, and organizational skills. It is important, especially in schools where leadership talent may be obscured, that prospective facilitators receive leadership training to increase their effectiveness.

- Principals should look for and capitalize on ways to build capacity. For example, many facilitators were selected because of seniority linked with expertise, but this usually also meant they were close to retirement age. Unfortunately, their capacity to contribute to future reform efforts and school improvement (both personally and schoolwide) was commonly lost after reform efforts ended because of retirements.
- Principals may support the work of teacher leaders and continue to build leadership capacity along the way. They may also identify ways and encourage teachers to engage in networking and information sharing at the school level and beyond.
- School leaders should look for ways to recognize and celebrate gains and other successes resulting from improvement efforts.
- School leaders should anticipate and begin preparing reform sustainability before the time of transition away from a formal relationship with model providers. To enhance efforts of sustainability, the reform facilitation should be distributed and reduced systematically over time to promote ongoing staff buy-in, leading to their fuller assumption of responsibility for change in their schools.

External Reform Providers

External reform developers and providers have an enormous role in the process of school improvement. What appeared to have been absent from the selection process as schools in this study shopped for and adopted whole-school reform models was a *needs assessment* conducted by reform providers in conjunction with school decision makers. Schools used the resources and information they had to seek out what they perceived to be the most appealing or suitable reform model for adoption. However, it seems that most of them were entirely unaware of the nuances that would affect teacher commitment, implementation, effectiveness, and sustainability. Whether the model design emphasized cultural, professional, or procedural control (Rowan & Miller, 2007) went completely unnoticed.

- External reform providers should share responsibility in informing schools of the realistic potential of their improvement strategies in relation to meeting the needs of the school. It would be productive and entirely appropriate for reform providers to conduct their own matching process, or system analysis of sorts, regarding the ways schools would or would not benefit most from what they offer in the way of reform strategies. Indeed, reform providers have a moral, ethical responsibility to their clientele.

In this study, schools argued that reform providers needed to be more forthright in dealing with the school, practice stronger communication patterns, have greater involvement with the school in professional development, and deliver on service provision that schools were led to believe they would receive during the adoption phase.

- Reform providers should have greater accountability to schools, respect the expertise of school users, find ways to learn from them, and acknowledge the key roles of the principal and the district office in school improvement efforts.

During the implementation process, schools found that reform providers would not acknowledge the linkages between model provision, fidelity, and instructional use among teachers. Rather than being overly focused on fidelity, providers should recognize that schools and teachers must make certain adjustments and modifications to promote greater consistency in their local or state context.

- Reform providers should tolerate a certain amount of adaptation and proactively guide (rather than admonish) schools in how to do this in ways that result in greater compatibility between the model and the school context and, ultimately, greater advantages for teachers and their schools. Repeated patterns of adaptation over time and across schools would suggest that reform providers periodically should reevaluate and modify the alignment of the reform with state and district contexts to meet the identified needs of schools.

Finally, in this study, schools complained that reform providers dropped them toward the end of their funding grants before they had the chance to drop the model.

- Reform providers should develop more coherent strategies for districts and schools to help smooth the transition from funded implementation to unfunded sustainability. They should also further develop strategies for sustaining reform and continuous improvement.

The future of national school reform, such as NCLB, is unclear. What does seem certain is that reform efforts in the upcoming years will undoubtedly continue to address school improvement in coherent, integrated ways that are standards based, build capacity at each level of the educational system, solicit and depend on teacher input, promote teacher quality through innovative professional training and development, and rely on accountability systems to measure student growth and school success. Sustaining change in schools is a multidimensional undertaking that requires a strong state infrastructure, a supportive district, effective school leadership, a committed faculty, and, finally, a change mechanism or reform program that is worth committing to. Clearly, sustaining improvement is a collaborative challenge in which each level or entity affects conditions that are conducive to lasting change at other levels. When it occurs in this holistic context, it is likely that school improvement will result in change for good.

Resource

Methodology

DESIGN OF THE STUDY

The data for this project were collected as part of a longitudinal study examining the implementation, effects, and sustainability of school improvement strategies resulting from federal funding through the comprehensive school reform (CSR) in public schools across Kentucky. The study began in fall of 2001, when schools were starting the third of a three-year grant cycle and concluded four years later in fall of 2005. It was funded as a Field Initiated Study, Office of Education Research and Improvement, U.S. Department of Education.

At the time this research began, numerous studies had examined the implementation and effects of whole-school reform models quantitatively. The findings of those studies were mixed in detecting any measurable gains in schools resulting from the reform experience. Much of the research neglected to address questions related to processes and effects that were less easily identifiable or qualitatively measured. Strikingly absent from the literature were studies designed to assess the sustainability of reform efforts over time.

To understand more fully the potential of reform it was imperative to recognize the efforts of schools and the context in which they operated. This was especially relevant in a state such as Kentucky where many schools are rural, small, geographically isolated, and, as a result, largely misunderstood. Ethnographic methods promised to be particularly effective in enabling us to contextualize processes of school reform, assess implementation strategies, and better clarify and explain the extent to which they were sustained (Brown, 2005).

Quantitative data sets that included Commonwealth Accountability Testing System (CATS) index scores by school, student test scores, structural and organizational features of schools, teacher characteristics, and so forth were assembled. Meshing together data from the two methods would provide the clearest, most holistic picture of what actually was occurring in schools during the CSR movement. Quantitative data were used to inform the data collected qualitatively and vice versa.

RESEARCH QUESTIONS

This study asked the following research questions:

1. What are the processes through which schools selected, introduced, and implemented change with CSR models? And which processes effectively lead schools to more successful outcomes?

2. How are schools' responses to model characteristics involving school organization, support, leadership, professional development, school climate, and funding allocation related to school performance and sustainability of reform efforts?

3. What are the ways and extent to which CSR models are effective in improving schools serving middle-grade populations?

4. What are the patterns of sustainability of CSR in schools after termination of CSR funding?

A longitudinal study over multiple years allowed my colleague Wayne Usui and me to address these research questions by capturing the perceptions of participants as they recollected and recounted the process of reform in their schools over the previous two years and, at the same time, detect patterns in schools while they still were implementing reform changes with CSR funding. Further, going into schools in the final year of the funding cycle enabled us to ascertain the extent schools intended and prepared to sustain school reform efforts without CSR funding for the upcoming year. Finally, by revisiting schools and analyzing quantitative data sets derived from state testing results two years after CSR funding expired, the schools had more time to realize the maximum effects of the CSR experience, particularly positive gains in performance as measured by CATS.

SELECTION OF SCHOOLS

When this study began in 2001, middle-school populations across Kentucky scored lower on standardized achievement tests than did elementary or high school populations. The results from a testing cycle at that time identified nearly 80 out of approximately 350 middle-level schools as low performing. Similarly, these schools also registered disappointing results on other performance indicators. The Kentucky Board of Education had established middle-school improvement as a highest priority. Thus, this study addressed patterns as they pertained to schools serving middle-level populations.

To examine the processes, effects, and sustainability of school reform efforts, we identified 74 schools, each of which served a seventh and eighth grade, to participate in this study. The schools were divided into three nonequivalent comparison groups. The first group, Group A, included all 18 schools that received CSR funding beginning in the 1999–2000 school year through the 2001–2002 school year. The second group, Group B, was comprised of the 13 schools that applied but did not receive CSR funding that same year. The third group, Group C, consisted of an additional 43 schools that were eligible to apply for funding but did not apply. These schools were included for purposes of comparison in quantitative analysis and allowed us to examine the extent to which schools with CSR models differ from schools that did not pursue CSR funding. If a school applied for or received funding in any subsequent year, it was excluded from our list of schools. A school was also excluded if it had reconfigured since 1998. Table A.1 indicates the descriptive characteristics of the 74 schools in this study by Group.

Among schools awarded CSR funding beginning in 1999 (Group A), the mean age of teachers was 41.8 and their mean years of experience was 13.3 years. Nearly 75% of faculty members were female and 25.1% male. Finally, 93.8% of the faculty members were white and 6.2% were of other racial or ethnic backgrounds. Most of the teachers of color were employed in urban schools, whereas racial diversity among teachers was absent in rural schools.

DATA COLLECTION METHODS

The qualitative portion of the study underpinning this book focused on the experiences of the 18 CSR-funded schools. It consisted of field observation, in-depth interviewing, and document analysis which were conducted in first year of the study and again in the third year. The research was conducted overtly and, when possible, school personnel were encouraged to contribute to the planning of data collection and analysis. These strategies increased teacher satisfaction with the researcher's presence in the school (Corsaro, 1985); allow the researcher to gain acceptance, rapport, and credibility with principals and teachers more rapidly (Evans-Andris, 1996); and enhance the overall research effort (Becker, 1970; Pitman & Maxwell, 1992).

Gaining Access to Schools

Ordinarily, we contacted each school by phone in advance of our anticipated arrival to present a brief overview of the study to the principal and,

Table A.1   Descriptive Characteristics of 74 Schools by Reform Status

| | Comprehensive School Reform Group | | | | | | | | | | | |
| | Group A | | | Group B | | | Group C | | | Total | | |
	Mean	*N*	*Standard Deviation*	*Mean*	*N*	*Standard Deviation*	*Mean*	*N*	*Standard Deviation*	*Mean*	*N*	*Standard Deviation*
Mean teacher age 98–99	41.81	18	3.00	39.73	13	2.12	40.92	43	3.02	40.93	74	2.92
Percentage male teachers 98–99	25.17	18	10.39	25.47	13	10.47	26.18	43	11.76	25.81	74	11.09
Percentage white teachers 98–99	93.86	18	9.26	96.16	13	6.61	96.75	43	5.88	95.94	74	6.97
Mean teacher experience 98–99	13.27	18	2.83	12.29	13	2.03	12.83	43	2.38	12.84	74	2.43
Combined 7th and 8th grades 1999	255.00	18	189.53	268.17	13	189.59	266.66	41	206.18	263.96	71	196.70
Rural	0.78	18	0.43	0.46	13	0.52	0.55	42	0.50	0.59	73	0.50
Schoolwide Title I (dummy)	0.94	18	0.24	0.92	13	0.28	0.76	42	0.43	0.84	73	0.37
Percentage nonwhite	11.69	18	19.40	10.55	13	13.69	7.20	43	13.80	8.88	74	15.23
Percentage free or reduce lunch	72.51	18	14.86	68.11	13	14.09	67.77	43	17.78	68.98	74	16.43
Attendance rate 1999	92.73	18	2.20	93.23	13	1.79	93.25	40	1.33	93.11	70	1.66
Dropout rate 1999	0.35	18	0.57	0.81	13	0.70	0.83	40	1.60	0.70	70	1.28
Retention rate 1999	2.40	18	3.54	3.20	13	3.44	2.09	40	2.61	2.36	70	3.00

Source: Evans-Andris, M. & Usui, W. (2004a).

with their cooperation, to schedule a meeting to discuss our plans in detail. Principals most often welcomed the idea of participating and readily agreed to accommodate our schedule. They commonly made comments like, "We can use all the help we can get." As this suggests, it is likely that many schools participated in hopes of gaining feedback about their school's performance. Overall, 100% of the schools invited to be in this study agreed to participate.

Typically, rural schools required less advance notice of our intent to come to their schools than did those in urban areas. In fact, on two occasions, in their eagerness to support our work, principals in rural schools persuaded other principals to allow me to come to their schools at a moment's notice. In the first instance, I had been misinformed about which schools in a given district had a CSR-funded reform model. As I was leaving one school the principal, assuming that I was heading to another CSR site in that district, commented for me to say hello to that school's principal when I got there. When I hesitated on learning of the additional school, the principal told me, "Oh, just go on over there anyway. She wouldn't like it if she was left out." He then proceeded to call ahead and more or less "pave the way" by presenting a synopsis of my fieldwork to his colleague and emphasizing the importance of her school's participation in the study. In the second instance, I was not aware of the proximity of one school to another. Again, a principal encouraged me to visit the school and phoned its principal to inform her of my work and to expect my visit.

On several occasions, plans to begin working in a school were delayed. Only twice were these delays attributable to concerns about participation in the study. In the first case, the superintendent of a rural district wanted an endorsement of the school board in place prior to us beginning our work, and in the second, a principal requested that we postpone our visit until she had the opportunity to learn more about and discuss our study with her school's model facilitator. She explained that the school had been approached by researchers numerous times in recent years, causing them to become more scrutinizing. In both cases, we ultimately gained approval and full cooperation of the schools. More commonly, principals had us postpone our target date to begin data collection to avoid interfering with the school's preparation for state testing. In one instance, a principal asked that we split data collection in her school—observe before testing and interview afterward—even though our request to study in that school was months ahead of the testing window. Although this request was extreme, it was clear that testing was an overriding concern of many educators.

We followed a predetermined routine in each school. First, we would meet with the principal to more fully explain the project, answer questions, and clarify any concerns about the school's participation in the study. We then would secure formal consent to participate in the study. Afterward, we were given a quick tour of the building and a master schedule to facilitate our planning. We would also request permission to navigate a school building to collect data as our schedules and interests determined. Most principals granted this permission. In a few cases, more directive principals or their model facilitators would map our route and draw up a schedule for us which we would follow long enough to gain confidence from the administrators and then, with their permission, branch out on our own.

After these introductory sessions, on three occasions in rural districts, I was offered informal driving tours of local school communities, each of which lasted more than an hour. They provided an excellent opportunity to see the districts and learn more about the schools, the principals, and other notable features of the broader school communities. Probably, the individuals who extended those offers to me recognized that to more fully grasp and appreciate the challenges of school reform facing their schools, it was important to be exposed to the geographic and socioeconomic contexts in which they operated.

Establishing Rapport

Establishing rapport and gaining the trust of study participants generally enables the researchers to conduct their business more thoroughly and with greater validity. Moreover, it makes gathering data in schools more enjoyable. To begin this process we asked that principals notify their teachers that we would be in the building prior to our arrival. Consequently, in most school, we were greeted with welcome and hospitality. A few times, for one reason or another, the principal neglected to announce our presence so we sometimes found ourselves having to make quick introductions and explanations to teachers as we encountered them throughout the school. A stipulation of the CSR grant subjected the schools in this study to periodic evaluations conducted by an outside agency, which involved cursory classroom observation, questionnaires, and brief teacher focus groups. School personnel were accustomed to such visits from program evaluators and, at the outset, expected us to conduct our business similarly. When they realized we were not evaluating them and not using the same data collection strategies or rubrics as the evaluation teams, they seemed more willing to share information and often readily took us into their confidence.

Perhaps because of their skepticism of evaluation teams, rapport with teachers was not automatically forthcoming. We looked for opportunities to build positive relationships. When teachers are not engaged in direct teaching is a good time to talk casually with them and begin establishing rapport. We spent time chatting with small groups in the teachers' lounge or, when possible, ate lunch with them. During those times, teachers talked about their families, trips they had taken together to conferences, students who had fallen on hard times with drugs, sex, parenthood, and other various topics. They told us about their professional interests and aspirations. We also learned of personal hobbies, and frequently, we were provided with insider information regarding the best nearby restaurants, fishing holes, or notable local hiking trails.

Another way we built rapport was by offering limited assistance or performing small favors when we could, assuming it did not jeopardize our role as researcher or preclude our ability to collect data. For instance, we uniformly refused infrequent requests from teachers to act as substitutes or classroom aides. On the other hand, we provided assistance in other ways. For example, one day, a school's model facilitator needed someone with technical expertise to assist her at a meeting that evening. My colleague, who was spending several days in the school district, volunteered to attend the meeting and run the equipment. The facilitator was grateful and even remarked about it during an interview two years later. Another time, I arrived at a school earlier than expected and found the model facilitator rushing to complete several duties so she could meet with me later. I gladly volunteered to perform one of those tasks for her. Later, while accompanying her on an errand, I learned more about the local community and her involvement in it. Finally, a group of teachers in a rural school informed me that they would be bringing their eighth graders on a class trip to our city. I arranged for them to be the guests of the university to tour the campus and visit the planetarium and the library. In each of the cases described here, the participants were grateful for our contribution and rapport was enhanced. Another sign that we gained tremendous rapport with study participants was their students entertained us with songs or demonstrations as a way of saying good-bye on our departure. Also, we received a number of invitations to return to schools for pageants, talent shows, sporting events, and even faculty holiday parties.

Infrequently, we detected signs suggesting a lack of rapport or trust. For example, during observations teachers might "perform" rehearsed lessons, give period-long tests, or assign passive seatwork such as silent reading for the entire session. On these rare occasions we made a point to ask about these classroom assignments during interviews so that we could determine more accurately whether the assignment was routine or in response to our presence.

Over four years, schools are confronted with many challenges such as closings, reconfigurations, low-testing cycles, funding issues, and so forth. We attempted to remain autonomous from any such circumstance. For the most part, we succeeded in this objective. Several times, however, schools sought information involving funding sources and grant awards. When it became clear to us that a few schools hoped we would leverage consideration on their behalf at the district or state level, we assertively reminded them that our findings were confidential and we were not in a position to lobby on behalf of any school.

Observation

To facilitate data collection and increase the validity of field observation, we made every attempt to interact with school participants and to encourage them to share relevant experiences, perceptions, and opinions with us. In smaller schools, we normally were able to observe and talk with each faculty member, whereas in larger schools we had to choose which classes to visit. We made a point to observe teachers in each of the four main content areas and upper-grade levels (seventh and eighth grades) and tried to observe teachers in itinerant classes including music, computer, and so forth. Generally, we observed several times in each classroom that we went to. In all, only one teacher asked that I not come in her room, explaining that she felt overwhelmed and behind schedule because of a visit from external program evaluators the previous week.

We spent approximately 15 hours over two weeks in each school in the first year and again in the third year of the study observing in classrooms, lounges, learning labs, and resource centers. During that time, we were particularly attuned to the following:

- Patterns of implementation of model components in the school and classrooms
- School leadership and support as they pertained to reform implementation
- Attitudes of teachers and others toward CSR model components in schools
- Indications of CSR model adoption, implementation, and sustainability

While observing, we also documented objectives set for any given classroom session, teaching strategies/pedagogy, extent to which teachers demonstrated rapport and respect toward students and vice versa, classroom management, classroom disruptions, instructional time devoted to test-taking strategies, and so forth. Observation also provided rich information pertaining to patterns of school and classroom climate, vision and leadership, decision making, resource distribution, professional development, and parental involvement and support.

We ended observation sessions in schools either when it seemed that the data were reaching a saturation point, that is, that the observations were repetitious and providing no new insight or information or when we had exhausted the potential participant pool by observing everyone who taught seventh graders. The data informed the ways that reform models functioned uniquely in each school and allowed us to compare the relative differences of instructional strategies and components of implementation across classrooms and across schools. Finally, during this phase we established contacts for subsequent interviews.

Interviewing

In the first year of the study, we conducted up to six in-depth formal interviews in each of the 18 schools. In the third year of the study, this process was repeated as a means of follow-up with the same respondents who participated in the first year. The interviews were audiotaped, lasted about 40 to 75 minutes, and normally were conducted in offices, empty classrooms, or other quiet places in the building.

We selected respondents based on their likelihood to possess, relate, and clarify general levels of information, in addition to personal experiences regarding CSR adoption and implementation in their schools. With few exceptions, only teachers we observed were invited to be interviewed. Additional respondents included principals, in-school model facilitators, and occasionally a resource teacher. For purposes of triangulation, we also interviewed external model providers, district administrators and, in some instances, state personnel.

The interviews were semistructured allowing the interviewer the greatest flexibility in obtaining useful information. This strategy offers the researcher the opportunity to gain complete information by encouraging the respondent to elaborate and provide additional description when appropriate (Gordon, 1980; McCracken, 1988). The respondents discussed the following issues:

- Their account of how their school selected and gained a CSR model
- Their understanding of their role in the process of change
- The ways and degrees to which specific model components were implemented (or not) in their school and in their work routines
- The effects of the model (if any) on their work, teaching strategies, and patterns of leadership
- The extent to which CSR strategies were sustained after funding expired
- The optimal model implementation strategies based on their observations and experience

Documents

Besides conducting extensive field observation and interviewing, with the consent of the principal, we also obtained documents from each school, each of which potentially was relevant to patterns of CSR implementation and sustainability. These included the school's original CSR grant application, the school's consolidated plan, the annual school report card, the school improvement plan, any performance assessments and evaluations provided to the school either by the model provider or the outside agency charged with evaluating CSR implementation in each school, and, finally, the scholastic audit report in the event that the school had undergone this process.

Exiting the Field

The longitudinal nature of this study necessitated us leaving or exiting schools more than one time. On completion of data collection in a school during any given year, we normally made a point to thank the teachers who had participated in the study and remind them we would return to see them at some point during the following year. We also conducted an exit session with the principal to discuss our findings in general terms, answer questions, and solicit his or her suggestions for future methodological issues. After completing our visits, we sent the principals a formal letter of thanks and a copy of our annual report summarizing study findings across all schools. This strategy worked well, and over time, it became evident that many schools became accustomed to our procedures. For example, when returning to a school one year later, a teacher came to his classroom door to greet me and said, "You promised you'd be here again, and look, here you are!" Additionally, principals advised us of anticipated changes affecting our data collection routine or told us if they or teachers who worked for them planned on retiring or switching schools.

Flexibility

Ethnographic field methods employed in this study demanded flexibility on both the part of the investigators and the schools. Unanticipated disruptions occur with great frequency in schools because of inclement weather, power outages, plumbing mishaps, and so forth. Bouts of severe weather, particularly in rural areas, hindered our study enormously. Schools were plagued by ice, snow, flooding, and even tornados, requiring several to be closed off and on for up to 30 days in one year. Such incidents caused us to make several fruitless trips to districts far from our home base. For example, one time, I had just begun a three-day observation session in a rural district when the principal rushed in to inform me that the school would be closing in the hour because of an impending snowstorm. As the school was located in a mountainous region more than three hours from the university, I decided to leave and schedule a return trip to the school later. The most extreme episode occurred in late spring during the first year of the study when a research assistant had driven several hours to a rural school district only to arrive in time for a tornado warning. A tornado did in fact touch down causing observations to be suspended until the following autumn.

RELIABILITY AND VERIFICATION

Patton (2002), Cresswell (1997), and others suggest that the reliability and verification of data collected through qualitative field methods is increased when researchers are experienced, spend long periods in the field, and employ triangulation. Each of these is described next.

Our previous experience in field methods varied. At the time of the study, I had more than 10 years of experience conducting ethnographic research in schools. The coinvestigator was less experienced in field methods but had tremendous expertise in quantitative data analysis. Also, at most times over the four years, we had assistance from graduate students who contributed to the organization and management of the project and, depending on their coursework and experience, occasionally collected data.

Our prolonged engagement in the field also increased the validity and reliability of this study. In 2001–2002 school year, we studied in 23 schools including the 18 CSR-funded schools and, for purposes of comparison, four schools that applied but were not funded, and 1 school that was eligible but did not apply for funding. In 2003–2004 school year, we revisited 20 of the original schools. As described earlier, during our visits to schools we observed and interviewed teachers and administrators. For follow-up in the third year, we observed and interviewed as many of the original participants as possible to compare the perceptions and strategies of the participants and the residual effects of the CSR program over time and to ascertain effects of changes in schools involving personnel, leadership, and so forth. Altogether, over the two periods, we conducted approximately 630 hours of field observation, which translated to about 1,400 pages of typed field notes and more than 255 interviews rendering 2,800 pages of transcription.

Third, our use of triangulation increased the verifiability of the data. Data were triangulated by interviewing other key respondents, such as external model providers, district superintendents, highly skilled educators, personnel employed by the Kentucky Department of Education who were instrumental in the CSR program statewide, and so forth. Occasionally, personnel from other schools were asked questions to clarify or otherwise provide insight to issues raised in interviews or observations. Data were also compared with information culled from documents.

DATA ANALYSIS

The ethnographic methods used in the study provided a means to generate analytic categories and explore the complex relationships between them (Denzin & Lincoln, 1994; Glaser & Strauss, 1967; McCracken, 1988; Strauss & Corbin, 1990). Mostly, I reviewed the field notes and interview transcripts on a continual basis, employing the principle of constant comparison whereby the data were compared with previously collected data in search of similarities, differences, and negative cases. I met frequently with the coinvestigator to compare our field experiences, discuss preliminary findings, and explore competing explanations. We also sought input regarding methodological issues and preliminary findings from outside sources several times each year through discussions with the study's two consultants, both of whom were knowledgeable with issues of educational research, school improvement, and the CSR movement.

Interviews and observational field data were coded, and ultimately, I built a comprehensive outline of each school that merged the data from the two sources. These provided the basis for case studies. The cases were then analyzed using initial research questions as well as themes that emerged from the analytic process. I identified themes across cases and identified patterns and theoretical categories involving model components, implementation processes, and sustainability of reform efforts. This process was repeated in the third year of the study, which then allowed for comparison of each case and the stability of themes over three years. Finally, we compared findings across methods so that quantitative outcomes relating to school performance and student achievement over six years both informed and were informed by qualitative findings.

ETHICAL CONSIDERATIONS

Gallant (2002) argues that qualitative studies such as this one pose multiple risks to participants including breeches of confidentiality, violations of privacy, and the presentation of results in a way that does not respect the subjects' interests. It is the responsibility of the researcher then to protect the rights of subjects to the fullest extent possible. In this study, we went to great lengths to protect and secure the data that we collected over the years. Early on in the study, we became aware of networks or family ties among educators that frequently crossed school and district borders. For example, different family members may work in different schools in one district. Our recognition of these networks served as a reminder for us to be cautious and guarded in conversations and interviews so as not to violate confidences of study participants. Occasionally, principals would ask us questions about their school's progress or status as compared to that of another school in their district or in our study. If we were able, we would answer questions about the school but not in comparison to any other particular school.

The findings generated from the methods detailed in this Resource are illuminating and critical to further understanding about how reforming schools implemented and sustained improvement efforts over time and outcomes related to their reform behaviors.

References

Allen, D. (2000). Doing occupational demarcation: The "boundary-work" of nurse managers in a district general hospital. *Journal of Contemporary Ethnography, 29*(3), 326–356.

Beath, C. (1991). Supporting the information technology champion. *Management Information Systems Quarterly, 15*(2), 355–370.

Becker, H. S. (1970). *Sociological work: Method and substance.* Chicago: Aldine.

Bennett, N., Wise, C., Woods, P., & Harvey, J. (2003). *Distributed leadership.* Nottingham, Great Britain: National College for School Leadership.

Berends, M. (2000). Teacher-reported effects of New American Schools designs: Exploring relationships to teacher background and school context. *Educational Evaluation and Policy Analysis, 22*(1), 65–82.

Berends, M., Bodilly, S., & Kirby, S. (2002a). Facing the challenges of whole-school reform: New American Schools after a decade. (MR-1498-EDU). Santa Monica, CA: RAND.

Berends, M., Bodilly, S., & Kirby, S. (2002b). Looking back over a decade of whole-school reform: The experience of New American Schools. *Phi Delta Kappan, 84*(2), 168–177.

Berends, M., Heilbrunn, J., McKelvey, C., & Sullivan, T. (1999). *Assessing the progress of New American Schools: A status report.* (MR-1085-EDU). Santa Monica, CA: RAND.

Berman, P., & McLaughlin, M. (1978). *Federal programs supporting educational change, Vol. VIII: Implementing and sustaining innovations.* (R-1589/8-HEW). Santa Monica, CA: RAND.

Bidwell, C. (1965). The school as a formal organization. In J. March (Ed.), *Handbook of organizations* (pp. 972–1022). Chicago: Rand McNally.

Bidwell, C. (2001). Analyzing schools as organizations: Long-term permanence and short-term change. [Special Issue]. *Sociology of Education,* 100–115.

Billig, S. (1997). Title I of the Improving America's Schools Act: What it looks like in practice. *Journal of Education for Students Placed at Risk, 2*(4), 329–343.

Billig, S., Perry, S., & Pokorny, N. (1999). School support teams: Building state capacity for improving schools. *Journal of Education for Students Placed at Risk, 4*(3), 231–240.

Bodilly, S., Keltner, B., Purnell, S., Reichardt, R., & Ikemoto, G. (1998). Lessons from New American Schools' scale-up phase: Prospects for bringing designs to multiple schools. (MR-942-NAS). Santa Monica, CA: RAND.

Bogler, R., & Somech, A. (2004). Influence of teacher empowerment on teachers' organizational commitment, professional commitment and organizational citizenship behavior in schools. *Teaching and Teacher Education, 20,* 277–289.

Borman, K., Carter, K., Aladjem, D., & Le Floch, K. (2004). Challenges for the future of comprehensive school reform. In C. Cross (Ed.), *Putting the pieces together: Lessons from comprehensive school reform research* (pp. 109–150). Washington, DC: George Washington University Press.

Borman, G., & Hewes, G. (2002). The long-term effects and cost-effectiveness of Success for All. *Educational Evaluation and Policy Analysis, 24*(4), 243–266.

Borman, G., Hewes, G., Overman, L., & Brown, S. (2002). Comprehensive school reform and achievement: A meta-analysis (Report 59). Baltimore: Center for Research on the Education of Students Placed At Risk (CRESPAR).

Borman, G., Hewes, G., Overman, L., & Brown, S. (2003). Comprehensive School Reform and achievement: A meta-analysis. *Review of Educational Research, 73*(2), 125–230.

Borman, G., Slavin, R., Cheung, A., Chamberlain, A., Madden, N., & Chambers, B. (2005a). Success for All: First-year results from the national randomized field trial. *Educational Evaluation and Policy Analysis, 27*(1), 1–22.

Borman, G., Slavin, R., Cheung, A., Chamberlain, A., Madden, N., & Chambers, B. (2005b). The national randomized field trial of Success for All: Second-year outcomes. *American Educational Research Journal, 42*(4), 673–696.

Brewer, G., & DeLeon, P. (1983). *The foundations of policy analysis.* Chicago: Dorsey Press.

Brown, K. (2005). C'mon, tell me . . . Does school ethnography really matter? *Educational Researcher, 34*(9), 29–34.

Camburn, E., Rowan, B., & Taylor, J. (2003). Distributed leadership in schools: The case of elementary schools adopting comprehensive school reform models. *Educational Evaluation and Policy Analysis, 25*(4), 347–373.

Carlson, R., & Buttram, J. (2004). *Case studies of rural schools implementing comprehensive school reform models.* Paper presented at the annual meeting of the American Educational Research Association, San Diego, CA.

Cavell, L. (2002). *Unlocking the eleven components of CSR.* Washington, DC: National Clearinghouse for Comprehensive School Reform.

Clements, S. (1998). *The changing face of common schooling: The politics of the Kentucky Education Reform Act of 1990.* Unpublished doctoral dissertation, University of Chicago.

Clements, S. (2000). Linking curriculum and instruction to performance standards. In R. Pancratz & J. Petrosko, *All children can learn: Lessons from the Kentucky reform experience* (pp. 98–115). New York: Wiley and Sons.

Coburn, C. (2001). Collective sensemaking about reading: How teachers mediate reading policy in their professional communities. *Educational Evaluation and Policy Analysis, 23*(2), 145–170.

Coburn, C., & Russell, J. (2008). District policy and teachers' social networks. *Educational Evaluation and Policy Analysis, 30*(3), 203–235.

Coleman, J., & Hoffer, T. (1987). *Public and private high schools: The impact of communities.* New York: Basic Books.

Cooper, R., Slavin, R., & Madden, N. (1998). Success for All: Improving the quality of implementation of whole-school change through the use of a national reform network. *Education and Urban Society, 30*(3), 385–408.

Copland, M. (2003). Leadership of inquiry: Building and sustaining capacity for school improvement. *Educational Evaluation and Policy Analysis, 25*(5), 375–395.

Cotner, B., Herrmann, S., Borman, K., Boydston, T., & LeFloch, K. (2005). *A deeper look at implementation: School-level stakeholders' perceptions of comprehensive school reform.* A paper presented at the annual meetings of the American Educational Research Association, Montreal, Canada.

Corsaro, W. (1985). *Friendship and peer culture in the early years.* Norwood, NJ: Ablex.

Cresswell, J. (1997). *Qualitative inquiry and research design: Choosing among five traditions.* Thousand Oaks, CA: Sage.

Cuban, L. (2001). *Oversold and underused: Computers in the classroom.* Cambridge, MA: Harvard University Press.

Daft, R., & Becker, S. (1978). *Innovation in organizations.* New York: Elsevier.

Darling-Hammond, L., & McLaughlin, M. (1995). Policies that support professional development in an era of reform. *Phi Delta Kappan, 76*(8), 597–604.

Datnow, A. (2000). Power and politics in the adoption of school reform models. *Educational Evaluation and Policy Analysis, 22*(4), 357–374.

Datnow, A. (2004). Happy marriage or uneasy alliance? The relationship between comprehensive school reform and state accountability systems. *Journal of Education for Students Placed at Risk, 10*(1), 113–138.

Datnow, A. (2005). The sustainability of comprehensive school reform models in changing district and state contexts. *Educational Administration Quarterly, 41*(1), 121–153.

Datnow, A., & Castellano, M. (2000). Teachers' responses to Success for All: How beliefs, experiences, and adaptations shape implementation. *American Educational Research Journal, 37*(3), 775–799.

Datnow, A., & Castellano, M. (2001). Managing and guiding school reform: Leadership in Success for All schools. *Educational Administration Quarterly, 37*(2), 219–249.

Datnow, A., Hubbard, L., & Mehan, H. (2002). *Extending educational reform: From one school to many.* New York: RoutledgeFalmer.

Datnow, A., McHugh, B., Stringfield, S., & Hacker, D. (1998). Scaling up the Core Knowledge sequence. *Education and Urban Society, 30*(3), 409–432.

Datnow, A., & Stringfield, S. (2000). Working together for reliable school reform. *Journal of Education for Students Placed at Risk, 5*(1), 183–204.

Denzin, N., & Lincoln, Y. (Eds.). (1994). *Handbook of qualitative research.* Thousand Oaks, CA: Sage.

Desimone, L. (2002). How can comprehensive school reform models be successfully implemented? *Review of Educational Research, 72*(3), 433–480.

Dewees, S. (2000). *Participation of rural schools in comprehensive school reform demonstration program: What do we know?* Charleston, WV: Appalachian Educational Laboratory.

Evans, R. (1996). *The human side of school change: Reform, resistance, and the real life problems of innovation.* San Francisco: Jossey-Bass.

Evans-Andris, M. (1996). *An apple for the teacher: Computers and work in elementary schools.* Thousand Oaks, CA: Corwin.

Evans-Andris, M., & Usui, W. (2001). *Comprehensive school reform and educational dynamics in Kentucky middle schools.* Proposal for research funded by the U.S. Department of Education, Office of Educational Research and Improvement.

Evans-Andris, M. & Usui, W. (2004a). *Comprehensive school reform and performance in Kentucky middle schools.* Presented at the annual meetings of the American Education Research Association. San Diego, CA.

Evans-Andris, M., & Usui, W. (2004b). *Comprehensive school reform and sustainability in Kentucky middle schools.* Paper presented at a conference of the National Clearinghouse for Comprehensive School Reform, Washington, DC.

Evans-Andris, M., & Usui, W. (2008). Comprehensive school reform and student achievement in Kentucky middle schools. *Middle Grades Research Journal, 3*(2), 51–69.

Fink, D., & Brayman, C. (2006). School leadership succession and the challenges of change. *Educational Administration Quarterly, 42*(1), 62–89.

Fullan, M. (1991). *The new meaning of educational change.* New York: Teachers College Press.

Fullan, M. (2001). *Leading in a culture of change.* San Francisco: Jossey-Bass.

Fullan, M. (2005). *Leadership and sustainability: System thinkers in action.* Thousand Oaks, CA: Corwin.

Fuller, B., Wright, J., Gesicki, K., & Kang, E. (2007). Gauging growth: How to judge No Child Left Behind? *Educational Researcher, 36*(5), 268–278.

Furney, K., Hasazi, S., Clark-Keefe, K., & Hartnett, J. (2003). A longitudinal anlaysis of shifting policy landscapes in special and general education reform. *Exceptional Children, 70*(1), 81–94.

Gallant, D. (2002). Qualitative social science research. In R. Amdur & E. Bankert (Eds.), *Institutional review board: Management and function* (pp. 403–406). New York: Jones and Bartlett.

Garet, M., Porter, A., Desimone, L., Birman, B., & Yoon, K. (2001). What makes professional development effective? Results from a national sample of teachers. *American Educational Research Journal, 38*(4), 915–946.

Giles, C., & Hargreaves, A. (2006). The sustainability of innovative schools as learning organizations and professional learning communities during standardized reform. *Educational Administration Quarterly, 42*(1), 124–156.

Glaser, B., & Strauss, A. (1967). *The discovery of grounded theory.* New York: Aldine.

Goertz, M. (2005). Implementing the No Child Left Behind Act: Challenges for the states. *Peabody Journal of Education, 80*(2), 73–89.

Gordon, R. (1980). *Interviewing: Strategy, techniques, and tactics.* New York: Dorsey.

Graczewski, C., Ruffin, M., Shambaugh, L., & Therriault, S. (2007). Selecting and implementing whole school improvement models: A district and school administrator perspective. *Journal of Education for Students Placed at Risk, 12*(1), 75–90.

Hanson, E. M. (1981). Organizational control in educational systems: A case study of governance in schools. In S. Bacharach (Ed.), *Organizational behavior in schools and school districts* (pp. 245–276). New York: Praeger.

Hargreaves, A. (1994). *Changing teachers, changing times: Teachers' work and culture in the postmodern age.* New York: Teachers College Press.

Herman, R., Aladjam, D., McMahon, P., Masem, E., Muligan, I., Smith, O., et al. (1999). *An educators' guide to schoolwide reform.* Arlington, VA: Educational Research Service.

Hodson, R. (1991). The active worker. *Journal of Contemporary Ethnography, 20*(1), 47–78.

Holdzkom, D. (2002). *Effects of comprehensive school reform in 12 schools: Results of a three year study.* Charleston, WV: Appalachian Education Laboratory.

Hurley, E., Chamberlain, A., Slavin, R., & Madden, N. (2001). Effects of Success for All on TAAS reading: A Texas statewide evaluation. *Phi Delta Kappan, 82*(10), 750–756.

Ingersoll, R. (2001). Teacher turnover, teacher shortages: An organizational analysis. *American Educational Research Journal, 38*(3), 499–534.

Ingersoll, R. (2003). *Who controls teachers' work? Power and accountability in America's schools.* Cambridge, MA: Harvard University Press.

Johnson, S., Birkeland, S., Donaldson, M., Kardos, S., Kauffman, D., Kiu, E., et al. (2004). *Finders and keepers: Helping new teachers survive and thrive in our schools.* San Francisco: Jossey-Bass.

Kannapel, P., & DeYoung, A. (1999). The rural school problem in 1999: A review and critique of the literature. *Journal of Research in Rural Education, 15*(2), 67–79.

Kanter, R. (1983). *The change masters.* New York: Simon and Schuster.

Karen, D. (2005). No child left behind? Sociology ignored! *Sociology of Education, 78*(2), 165–170.

Kirby, S., Berends, M., & Naftel, S. (2001). *Implementation in a longitudinal sample of NAS: Four years into scale-up.* (MR-1413-EDU). Santa Monica, CA: RAND.

Kirby, S., Berends, M., & Bodilly, S. (2002). *A decade of whole-school reform: The New American Schools experience.* (RB-8019-EDU). Santa Monica, CA: RAND.

Kidron, Y., & Darwin, M. (2007). A systematic review of whole school improvement models. *Journal of Education for Students Placed at Risk, 12*(1), 9–35.

Laine, S. (2004). *CSR in schools and classrooms: Implications for teachers and teaching.* Naperville, IL: Learning Point Associates.

Land, D., & Legters, N. (2002). The extent and consequences of risk in U.S. education. In S. Stringfield & D. Land (Eds.), *Educating at-risk students.* (pp. 1–28). Chicago: University of Chicago Press.

Lane, B., & Gracia, S. (2004). State-level support for comprehensive school reform: Implications for policy and practice. *Journal of Education for Students Placed at Risk, 10*(1), 85–112.

Lee, V., & Burkam, D. (2002). *Inequality at the starting gate*: Social background differences in achievement as children begin school. Washington, DC: Economic Policy Institute.

Lee, V., & Smith, J. (1993). Effects of school restructuring on the achievement and engagement of middle-grade students. *Sociology of Education, 66*(3), 164–187.

LeFloch, K. C., Taylor, J., & Thompson, K. (2005). *The implications of NCLB accountability for comprehensive school reform.* A paper prepared for the annual meeting of the American Educational Research Association, Montreal, Canada.

LeFloch, K., Zhang, Y., & Herrmann, S. (2005). *Adoption: Exploring the initiation of comprehensive school reform models.* A paper presented at the annual meeting of the American Educational Research Association, Montreal, Canada.

Leithwood, K. (1992). The move toward transformational leadership. *Educational Leadership, 49*(5), 8–12.

Leopold, G., Childers, R., & Hawley-Rowe, C. (2000). *Rural school principals' views on the comprehensive school reform demonstration program application process.* Charleston, WV: Appalachian Education Laboratory.

Levin, H. (2006). Can research improve educational leadership? *Educational Researcher, 35*(8), 38–43.

Lewis, A. (2002). A horse called NCLB. *Phi Delta Kappan, 84*(3), 179–180.

Lieberman, A. (Ed.). (1995). *Work of restructuring schools: Building from the ground up.* New York: Teachers College Press.

Lieberman, A., & Miller, L. (1990). Teacher development in professional practice schools. *Teachers College Record, 92*(1), 105–122.

Lippman, L., Burns, S., McArthur, E. (1996). *Urban schools: The challenge of location and poverty.* NCES 96864. Washington, DC: National Center for Education Statistics.

Lipsky, M. (1980). *Street-level bureaucracy: Dilemmas of the individual in public services.* New York: Russell Sage Foundation.

Little, J. (1993). Teachers' professional development in a climate of educational reform. *Educational Evaluation and Policy Analysis, 15*(2), 129–151.

Little, J. (2003). Constructions of teacher leadership in three periods of policy and reform activism. *School Leadership and Management, 23*(4), 401–419.

Lortie, D. (1975). *Schoolteacher: A sociological study.* Chicago: University of Chicago Press.

Louis, K., Febey, K., & Schroeder, R. (2005). State-mandated accountability in high schools: Teachers' interpretations of a new era. *Educational Evaluation and Policy Analysis, 27*(2), 177–204.

Lytle, J. (2002). Whole-school reform from the inside. *Phi Delta Kappan, 84*(2), 164–167.

MacIver, M., & Farley-Ripple, E. (2008). *Bringing the district back in: The role of the central office in instruction and achievement.* Alexandria, VA: Educational Research Service.

Malen, B., & Fuhrman, S. (1991). The politics of curriculum and testing: Introduction and overview. In S. Fuhrman & B. Malen (Eds.), *The politics of curriculum and testing: The fourth annual yearbook of the Politics of Education Association* (pp. 1–9). New York: Falmer Press.

Mangin, M. (2007). Facilitating elementary principals' support for instructional teacher leadership. *Educational Administration Quarterly, 43*(3), 319–357.

May, H., & Supovitz, J. (2006). Capturing the cumulative effects of school reform: An 11-year study of the impacts of America's choice on student achievement. *Educational Evaluation and Policy Analysis, 28*(3), 231–257.

May, H., Supovitz, J., & Perda, D. (2004). *A longitudinal study of the impact of America's Choice on student performance in Rochester, New York, 1998–2003.* Philadelphia: University of Pennsylvania, Consortium for Policy Research in Education.

McAndrews, L. (2006). *The era of education: The presidents and the schools 1965–2001.* Chicago: University of Illinois Press.

McCracken, G. (1988). *The long interview.* Newbury Park, CA: Sage.

Meyer, J., & Rowan, B. (1977). Institutionalized organizations: Formal structures as myth and ceremony. *American Journal of Sociology, 83*(2), 340–363.

Moffett, C. (2000, April). Sustaining change: The answers are blowing in the wind. *Educational Leadership, 57*(7), 35–38.

Muncey, D., & McQuillan, P. (1996). *Reform and resistance in schools and classrooms.* New Haven, CT: Yale University Press.

Munoz, M., Ross, S., & McDonald, A. (2007). Comprehensive school reform in middle schools: The effects of Different Ways of Knowing on student achievement in a large urban district. *Journal of Education for Students Placed at Risk, 12*(2), 167–183.

Murphy, J., & Datnow, A. (Eds). (2003). *Leadership lessons from comprehensive school reforms.* Thousand Oaks, CA: Corwin.

National Commission on Excellence in Education. (1983). A nation at risk: The imperative for educational reform. (ED 226 006). Washington, DC: U.S. Government Printing Office.

National Writing Project. (1999). *Annual report.* Berkley: University of California.

Natriello, G., McDill, E., & Pallas, A. (1990). *Schooling disadvantaged children: Racing against catastrophe.* New York: Teachers College Press.

Newmann, F., Smith, B., Allensworth, E., Bryk, A. (2001). Instructional program coherence: What it is and why it should guide school improvement policy. *Educational Evaluation and Policy Analysis, 23*(4), 297–321.

Nir, A. (2002). School-based management and its effect on teacher commitment. *Leadership in Education, 5*(4), 323–341.

Olson, L. (2000). Blue-ribbon panel to set standards for reform models. *Education Week, 19*(22), 10.

Pankratz, R., & Petrosko, J. (Eds). (2000). *All children can learn: Lessons from the Kentucky reform experience.* San Francisco: Jossey-Bass.

Patton, M. (2002). *Qualitative research and evaluation methods.* Thousand Oaks, CA: Sage.

Pitman, M. A., & Maxwell, J. (1992). Qualitative approaches to evaluation: Models and methods. In M. LeCompte, W. Millroy, & J. Preissle (Eds.), *The handbook of qualitative research in education* (pp. 729–770). San Diego: Academic Press.

Poggio, J. (2000). Statewide performance assessment and school accountability. In R. Pankratz & J. Petrosko (Eds), *All children can learn: Lessons from the Kentucky reform experience* (pp. 75–97). San Francisco: Jossey-Bass.

Pogrow, S. (2000). Success for All does not produce success for students. *Phi Delta Kappan, 82*(1), 67–80.

Pogrow, S. (2002). Success for All is a failure. *Phi Delta Kappan, 83*(6), 463–469.

Rosenzweig, E., O'Brien, J., & Collins, D. (2004). *Comprehensive school reform models: Gauging changes in teacher instructional practice.* Unpublished manuscript, The Education Alliance at Brown University, Providence, RI.

Ross, S. (2001). *Creating critical mass for restructuring: What we can learn from Memphis.* Charleston, WV: Appalachian Educational Laboratory Policy Briefs.

Ross, S., Sanders, W., & Stringfield, S. (1998). *The Memphis restructuring initiative: Achievement results for years 1 and 2 on the Tennessee value-added assessment system (TVASS).* A special report prepared for Memphis City Schools.

Ross, S., Wang, M., Weiping, L., Alberg, M., Sanders, W., Wright, S., et al. (2001). *Fourth-year achievement results on the Tennessee value- added assessment system for restructuring schools in Memphis.* Paper presented at the annual meeting of the American Educational Research Association, Seattle, WA.

Rowan, B. (1990). Commitment and control: Alternative strategies for the organizational design of schools. In *Review of Research in Education, 16*(1), 353–389.

Rowan, B., & Miller, R. (2007). Organizational strategies for promoting instructional change: Implementation dynamics in schools working with comprehensive school reform providers. *American Educational Research Journal, 44*(2), 252–297.

Sarason, S. (1996). *Revisiting "the culture of the school and the problem of change."* New York: Teachers College Press.

Schon, D. (1987). *Educating the reflective practitioner.* San Francisco: Jossey-Bass.

Sherwood, T. (1999). *A practical look at comprehensive school reform for rural schools.* Charleston, WV: ERIC Clearinghouse on Rural Education and Small Schools.

Slavin, R. (1996). Reforming state and federal policies to support adoption of proven practices. *Educational Researcher, 25*(9), 4–5.

Slavin, R. (2002). Mounting evidence support the achievement effects of SFA. *Phi Delta Kappan, 83*(6), 469–473.

Slavin, R. (2004). Built to last: Long-term maintenance of Success for All. *Remedial and Special Education, 25*(1), 61–66.

Slavin, R. (2008). What works? Issues in synthesizing educational program evaluations. *Educational Researcher, 37*(1), 5–14.

Smith, M., & O'Day, J. (1991). Systemic school reform. In S. Fuhrman & B. Malen, (Eds.), *The politics of curriculum and testing: The fourth annual yearbook of the Politics of Education Association* (pp. 233–267). New York: Falmer Press.

Smylie, M., Conley, S., & Marks, H. (2002). Exploring new approaches to teacher leadership for school improvement. In J. Murphy (Ed.), *The educational leadership challenge: Redefining leadership for the 21st century.* Chicago: University of Chicago Press.

Smylie, M., & Denny, J. (1990). Teacher leadership: Tensions and ambiguities in organizational perspective. *Educational Administration Quarterly, 26*(3), 235–259.

Smylie, M., Wenzel, S., & Fendt, C. (2003). The Chicago Annenberg Challenge: Lessons on leadership for school development. In J. Murphy & A. Datnow (Eds.), Leadership lessons from comprehensive school reforms. Thousand Oaks, CA: Corwin.

Spillane, J., Camburn, E. & Pareja, A. (2007). Taking a distributed perspective to the school principal's workday. *Leadership and Policy in Schools, 6*(1), 103–125.

Spillane, J., Diamond, J., & Jita, L. (2000). *Leading instruction: The distribution of leadership for instruction.* Paper presented at the annual meeting of the American Educational Research Association, New Orleans, LA.

Spillane, J., Halverson, R., & Diamond, J. (2001, April). Investigating school leadership practice: A distributed perspective. *Educational Researcher, 30*(3), 23–28.

Stanton-Salazar, R., & Dornbusch, S. (1995). Social capital and the reproduction of inequality: Information networks among Mexican-origin high school students. *Sociology of Education, 68*(2), 116–135.

Stecher, B., & Barron, S. 2001. Unintended consequences of test-based accountability when testing in "milepost" grades. *Educational Assessment, 7*(4), 259–281.

Sterbinsky, A., Ross, S., & Redfield, D. (2006). Effects of comprehensive school reform on student achievement and school change: A longitudinal multi-site study. *School Effectiveness and School Improvement, 17*(3), 367–397.

Strauss, A., & Corbin, J. (1990). *Basics of qualitative research: Grounded theory procedures and techniques.* Thousand Oaks, CA: Sage.

Sui-Chu, E., & Willms, D. (1996). Effects of parental involvement on eighth-grade achievement. *Sociology of Education, 69*(2), 126–141.

Taylor, J. (2005). *Sustainability: Examining the survival of schools' comprehensive school reform efforts.* Paper presented at the annual meeting of the American Education Research Association, Montreal, Canada.

Tushman, M. (1977). Special boundary roles in the innovation process. *Administrative Science Quarterly, 22,* 587–605.

Tyack, D., & Cuban, L. (1995). *Tinkering toward utopia: A century of public school reform.* Cambridge, MA: Harvard University Press.

Wagner, J., & Hollenbeck, J. (1995). *Management of organizational behavior.* Englewood Cliffs, NJ: Prentice Hall.

Weick, K. (1976). Educational organizations as loosely coupled systems. *Administrative Science Quarterly, 21*(1), 1–17.

West, A. (1999). *Comprehensive school reform: Five lessons from the field.* Denver, CO: Education Commission of the States.

Whitford, B. L., & Jones, K. (2000). *Accountability, assessment, and teacher commitment.* Albany, NY: State University of New York Press.

Whitmore, R. (2000). Schools grant program alarming researchers. Gannet News Service, http://www.ewa.org/infocenter/reporters/lightspan.htm. (No longer available)

Wong, K., & Meyer, S. (1998). Title I schoolwide programs: A synthesis of findings from recent evaluation. *Educational Evaluation and Policy Analysis, 20*(2), 115–136.

Yonezawa, S., & Stringfield, S. (2000). *Special strategies for educating disadvantaged students follow-up: Examining the sustainability of research based school reforms.* Baltimore: Johns Hopkins University.

Zhang, Y., Shkolnik, J., & Fashoa, O. (2005). *Evaluating the implementation of comprehensive school reform and its impact on grown in student achievement.* Paper presented at the annual meeting of the American Educational Research Association, Montreal, Canada.

Index

www.ingramcontent.com/pod-product-compliance
Ingram Content Group UK Ltd.
Pitfield, Milton Keynes, MK11 3LW, UK
UKHW052218050726
472866UK00007B/178